THE
MORNINGSIDE
PAPERS

THE
MORNINGSIDE
PAPERS

PETER
GZOWSKI

McClelland and Stewart

McClelland and Stewart Limited
The Canadian Publishers
25 Hollinger Road
Toronto, Ontario
M4B 3G2

Canadian Cataloguing in Publication Data

Gzowski, Peter.
  The Morningside papers

Commentary on and correspondence to the CBC radio program Morningside.
ISBN 0-7710-3743-0

1. Morningside (Radio program). I. Morningside
(Radio program). II. Title.

PN1991.3.C3G99 1985   791.44'72   C85-099081-5

Printed and bound in Canada by Webcom Limited

Typeset in Kennerley Old Style by Compeer Typographic Services Ltd.

Contents

Introduction 7

1 City Mice and Country Mice 15

2 "I've Got a Little (Canadian) List" 45

3 Nicaraguan Journal 53

4 Arguments 65

5 Memorable Meals: A First Course 87

6 Different Generations 107

7 Out of Work 115

8 Bears 135

9 The Closet 157

10 On Grannies and the Need for Mustard Plasters 161

11 Getting Sober 165

12 People and Their Machines – and Vice Versa 175

13 Our Man in Africa 195

14 A Lady Musician Named Joan 205

15 Fighting Back 209

16 Spring, Happy Spring 219

17 Violence in the National Game 227

18 Memories 233

19 Our Woman in Greece 257

20 Occasions in the Life of a Host 267

21 The Other Solitude 279

22 The Morningside Book of Slightly Amended, Nearly Always Canadian, Verse 295

23 Memorable Meals: The Second Course 303

24 The Language Judge 319

25 The Things You Figure Out 327

Index of Authors 350

A hint about making your way through this book

Unless you read books very differently from the way I do, you will probably not simply begin at the beginning of *The Morningside Papers* and carry on straight through, but will instead browse and sample, linger here, return there, and generally, I hope, treat these pages more as a companion – I am partial to the bedside myself, but will not be offended if you choose the bathroom – than a volume you can't put down. If you do use it that way, you may have some difficulty figuring out just who has written what. Here is the key: The chapters that are all written by one person – by Chris Brookes, for example, or Glen Allen, or, for that matter, by me – are straightforward. If they are a mixture of what I've written and the listeners' responses, my stuff usually runs first, as it was heard, and I've put my initials to sign off; after that, a little ✉ indicates the beginning of a letter. If the chapter is comprised entirely of letters – as Arguments is, for example – there's a ✉ at the beginning of everything. Anyway, don't worry; it's simpler than I've made it sound.

A note on permissions

In preparing these papers, I wrote to all my fellow authors, using the addresses on their original letters. Nearly all of them replied, granting me permission to publish what we'd already broadcast. But in spite of my best efforts, there were some people I just couldn't track down. Presuming they would follow the same pattern as those I could, I have included some of their letters. I apologize for this presumption, and would be delighted to hear from anyone who is surprised to see his, or her, work here. I'd rather have risked annoying them this way than by leaving them out.

And a word of dedication

This book is for my daughter Alison, with a slight apology for the number of times I mentioned her, or quoted her, on the air, with, as well, profound thanks to Nicole Bélanger, who brought me back to *Morningside*, and to Gloria Bishop, who kept me there.

Introduction

The people who work with me at *Morningside*, the daily CBC radio program for which the documents in this collection were originally prepared, are my friends. I see them every day, and know their habits and idiosyncracies. I know their marital situations and what they like for lunch. I know that Richard Handler, the brilliant expatriate American who produces, among other items, nearly all our scientific and medical pieces, is a dedicated hypochondriac; that Jim Handman, the son of a man I used to work with on magazines, who covers the theatrical scene for us (again among many other items, since all *Morningside* producers are perforce generalists as well as specialists), is himself as good an actor as many of the guests he brings to our studios; and that Tina Srebotnjak, the beautiful ex-newspaper writer whose beat includes Quebec and Newfoundland (Tina has lived in both those provinces and speaks each of their languages), has a mother who listens each Friday as I read the credits to make certain I say Tina's name and who also tunes in ahead of time in case, as she says, we start early. I can parody the Groucho-Marxian walk of Alan Guettel, our other ex-American, who produces our live music (and who is also, as we learned at the picnic that closed our third season together, an awesome softball player) and the sometimes scholarly prose of Peter Puxley, the gentlemanly former NDP researcher from Alberta who supervised, aside from his daily work, our dramatic retrial of Louis Riel in the spring of 1985. I know and forgive their occasional lapses, for I also know, for instance, that when I have taken home too many books to read at the height of the publishing season Hal Wake, a doctor's son from Ottawa who gave up his own on-air career in British Columbia to look after *Morningside*'s literary beat, will have read and absorbed what I haven't, and that, leaning on his research and his long and thoughtful background essays as I lean on the work of all my colleagues, I will somehow stagger through the morning's interviews. We will bring it off, as we bring off so much of the program, together.

In the world of broadcasting, of course, this is not an unusual phenomenon. Radio programs of the sort we do are group efforts, and both the success and the shortcomings of those of us who get to talk on the air are not nearly so much our own doing as the listener is sometimes led to believe. But at *Morningside*, I think, we are particularly close, if for no other reason than the extraordinary number of hours we spend in each other's company, from the long weekend we steal from our holidays each summer to plan the next season through forty-two weeks of shaping, organizing, researching and presenting a dozen or so items each day and on to the last morning of our broadcast year, a morning that arrives with a mixture of relief and sadness, much like the last day of school, and ends, as on the day Alan Guettel showed his ability to hit the long ball, in communal celebration.

We are, I suppose, more like a family than a group of acquaintances, and like all families we sometimes squabble and sometimes bicker and sometimes play jokes on each other. Early in my own career at *Morningside*, for instance, when my grave discomfort with anything erotic on the air was evident to my new colleagues, the spritely and dark-haired Talin Vartanian, who handles fads and fashions (as well as, by the way, our most popular serious feature, the weekly kaffee klatch among Dalton Camp, Eric Kierans and – now – Dave Barrett), sat up late one evening to leave, for my morning arrival, all the preparation for an apocryphal interview with an expert on brassieres, including instructions for fondling the material and describing a live model.

We are, as I say, friends, and when, on the occasions of the ACTRA awards they have all won for me (as they have some other honours), I have singled out for public thanks only the two executive producers who have presided over my term as host, or have mentioned only the arrival of two new listeners to our crew – Richard Handler's son Aaron and Beatrice Schriever's Gabriel – the others have understood. Or so I hope, for I love them all.

My relationship with the people whose work appears in these pages is a more complex one. My co-authors and I are ... not strangers, for strangers, except perhaps in passing encounters on trains or airplanes, do not share intimacies ... but not friends either, in the sense that friends see each other and know each other well. Of all of them, in fact – and there are one hundred and fifty-six people other than myself whose work appears here – I have met only a handful. I know Myrna Kostash, who writes from Greece, from our mutual days in the magazine business, and I have worked as an editor for Bill Stephenson, who had the memorable encounter with Albert Schweitzer, and with Dave Scott – or D.B. Scott as I see he signs himself – who sent in a clever parody of Koko's little list for our Mikado contest. Paul McLaughlin, another successful entrant in that contest (Paul came in and sang his version on the air) has sometimes worked as a producer for us, and Catherine Edward, who offers an argument about raising children, was – long before she became a mother – an announcer at the CBC in Toronto. Grace Lane and Ann Pappert, the two women who write to each other across the generation gap, I know from the circumstances I describe in the preface to their exchange. Chris Brookes, our Nicaraguan correspondent, dropped into the *Morningside* office one day on his way back to Newfoundland, and Jerry Kambites, as I say in my notes on his letters from Uganda, has also visited us. But there are others I might be expected to know whom I have not met. Glen Allen, for instance, who writes so grippingly about his battle to get off alcohol, is the son of Ralph Allen, my hero and mentor at *Maclean's*, but Glen and I (and I am delighted to report that, still dry, he has joined the staff of the magazine his father and I once edited) have, as this is written, not yet been introduced. I met Isabel Huggan, who writes on rain here and who has published a book of short stories, when she was on her publicity tour, and Carolann Johnson (machines), who used to host a television program in Edmonton, when I was on one of mine. But other than that, and with the possible exception of Mark Leier, who lives in Burnaby, British Columbia, and who, along with the note he wrote granting me permission to run his memorable meal, enclosed a newspaper clipping about the same romantic episode in his life in which he was described as (aged twenty-five) having "blonde hair to his shoulders, a beard and blue, blue eyes," all I know about the people who have joined me writing *The Morningside Papers* is what you will know when you have read their entries.

And yet, I cannot help thinking – and I imagine you will not be able to help thinking – my co-authors and I are close to each other too.

Morningside receives an almost unbelievable amount of mail, some of it solicited, of course, as in the contests whose results are summarized in this collection, but much of it just over the transom, as publishers say – letters, or in some cases essays (or even poems) inspired by something the writer has heard on the program or noted in the news. My habit, evolved over the years, is to begin my day with it. My alarm goes off at 4:44 AM – I rather like the symmetry on my digital clock – and after a quick shower and a coffee I make my way through the dark streets to the rambling old building in mid-Toronto from which so much of the fibre of Canada has been broadcast over the years. I am alone for the first hour or so. I unlock the door and turn on the lights in the musty air, too hot in the winter, too draughty in the spring. I have brought more coffee and a briefcase full of the previous evening's work, and I have picked up the morning papers on my way. The notes and format for today's edition – we call them "greens," after the five-copy paper on which they're typed – await me, with outlines for the questions I will ask and introductions and links to tie the show together. This is the producers' work, often done after I leave in the afternoon but still a product of what we've talked over as we go. But the early time is my own. When Janet Russell, our quiet and efficient script assistant, arrives at 6:30, we will play the day's records and talk over possible technical problems; later, when the director of the day arrives, the pace will heat up as we count down toward the opening theme – "In five, four . . ." "Good morning, I'm Peter Gzowski and this is *Morningside*" – but for now there's time to think, to cherish the history of the creaky old building and the men and women who have sat behind its microphones or gestured from the other side of the glass: Max Ferguson and Allan McFee (Max still comes in on weekends and the incomparable Allan tapes *Eclectic Circus* down the hall), Andrew Allen, who died during my years at *This Country in the Morning*, where he provided such elegant essays, and Esse W. Llungh – or "Young," as I was sure it was spelled when I sat in Timmins or Moose Jaw or Chatham, engrossed in the old *Stage* series – and John Drainie and Barbara Frum and W.O. Mitchell's *Jake and the Kid* and Bob Weaver's *Anthology* and *Trans-Canada Matinee* and Byng Whitteker and June Dennis and Lorne Greene and all the other great announcers and actors and writers and performers and reporters and stars who appeared over the years, with music composed and conducted by Lucio Agostini, whose presence is often still there, too, on our *Morningside* drama. And now it's *Morningside*, with *As It Happens* in the evening and *Sunday Morning* on the weekend, and we carry the torch.

The mail is on my typewriter, opened – except for the personal – the night before, and every morning, before the light breaks on the window, with my cardboard container of coffee in my hand and the local morning show chattering quietly on a monitor in the background, I settle in with it. There are ten or twenty and sometimes thirty and more a day: arguments, thank-yous, grievances, corrections, praise, criticism, challenges, jokes, travel notes, clippings, invitations, and often just hello, how are you doing? I read it all – partly, I suppose, because it informs or inspires me (there is scarcely an edition of *Morningside* that does not carry a story suggested by the mail or introduce a guest drawn to our attention by a listener), but mostly because, day after day, it reminds me of who we're broadcasting to, of how well-informed they are and how alert to artifice and affectation. Slightly more than a million Canadians a week now tune in regularly to *Morningside* and, I am convinced, they are the smartest million there are. If I am going to continue to perform the job they pay me to perform, I am reminded every morning, I had damn well better be on my toes.

On the air, though, I never think of the million. If there is one thing I have learned in the years on radio that started with *This Country in the Morning* in 1971 (actually, as someone will certainly point out, they started before that with a program called *Radio Free Friday* – where I first met Catherine Edward – but *This Country* was my first daily gig), it is that this is the most personal of media. A generation ago, perhaps, people may have got together to listen to the radio on

Saturday evenings, gathering around the flickering green light. If they gather now, it is for television. When they listen to the radio they listen alone, in a car or while they're doing the housework, in the background at the office or on earphones on the tractor – but by themselves. Radio is as one-to-one as the telephone, and when I talk on it, and try to think of what the *person* listening would like me to ask next, I try to remember that.

And that, I think, may explain the mail. I was the host of *This Country in the Morning* for three years. After I left it, I tried for a while and with a stupendous lack of success to do on late-night television some of the things that had made morning radio work. Among the reasons I failed, I think, is that television, or at least the kind of television we were trying to do, is essentially show business, and radio is not. On television, no one notices what you say, but everyone notices how you look while you're saying it. Television is style; radio is content. And people, as I hope this book demonstrates, respond to content.

The Morningside Papers are not an attempt to recreate the program in print. *Morningside* is, after all, made for the ear, three hours of largely spontaneous (if pre-planned) conversation and interviews (not always the same thing) and reports and games and panels and music and phone calls. The *Papers* are the exception: things I've written and things others have written. A few – notably the notes from Nicaragua and Greece, Don Myers's diary of his time out of work and the exchanges between Grace Lane and Ann Pappert and between Mark O'Neill and Mary McKim – were commissioned, and the piece by Charles Haines was, of course, in answer to my request that he summarize some of the weekly thoughts on language that he had presented conversationally on the air. But virtually all the rest came from the morning mail. As you make your way through their printed form, you will discover them as I discovered them, and I hope they will give you some of the same pleasure.

Before I turn you over to them, I want to tell you about Eve McBride and to thank her as best I can for what she has contributed to my ability to deal with the *Morningside* mail and to this book.

I returned to CBC radio in the autumn of 1982. Negotiations over management's invitation to succeed Don Harron at the program now called *Morningside* took about three minutes. Did I want to come back? they asked (after Nicole Bélanger, then the executive producer, had cleared the way), and I replied, Yes, with all my heart, leaving out the part about how I had wanted to come back since almost the day I left, eight years ago. The single reservation I had was that never in my time at *This Country in the Morning* had I figured out satisfactorily how to handle the mail. People who wrote to me, I had always thought, deserved at least the kind of answer that would let them know I'd read their effort. Yet without a secretary – and perhaps even with one – there simply weren't enough hours in the day to do that and to continue to do the kind of radio that was engendering the mail in the first place. Oh well, I thought when I pondered returning, perhaps the mail wouldn't be as heavy.

It was. If anything it was heavier, not only greater in quantity but more reflective, more challenging, more stimulating – and more deserving of reply.

Eve turned out to be the solution. One morning early in the fall of my first season at *Morningside*, the mail included a letter from her, neatly typed and full of the kind of thoughtful comment that was already swamping me. I cannot now remember what Eve's letter was about, but I learned from it that although she had grown up in Port Hope, Ontario, and was now living just around the corner from the CBC in Toronto, she had spent the last few years in the Yukon with her lawyer-husband, raising their four daughters, working in an art gallery, trying to write a novel and listening to the CBC. I called her. She understood my need and how important it was. Together we made a deal with Nicole, and every morning since, Eve has come in to translate my scribbled notes on the margins of the mail and to compose from them, after more conversation, the kind of responses the authors have deserved. Or, again, that's what I hope – for I love my correspondents, too.

Twice a week, as well, Eve has joined me on the air to read from the mail, and after doing that she has filed and catalogued it, and noted my marginal musings that someday we ought to put a book together. Editing that book, whittling down some twelve thousand entries to what you now hold in your hand, has been an enormous task. The final choices are, of course, mine; these are the pieces that pleased me most in my first three years at *Morningside*, that seemed to me, as opposed to so many other worthy contenders that spoke to passing issues of the day, to say something worth recalling, to speak from the heart and to the personal experiences of being a Canadian in the 1980s – or, simply, to be fun, or moving, to read again. But in selecting them and preparing them for publication, I had a lot of help, and I am grateful to Lynn Cunningham, to Gillian Howard, to Penny Gerie, to Edna Barker, and to Alison Gzowski, all of whom for various reasons and at various times pencilled, typed, typed and pencilled again, chopped and clarified, advised and consented, fought for their favourites and against those I liked for the wrong reasons, or simply joined in the process. But most of all, I am grateful to Eve McBride, my letters lady. The novel she started in the Yukon has not yet been published, but *The Morningside Papers* would not exist without her.

PETER GZOWSKI
Spring 1985

CITY MICE AND COUNTRY MICE

The "contests" we ran during my first three years on
Morningside were really exchanges. I would start
writing about something and listeners would respond.
When those exchanges worked best, it seemed to me,
they arose out of something that had transpired in my
own life and had been on my mind, as opposed to the
few occasions when I simply set out to get something
going. This one, for example, which began on my first
day back and stretched out through much of the fall of
1982, grew very directly from the fact that for the five
years preceding my return to radio I had been living in
a small, old stone house on the edge of the village of
Rockwood, Ontario, and, because of *Morningside*, had
just returned to Toronto. The responses came from all
over the country, and expanded on all my themes. One
person, in fact – David Sims – wrote twice, and I have
included both his letters in my selection here. This is
how it all started.

I

At one time or another during the past few days I have done, at least once, each of the following things:

I have had Chinese food delivered to my house. Barbecued chicken wings, honey-and-garlic spare ribs, beef and snow peas and an order of steamed rice, with extra mustard and plum sauce. Not very good, as it turned out, too bready and tasting of rewarmed cardboard – but delivered right to my door.

I have played with the converter on my rented cable TV, flicking and jumping between *Hollywood Squares* and a panel discussion on the nuclear holocaust, intercutting a young cable reporter's guide to the traffic courts with a concert of the Boston Pops, simultaneously watching a soccer game and the provincial news, checking up on the prices of stocks I cannot afford, the departure times of airplanes I'll never ride and the fluctuations in the costs of foods I do not care for, and never once, because of the magic control at my fingers, having to watch a commercial.

I have lurched to the door in the mornings and found my local paper lying soggy on my doorstep. I have summoned a taxi to the same door. I have shooed away someone who wanted to park his Volvo on the bricks that cover what once was the front lawn of the house I live in, bought a package of cigarettes at two in the morning, gone to a movie within three blocks of where I live, shovelled up the junk mail in my foyer, been wakened by the sound of breaking glass at four AM, worried if the neighbours can see me stride naked to the bathroom, locked my door at night, ridden the subway, bought a morning newspaper the night before, seen a major-league baseball game in a real – well, since it was in Toronto, almost real – major-league park and walked to work. And every day, my list of new adventures grows.

I have, you see, recently moved back to the big city. I was born here, and raised nearby, and after all the other places I've lived and worked I've always come back to it. But for the past five years I've really been away. During those years I made new friends and found new pleasures, and yet now I've come back again. This time, the city seems to have changed. Or maybe I have. I see it now through new eyes. In five years the city mouse has become a country mouse and now he sees his old turf differently.

In the country, I couldn't get Chinese food delivered, or watch the cable, or get the paper brought to my home. To go to a movie theatre has been a major excursion. What I needed to buy (or read) I bought by travelling, usually by car and always by daylight. Now, I'm having some difficulty adjusting to my new conveniences, and during the next few days I thought I'd ruminate out loud about some of the things I'm learning – as well as some of the things about my life as country mouse I'm already beginning to miss.

II

On the morning of the first Saturday I moved back to the city, I went shopping. In itself, this was not a new experience for me, for in the past five years, while I have lived as a country mouse, I have often spent Saturday mornings shopping. I have jumped in my car and driven to the local bakery for a dozen sticky Chelsea buns and a copy of the morning paper, which lacked, because of my distance from its printing presses, the previous evening's sports scores. Later, if I have needed stuff, I have cruised the local merchants, chequebook in hand, and driven twenty kilometres to the nearest bookstore, where I have kept a charge account, or the provincial liquor outlet for another jug or two of the wine I know goes well with fresh sweet corn.

In the city, though, I needed no car, and my chequebook would have been only slightly less useful than a walletful of *zlotys* or a necklace of wampum. In the city you need hard, cold cash – or the 1980s equivalent of cash: hard, cold plastic.

In the city, I live downtown, on the edge of what my friend Harry Bruce, who has since moved to Halifax, christened the land of the white-painters. There are more BMWs on the street where I walk than there are trees. The houses are closer together than seats on a subway train. As evening falls you can hear the Jacuzzis flush as if in unison, and right around the corner there are more stores than there were in all of Rome. Without crossing the street I could buy, if I had the money, a Cuisinart or the *New York Times*, vitamin B$_{12}$ or a quiche to go. There are three kinds of orange drink in my neighbourhood convenience store, and twenty-four kinds of doughnuts next door. I could have my suede cleaned, my fuel pump tuned, my walls hung or my aquarium stocked. If I did cross the street I could buy a silken kite or a Stilton cheese, a German knife, a Danish peppermill, a Swedish bar stool, a Hungarian table wine or a Mandarin orange. I could get egg bread or bread rolls, breaded veal or a well-bred parakeet. I could buy a marinated leg of lamb, a chocolate-coated cherry, Kiwi fruit, canned artichoke hearts, fresh lobsters, hot croissants and cold Heineken. I could take home a live Dieffenbachia or ice cubes made of glass, a wicker end table, the latest issue of a magazine I would not like my children to see me reading or a copy of the kind of book I used to carry under my arm at university, title-side out.

I could live my life in the neighbourhood I have moved to, I think, and never sample all its wares.

And yet, as Mordecai Richler says, and yet.

On Saturday morning I went to see if I could buy something that would make me a cup of cappuccino before I came to work. Cappuccino in the morning is one of my fantasies, although the only person I have met yet who can afford to drink it is Peter Pocklington. I went to my neighbourhood kitchenware store. (In the village I have just moved from, the equivalent is one corner of the Home Hardware, just behind the fertilizer.) A lady with a German accent came to help me. First she asked me how many cups I wanted to make, and when I just said one or two she gave me a one-sentence lecture about the need to entertain my friends. Then she showed me a machine that looked as if, were I to pull the right levers in the right order, it would leave in eight minutes for Brandon. When I said that was too complicated she showed me something automatic that, I think, would not only have made me a cappuccino but have served as the centrepiece for next week's exhibition on shapes of the future. When I demurred, my helpful storefrau led me to something that appeared to have been made for filling the gas tanks of model airplanes.

Nothing I saw cost less than $198.50.

And all I wanted was a cup of coffee.

I felt as my first-born son must have felt on the second Christmas of his life when, surrounded by half-opened packages and urged on by his loving parents to open more, more and more again, he burst into tears of sadness and being overwhelmed.

I went back to my rented house, past the parked BMWs, past the silent Jacuzzis, past the white-painted bricks, to my white-painted townhouse.

I had been gone for an hour and a half, window shopping in the casbah of the trendies, and I had bought . . . nothing. My plastic was intact.

III

On the first turn you take if you drive toward the city from the house I have been living in for the past five years is a pond. I'm not sure why it lies there; on a golf course it would be casual water, and you could move your ball from it, and on the prairies it would be a slough (a word unknown in the east). But beside Highway 7 in rural Ontario it is a pond; no river runs in, no stream out. A willow tree droops over one corner, and in the summer and early fall there are cat tails and bull rushes at its edges. Even when the wind is high, it is quiet and still. On the last morning I drove in from the country, a tall blue heron posed a dozen feet from its shore.

I stopped my car to stare; the heron did not move.

If I had dared to predict, when I moved to the country five years ago, how much I would become intrigued by birds, my friends would have laughed at me. I was a total city mouse then; I rode taxis and ordered meals in, and for adventure took my kids to the zoo. In the country, blue jays jabber at me outside my kitchen window, and I jabber back, and run out with a handful of Thompson's wild bird food, $1.39 the four-pound bag, to pacify them. I am their servant. My mornings are better when they start with a brilliant male cardinal, tiptoeing in to get food for his lady. In the afternoons, an oriole pipes from the black walnut and I stop work. One summer evening as I sat with the latest P.D. James in the garden a hummingbird hovered over my teacup. I have seen grackles and juncos, bluebirds and warblers, woodpeckers and flickers, jays, buntings, larks and nuthatches, chickadees, thrushes, whippoorwills and enough sparrows to start my own cathedral – all outside my windows, or just over the first rolling hill. I do not always know what they are, for I am not always quick enough to find the right page in Roger Tory Peterson, my copy of which is now as well-thumbed as a family Bible. One magic morning I watched in wonder as a college of mourning doves waddled up through the early mists.

I am a sucker for all of this, and during the years I lived in the country my books, binoculars and birdseed have become as much a part of my life as backgammon once was, or Beefeater gin.

And now, I think I'm going to miss it.

There are compensations for all this, I know. Better shopping and faster taxis – or, in my case, taxis at all. Strangely, I can walk to work in the city, where I had to drive for anything in the country – or anything except work, most of which I did at home, next to the chattering blue jays. The snow won't shut me in this winter, and I don't have to worry about the well freezing or the door blowing off the barn.

The country surprised me when I moved there, and the city is surprising me again. This morning on my way to it I saw four sparrows, a starling and one of the last robins of the fall. But what I thought about was the blue heron, standing still near his private pond.

IV

One of the things I have not yet had to do in the first days of living back in the city is fill the gas tank of my car. This is not a part of country living that I miss. In the country, I have had to buy gasoline almost as often – or so it has seemed – as I have had to change my socks, and the habit has come close to breaking me.

I don't know what gasoline cost when I used to live here. They sold it by the gallon then, and every couple of weeks I'd notice the tank was low and cruise in for a top-up. It cost ten dollars, or thereabouts, if I was empty. A nuisance. Now they sell it by the litre, and I know *exactly* what it costs. The car I drive is fuel-efficient, and I read the prices on the pumps before I buy, but it's twenty bucks minimum when I'm close to empty and I seem to be in gas stations more often than I'm in my kitchen. The nuisance has become a real factor in my fiscal affairs, and I am having no more luck with my budget than Allan MacEachen has had with his.

That's only one part of what, I've come to realize, my flight to the country has cost me in dollars. Another part is the phone. I know I talk on the phone a lot, and that phone calls are part of my work, but I never before realized that the rest of the world has lived in a place called long distance. If you had asked me my phone number any time over the past five years I would have begun my answer with my area code, and even my kids, now grown and living in the city, think my number begins with a one. While this has some advantages – one of them is that I know, when someone wants to interrupt my solitude, he has been willing to spend a dollar to do so – it makes my monthly letter from the Bell look like the stock-market columns in the Friday Report on Business.

I had not thought of any of this when I left. I thought of the country as a retreat, a quiet place, where life would be simple and pleasant and cheap, and where I could cut down on the need I have felt most of my adult life to make as much money as I could just to stay even. Well, quiet and simple and pleasant it has been, I assure you, but cheap? I might as well have bought a racehorse. I pay rent on my mailbox and a tax on my trees. Fertilizer costs money so the grass will grow long, and the local university student charges me to keep it, occasionally, short. The tomatoes I have tried to grow have been more expensive – if better – than those I could buy in a city supermarket, and I have not been able to put up the capital to buy equipment to do my own preserves. Even my daily newspaper, which I have to use gasoline to go to buy, costs me more than it would have cost in the city. At times I have looked at my city friends the way the have provinces have looked at the have-nots in a federal conference, as if I were subsidizing them and they didn't realize it.

Look, I know I've done lots of things wrong. I ought to have bought a sheep for the lawn and started making my own soap instead of driving four miles to buy it at inflated rural prices. In the winters, I ought to have huddled over an oil stove rather than watching the fireplace cheerfully crackling away with the last of my paperback royalties. I have not, I promise you, lived extravagantly, and the old stone house where I've been hiding out – once the home of a working quarry-master – is more cottage than estate, even though it burns more fuel than Premier Davis's private jet. But one of the strongest lessons I have learned in my time away from the life I grew up with is that being a country mouse is at least as expensive as being a city mouse, and I don't think city mice realize it.

Am I wrong about this? I don't think so. I don't think the city slickers know what it costs us hayseeds to stay where we want to stay. You may want to add to what I've discovered. Or argue with my conclusions. Or tell me what you know about saving money in the country that – short of trying to ride my sheep to the store on Saturdays – I didn't think of when I was there. If you do, please drop me a line. I'd ask you to call me, but I know the cost of long distance. Boy, do I know the cost of long distance.

P.G.

✉ In the six months I have lived in the country, and in the six months I have not lived in Saskatoon (or Edmonton, or Calgary), I have discovered an important distinction between city mice and country mice: there are more mice in the country. There are also more mosquitoes, more grasshoppers, more days when the rain washes our road away. And yes, there seem to be more sunsets, more northern lights, more intimate moments, but I am not sure I am happy, though I'm happier than I was in Saskatoon.

There is a line on my forehead that no longer smooths away, and I have dried blisters under my wedding ring. Sometimes we forget to brush our teeth. In the city we talked about politics or literature. We wrote letters to the CBC and we *cared* when Allen Maitland pronounced Z "zee." We still care, but somehow the letters are not often mailed. Our political discussions begin well, but more often than not they dwindle into personal anxieties: whether our sewer lagoon will hold water, whether our well won't; whether sparks from the smudge could catch in the pasture. We spend our lives afraid of the nature we want to live close to: too much wind blows away the topsoil; too much snow blows in the road; too much rain makes the crops mould; too much sun brings hail. We find nature excessive and dangerous and yes, just a little bit boring.

Sometimes I live in the country.

Sometimes I live in the town.

Sometimes I long for cappuccino, too.

Kim Dales
Batoche, Saskatchewan

✉ As I sit here in the sunny peace of my own quiet backyard, I find it hard to believe I have spent my morning in battle – for that's how it is – with the city.

This city – Calgary – is a living maze fraught with obstacles and constantly changing. I live less than two miles from the Federal Building, where I have some business that must be done. Fortunately it is not urgent; I have made four attempts to drive to my destination and find a parking spot. None of them was successful. The first couple of times I was thwarted by closed roads, new one-way streets or temporary detours. The third and fourth efforts failed simply from my discouragement. After forty minutes or so of navigation, and no place to park within several blocks, I gave up. I look on my objective now as a kind of challenge, something to try when I have some spare time.

Then there is the dilemma of which bank I should transfer my account to. There are five branches of my bank within a mile or so of our house. Do I choose the one that is closest (by all of three blocks)? Do I choose the one that is near my grocery store (for convenience)? Or do I choose the one that is most distant (less temptation to withdraw my savings)? I spend so much time finding out what my choices are, and then deciding which is most appropriate, that my free time, my time to sew, to draw, to read, seems to disappear.

The city has its good points, too. Yet for us they are the contrasts to the hustle-bustle. A canoe ride down the river, with trees, bushes, even some wild animals on the banks. A bicycle ride through the grassy treed parks, a walk down to Sandy Beach for an evening picnic. These are the things that give us pleasure, living in the city. Do you suppose country people come downtown and drive around in rush-hour traffic to relax?

Hope Smith
Calgary

✉ When I was one year old my grandparents bought a five-acre hobby farm in what was then "the country" (now within sound of the intersection of Islington and Eglinton). As a child I spent idyllic weekends with my younger cousins gathering eggs, chasing rabbits and chickens and goats, smelling pigs and waddling like a duck. Those nostalgic childhood memories prompted Ed and me to move to the real country two years ago. We had bought a forty-seven-acre farm about twenty kilometres north of Orangeville and we moved in when the leaves on all the maples around the football-field-sized lawn were showing off their fall colours under a brilliant sun.

Since then we have experienced culture shock, some aspects as sweet as the promise of childhood memories, some as harsh as an unexpected assault.

The sweeter aspects include hosting giant picnic parties with neighbours, family and friends, with old-fashioned bag races and balloons hanging from the gingerbread on the verandah and prize ribbons and tables full of pot-luck surprises. I remember children running through a low-lying meadow and catching fireflies in a jar, then one small boy crying in the dark beside his father's car because he didn't want to go home. I remember sitting in the dark on the verandah very late in the warm summer night staring up at the incredible brilliance and sharpness of a sky full of stars. I remember watching for the school bus and waiting on the driveway as Esther (our dog) greets the bus and the driver and all the other children as well as her special ones. I remember stopping for a rest last April after delivering a load of chicken manure to the vegetable garden and hearing an incredible, still-unidentified bird song like a trickle of water and climbing up to lie on the picnic table under the spell of the sun and the song.

It is good for one's ego to be able to sit down to dine on the fruits of one's own labours – ham, bacon, roast pork, eggs, strawberries, ice cream, pumpkin pie. I must give credit for an awe-inspiring amount of muscle power expended and sweat produced.

In retrospect it is also amazing that we have survived. Twice the children and I have been caught in the car within two miles of home in snow we couldn't see through. The first time, the snow was a monster in a nightmare. We were rescued by an angelic neighbour in a four-wheel-drive jeep. The second nightmare would have killed us if no one had been home at the nearest house. The wind was so strong it made the cold feel like stabbing knives.

Not only the elements are harsh. Three times rural contractors have ripped off the "rich" newcomers from the city. It was especially hard because one of them was a close neighbour, all smiles and friendliness in the beginning.

I guess life is a constant learning experience. I didn't know my strawberry plants would give me two crops this summer. Is this a reward for nipping off all the blossoms, as instructed, last summer? I didn't know a dog like Esther (mixed heritage but definitely a hunter) could catch and eat a groundhog a day. I didn't know chickens had such a wide vocabulary or that they could growl. I didn't know roosters were such violent rapists. I had no idea that a boar's sexual equipment was really that shape. I thought Ed was joking, until I saw for myself.

Merrily Walker
St. Catharines, Ontario

✉ Last year my oldest son was in a serious accident. For two weeks while he was in a coma we weren't sure if he would live. For two months, while he was being shunted from ward to ward of the hospital and I was virtually living there, we wondered when or if he would ever be able to resume anything like a normal life. I could write a book about the hospital experience and the wonderful revelation it was of the better side of human nature. But that's another story. Here's what the country mice did for us:

Starting the day of the accident, I didn't cook a meal for at least two weeks. Dinner would appear – delivered to me if I was home (which was rare) or to the kids, or just left at the door (could you do *that* in the city?) – with a note, a bouquet of wild flowers, a sprig of autumn leaves, a jar of homemade preserves. Unknown to me, my friends had set up a phone chain to provide the meals. So that they didn't intrude unduly on my few precious moments at home with the rest of the kids, there were phone chains that handled news of my son's progress. Now, almost a year later, my son is back at school – not a hundred percent but okay. People still ask after him and their concern is real – sometimes tearful.

One of the things the city mice find hardest to accept when they come to the country is the kind of jungle telegraph that exists. The community is aware of who you are, what you do, how much you make, even if you watch soap operas or like to do your housework in the nude. It seems nosy. Country mice know better. It's a caring that we seem to have lost in our cities with our transience, our desperate search for privacy in an urban world of high-rises, condos, tiny house lots and jammed, high-volume shopping malls. We have developed a sadly unhuman (not inhumane) capacity to experience profound emotional highs and lows and yet not touch minds with the person touching elbows with us. We evolved as social animals. It goes against our genes to live in isolation without the support of the group.

You can have your Chinese dinners, newspaper and mail delivered to your door by people you don't know and will probably never need to be concerned about. You can have your cable TV. Sometimes I envy you but I'll stick with my rural community, supported when I need to be, knowing I'll do the same for them so not worrying about being beholden. I'll accept the bad roads, the need to plan a shopping trip carefully so it doesn't have to be repeated, the frequent power failures, the dust, the flies, the lack of time to go to beauty parlours, chic food stores, boutiques, even concerts and plays (although that's not really beyond grasp). I wouldn't swap what we have here for anything the city has to offer.

Joan Baumber
Bragg Creek, Alberta

✉ I have lived in the country for two months but I'm quickly discovering that you have to be organized to do it. Nothing is convenient in the country.

In Los Angeles, where I lived for the past five years, I was within five minutes' walking distance of grocery stores, gas stations, a laundromat, a bookstore, a liquor store and a library. I lived entirely by whim. If I suddenly wanted a bowl of Rocky Road ice cream at eleven at night I only had to step outside. Every day the paper came, the mail came, the garbage went and the water flowed. In the city, I never had to think about the logistics of basic living.

Now I live fifteen kilometres outside of Brooks, Alberta. I plan menus days and weeks in advance. I'm learning to anticipate my whims (which detracts considerably from their charm), and I am trying to control my cravings for Rocky Road ice cream at eleven PM. I don't drive my car on empty and if I want something new to read I have to write it myself. I can't afford to drive into town every day to pick up my mail and I don't hop back into bed on the weekend with the morning paper. Instead of one large garbage can under the sink, I now have three small ones: cans, compost and combustible. I think before I throw. The only home delivery I get is the water for the cistern, which I use sparingly. Flushing the toilet is a rare treat. Country living is not romantic and carefree.

Even so, I like driving home slowly on country roads with all their potholes, stray cows and slippery gravel. It's easier on my nerves than freeways, traffic jams and sirens. I like to feel the wind sweeping out the sky and fluffing up the trees. I am trying to forget the smog-ridden sky in the city where breathing was a luxury I tried to live without. I like to be wakened up in the morning by the neighbour's roosters crowing, rather than by their cars warming up. I enjoy spying on the private lives of the birds outside my front window more than on the lives of my neighbours across the street.

Perhaps what I like most is not always being entirely surrounded by people. I feel no more lonely here than I did in the city and I seem to have more energy to pay attention to my family and friends.

Sally Swanson
Brooks, Alberta

✉ When we first moved out to a rented farm house at Salem Corners, my wife Trudie (from whom I'm now separated) and I decided to become chicken farmers. We bought about a dozen fowl – an assortment of Sussex and Bantam chickens and some ducks – from a woman near Janetville. She told us to clip their wings, but didn't tell us how to do it. I wouldn't like a chicken to clip my wings; therefore, I didn't clip theirs. As a result, no fence was high enough to contain our birds. Not that it mattered; we enjoyed watching the ducks fly – until they disappeared one day. They hadn't gone far. They'd joined a neighbour's larger flock.

The neighbour was a gruff, hirsute (like me), unsentimental homesteader who probably despised my reluctance to clip the birds' wings. He showed me how to do it.

With their wings clipped, the ducks, especially the drake, became bad-tempered, but not as bad-tempered as the Sussex rooster. One day I was in the kitchen watching Trudie at the chicken farm feeding the birds. Suddenly, she turned and ran toward the house, but tripped in the long grass. The rooster, in hot pursuit, jumped onto her back and did a triumphant dance. From then on it terrorized us all, though we quickly learned how to fight back. The compassion we'd felt for the unclipped birds gave way to the survival instinct. Sometimes I enjoyed getting a good kick in and sending the cock back to his corner.

Bird-brained though they were, it didn't take the hens and ducks long to figure out that if they wanted to keep their eggs, they'd have to hide them. Since our acre of the fifty-acre farm wasn't manicured regularly, there were plenty of hiding places. Our flock grew, despite unseen but active predators and the fatal hand of my good intentions. I put a baby bath full of water out for the first ducklings and photographed them swimming in it. They enjoyed themselves so much that they were still swimming there when I left. Next morning, they were still there – drowned. The distance between the surface of the water and the edge of the tub was too great for them to climb. They were the first birds I buried.

One day, as I arrived home from the school where I taught, I saw Pyevaquette, our dog, outside the chicken huts. She was barking excitedly. I'd caught her a few times chasing a bird, so expected her to be after one again. As I walked toward her, a neighbour's dog bolted out of one of the huts, scattering feathers as it streaked by. I had six corpses to bury that time.

In the winter, I closed the huts' doors at night. One morning, I found another half-dozen corpses – apparently drained of blood. Rats? Weasels? That winter was cold (what winter isn't?). One rooster stayed out overnight and became an ice statue. Spring and summer were more kind and the flock multiplied, although no purebred Sussexes had survived the winter. And so it went – spring and summer multiplication, winter decimation.

One spring, our most colourful Bantam rooster developed a limp. It seemed to limp only when it knew or seemed to know that it was being watched – surely, a bird with its tiny brain couldn't play the same tricks as a dog. Still the limp became increasingly pronounced, and we worried for the rooster's survival. At last, pity overcoming my fear of embarrassment, I stuffed the lame bird in a sack and drove it to the vet. Trudie chose to stay at home.

In the waiting room, there was the usual assembly of worm-ridden, unhappy cats and dogs. I shuffled over to a corner, watched closely by pets and their owners, and sat in a chair, the sack at my feet. When the receptionist called me over, I mumbled that I was concerned about my cock. She blushed and looked in the sack. The bird obligingly made some bird movements and sounds. Formerly tired dogs strained at their leashes. I was told to return to my seat and wait. The woman was not going to relieve me of my agony.

Eventually, Dr. Brown appeared at the door of the waiting room, smirked and told me to bring my rooster in. I picked up the sack and followed him, pretending not to hear the titters behind me.

The vet checked the bird out and found it to have a sound body if not a sound mind. His look suggested that he doubted the soundness of mind of someone who'd spend time and money nursing a bird that could make a good meal.

Half an hour later, I was home. I opened the sack. The rooster flew out and strutted around the yard. There was no suggestion of a limp.

David Sims
Toronto

✉ My observations on the relative merits of rural living:

You can see the Northern Lights (in season).

You can carry on loud outdoor arguments with your wife without letting the neighbours in on your prodigious command of colourful obscenities.

You can take a leak off your front verandah (in season) and not worry about being arrested.

You can leave your beer out on the back porch and no one will steal it.

You don't have to look in the newspaper for a crisis – there is usually a choice of several at hand. To wit: impassable lane; broken water pump; goats in garden; chickens in garden; goats and chickens not in garden, nor barn, nor in sight.

Grant Boyd
Thurso, Quebec

✉ We lived in the country for four years, and only recently returned to Toronto, where we lived all our lives until we moved to the farm.

I am not exactly sure of all the reasons for making that move initially, but it had something to do with feeling over-stimulated and wanting to live a more self-reliant, less chaotic life. We both had grand-fathers who were farmers and so we had both, in our childhood sum-mers, smelled the new-mown hay, drunk milk still warm from the cow, pumped our water directly from the well, played cards at night by the light of a coal-oil lamp.

When we made our decision (it was only after our younger son had gone off to college in another town), we intended to spend our time without the interruption of telephones, without the temptations that a city like Toronto holds. Instead we would respectively sculpt and perhaps write, paint and certainly improve musical skills long gone to seed.

We found a small – fifty-five acres – farm approximately one hour from the big city, on the crest of a hill, looking out across the country-side to a beautiful vista. We had the experience of designing our own home, as the existing farm house was only a tar-paper shack. With the large expanses of windows throughout the house we could al-ways be in touch with the outdoors and nature.

We became aware of birds (who would have guessed it?) and enamoured of them; we had bird feeders outside almost every win-dow. The highlight of our day was the appearance of some beauti-fully coloured species, and we, too, referred constantly to our Peterson. We felt particularly honoured by the annual visit of a bluebird fam-ily. Trees also became living things, with colours and shapes that held us in awe.

However, creativity somehow didn't quite take over in our daily lives.

While the farm was given over to the care of a real farmer, my hus-band found much of his time was spent grooming the five acres sur-rounding the house. He certainly had fun with his tractors and sundry pieces of farm-type equipment and of course he took to wearing plaid jackets and steel-toed construction boots. He even began dropping the s on most words and spoke of places being three or four "mile" down the road. We looked forward to the excitement of the weekly farm sale and worried about how the weather would affect the crops.

As for me, I found myself staring out the windows, almost mesmer-ized, or maybe drugged, by nature, watching for hours on end the light changing on the landscape from season to season. It was quite a show – but it didn't move either of us to sculpt, paint, produce music or in fact do anything very creative. After a few years I felt at times that my brain had stopped functioning. I could not seem to remember things I had learned in the past.

Winter, not my favourite season by far, began the first day of November and ended in April. We lived in the snow belt and were convinced that if only one snowflake fell in Ontario, it fell on our property. Often, by Christmas, the snow cleared by the ploughs was piled halfway up the hydro poles. Road conditions became crucial and we felt secure knowing that our trusty snowmobile sat in readiness.

There was, on the other hand, the absolutely breathtaking picture-postcard view of the wintry countryside that we took in from our cosy position before a roaring fire, and the crisp, sunny days of that same season when one could walk for miles and make the first imprint in the snow all the way.

When we first moved here, for months my sleep was interrupted by the absolute deadly silence and inky blackness of night. A branch brushing against the roof was enough to start my heart pounding and I frequently rose from my bed to peer out the windows into that endless and unbroken darkness, wondering if anyone or anything was out there, or if it had all disappeared.

But I became used to it and now, having returned to the city, I find myself awake at night and again peering through the windows, but for the opposite reason. It is extraordinary how noisy and well-lit our supposedly quiet residential street is. I know for sure that all the world is outside my door.

In the end, I think our experiment in tranquillity was defeated by the absence of kindred spirits. How I longed for an evening of stimulating conversation or gentle kibbitzing over a bridge game, a dinner shared by like-minded souls and the warm, happy feelings that result from such encounters.

It was not difficult to recognize loneliness looking out on those huge, unpeopled expanses of rolling hills. But if a feeling of loneliness overtakes me in Toronto, I need only cross the street into the park where young mothers push their small children on swings or coax them down the slide, where neighbours walk playful dogs and uniformed schoolgirls kick a soccer ball through their phys-ed class. In short, where there is life.

We think we now have the perfect solution: a townhouse in Toronto and a summer cottage on a beautiful lake. This should satisfy our need for both community and solitary living with just the balance we all seek.

The experience of living in a different milieu did change me. I see that now. I have become a person who, while needing the company of good friends, also cherishes privacy and quiet times alone or with my husband. The appreciation and delight in nature will never leave me and would not have been awakened had it not been for that move to the country.

Loretta Rosnick
Toronto

✉ My friend Tricia and I were once city mice, but long ago we forgot our city ways.

A week ago, I stepped out of my kitchen door onto a porch. Beside me, wild, untended roses competed successfully with maple saplings, burdocks, ragweed and goldenrod. From that porch, breathing untainted air, I surveyed classical pastoral beauty. In a day or two, those hills, those patterns of wheat, corn, fence rows, trees, those silos (which, when I first arrived, always made me think of Roman lookout towers), the five or six hillside farm houses, the spring river-summer creek ribboned along the valley – all would be lost, as non-existent as the sound of the philosopher's falling tree.

For seven years, I got up each morning in places rich with the silence of natural sounds and opened the bedroom blinds to look out onto fields, hills, valleys, woods and swamps onto scenes that changed subtly as shadows shortened, turned, lengthened, as the seasons rolled around. Now I wake to the surging drone of cars, open my curtains and look out onto a brick wall.

What have I done? So far, despite my good intentions to accept change as a valuable experience, I haven't gone through a single day without a few unconscious and many conscious groans. How can I help but think of the sweet smell of freshly mown hay, even of a manure-covered field, when I'm out running along streets thick with invisible but palpable poison. A few months ago, a startled deer ran by my side the length of a scrub field. I'd met other deer occasionally, groundhogs often, some porcupines, a muskrat or two; and always there were the birds, notably the redwing blackbirds, which sat on telephone wires or fence posts chirping their unmusical warnings as I ran by on one of my several three- or six-mile running routes, and the herons lifting gracefully out of the steaming swamp, more like prehistoric flying reptiles than birds. And, of course, there were the always-interested spectators, the milk-laden and the doomed cows.

Here in Toronto, morning steals like a shroud into our bedroom. There will be no direct sun for an hour or two to brighten these three gloomy rooms. I imagine the September sun in Sunderland, a concentrated, unshimmering red ball burning the morning mist over the eastern woods, which at this time of day appear merely as long, dark patches hovering over grey fields. Slowly, mist fades, and the sun, golden now, creates a landscape heavy with corn.

Back to Reality (with a capital R and fangs). My head hums, packed with indistinguishable noises. The "Enigma Variations" are sabotaged by the ceaseless sound of the city. Peace of mind and quietude have been banished. A part of me must keep fighting a defensive battle against ineluctable, ever-encroaching noise.

In our farmhouse kitchen (a room that was almost half as big as this apartment) we endured invasions of flies in the spring, troops of ants in the summer and families of field mice in the fall and winter. Here there are colossal silverfish and armies of small things that scuttle for cover when the light goes on.

We haven't been to a baseball game, nor have we walked to a movie, though we could easily do so; that is, we could walk to the cinema, but not through the doors. We had looked forward to going to movies, plays and art exhibits when we thought I was coming to a job. Instead, we walk to Loblaws and debate the comparative values of various brands of bread, while we count and recount our dwindling supplies of silver and spirit. No, I lie: Tricia's spirit, despite my efforts, is still high. Although she prefers living in the country, she is excited by the city, by the never-ending parade of people, by the conversion of our apartment into a home, by the fulfillment of a five-year dream to study jazz at Humber College. She sees things in perspective. To her, Toronto is not the scene of eternal damnation. It's a strange, brief but invigorating stage on a longer journey, most of which will take place against a rural backdrop.

I've always wondered if the neighbours in our mirror apartment across the alley could see me walking naked to the bathroom, but I've carried that small worry into the street where it's become the paranoid anxiety that the crowds can see me naked with huge U for unemployed (unemployable?) branded into my skin.

The city is the projection of my demons. In the country my angelic but quiescent nature was nourished. Perhaps the demons need this release – perhaps I need to feel their presence more sharply, so that when I do return to the country, I won't sleep.

David Sims
Toronto

✉ The farrier has just left, after trimming the horses' feet – the horses that our grown children still adore, seldom ride or groom and to whom I lug buckets of water through the storms and snow drifts to the distant barn. The horses I drive some twenty miles once a month to buy feed for. Would I be without them? Never! For their curious ears have more than a dozen times alerted us to grazing deer and running foxes.

Trimming of hooves every five weeks: $24. Winter feed and hay: $60 per month.

I watch now, sitting in the September sun, the hundreds of blackbirds gathering on the hydro wires that string the full length of our farm laneway. The laneway that oftentimes fills in four times a day during those nasty winter blizzards. The old tractor couldn't handle the heavy snows so we bought a backhoe (doesn't every family have one?) to remove the immense snow drifts and to gravel and grade the drive during the good months.

Backhoe: $10,000.

On Saturday I will load the four-wheel-drive with the week's accumulation of garbage and fall clean-up and drive to the township's disposal site – which used to be called the dump. There, on a windy hill, I will gather with residents and exchange "Howareyagittenons," discuss the weather and talk of who's running in the upcoming municipal elections . . . amidst the dust and flying pages of city newspapers.

Used four-wheel-drive: $2,500 – plus municipal taxes to allow one to dispose.

The farm's water supply is just fine, thank you! Still, out of habit and memories of a lack of the wonderful stuff, we share the bath water, space laundry loads and turn off the tap in between brushing and rinsing our teeth. We've been dry for up to two months and have put in two well systems since we moved here.

Two wells with pumps: $3,000.

The chief mouser, a twelve-year-old cat by the name of Slugger-guts (she's a fat fighter), quit and refuses to be replaced by a younger model. So we now have to trap the mice that mysteriously march into this old house in the fall.

Mouse traps: $6.50 for the season. Feeding retired mouser: $7 per month.

The new guard dog is delightful and eager to please but she is scared of thunderstorms, the dark and the strange sounds that fill the country air. So she lounges on the carpet by the fireplace and the old arthritic guard dog claims the chesterfield after we have gone to bed. Mildred, the new neighbour's hound, often stays over to do sentry duty – no charge.

Two dogs: $38 per month for feed and vet.

It is difficult getting a job in the country so my husband supported a business venture of mine for two years. Due to the economy, the business is now up for sale (or folded) after I spent $2,000 for gasoline alone. Capital investment I won't go into.

Cost of wife's financial independence: difficult to calculate.

Our fifteen-year-old son now has a "long-distance" girlfriend to whom each three-minute call costs fifty cents – he says he'll pay his charges from the part-time job miles and miles away I have to drive him to. At the end of each month when the phone bill arrives, I expect to get my walking papers from my husband – I occasionally talk to relatives in Gander and Halifax and to children in Toronto and neighbours just down the hill.

Telephone bill during a good month: $86.

Would I ever give all this up? Where else can you walk out to feed the animals or putter in the garden in pyjamas, or have a rip-roaring family argument that only those cowering assorted pets hear? And hang up the wash that perhaps isn't the cleanest in town? Would I – could I – move?

Only when I have to toboggan the groceries in from the main road during the winter do I think about a nice apartment at the Harbour Castle in Toronto . . . but then it's February, when most people are thinking about going south anyway!

Brenda LeDrew Keyes
Palgrave, Ontario

✉ I grew up in Northern Ontario, in a community of two thousand people. Although we lived in a village, my family spent much of its time in the rural environs of our town, including summer months at a secluded cottage. My first trip to "the city" – Toronto – must have come very early in my childhood, because I can't remember a time when I didn't feel that living "up north" meant missing something. In fact, growing up and getting older simply meant learning more and more about the outside world.

Our only tenuous links to the city were formed by the media: magazines, radio and later television – although I was eleven years old, in 1957, before we had regular, reasonably clear TV reception.

I don't think I was the classic country bumpkin when I came to Toronto, to go to university, in 1965, but I *was* wide-eyed. Nothing about my new urban home escaped my attention. I was literally dizzy with an appreciation of the diversity of city life. I saw poverty and wealth screaming contradictions at one another on almost every street corner. I walked through the old Holt Renfrew store on Bloor Street West with the same sense of marvel Margaret Mead must have felt seeing her first tribesman.

And when I went around the corner to Yorkville Avenue, I heard a folk singer eulogizing the death of civilization. I had to disagree with him. I was studying the poems of T.S. Eliot and the literary philosophy of Northrop Frye. I was seeing my first Impressionist paintings at the Art Gallery of Ontario and attending Harold Pinter plays at the Hart House Theatre. I could read the *New York Times* any morning in the library and see a first-run Hollywood movie any evening. Instead of feeling like the victim of social anorexia nervosa, I felt alive.

Certainly, as a young woman alone in the city, I experienced moments of terror and frustration, because my freedom of movement has always been restricted by the dangers of city darkness. And even though the *daylight* hours are no longer entirely safe in an urban centre like Toronto, I still love living in the city.

I battle traffic for the privilege of choosing among six different flavours of croissants. I stood in line for hours to see Judy Chicago's "The Dinner Party" at the art gallery, and I take night courses every winter. My only regret is that I can choose but one from the thousands that are offered.

I feel, however, that I must reveal what was at first a confusing turn of events. I have just recently started to work at writing short stories. What I'm finding out is that all of my characters, plots and settings are coming out of the north country. I can only conclude that, although I have an ongoing need for the stimulation of the city, where the products of other peoples' creativity are more readily available, I am turning back now to what I considered a cultural void in my youth, to discover a richness of first-hand experience that has not been equalled since.

Sandra Steele
Scarborough, Ontario

✉ The most striking thing about living in the country is just how graphic some things are. If I want water, I know exactly where it comes from: a well that's fifty feet from the house. My biffy is fifty feet the other way. Thank God. Once a year, I move it. I have to. Until recently, if I wanted light, I had to buy kerosene. I had to clean and fill the lamps every night. My point is that I can see how much energy I use; I can see how much waste I make. It is a lesson that is quickly learned up here, and, alas, it is a lesson that I manage to forget immediately when I go into town.

Another thing I've noticed is that my attitude toward firearms has changed. When I moved here I wouldn't have dreamed of owning a gun. Now I have two. I would never have killed anything. Now I have a hunting licence. It all started when a porcupine was eating one of the sills in my house. Right To Life for Porky or me living in a pile of lumber where this noble house once stood? I borrowed a gun and shot him.

Rick Jamieson
Collingwood, Ontario

✉ When my husband had to work this past fall, I spent an average of two hours a day splitting wood. The wood has to be stacked in a shed to keep dry and I'm sure I've carried more than four cords out of the woods, one piece at a time, over my shoulders. This does not include, of course, filling wood-boxes for a cooking and heating stove, hauling water by bucket (good, clean, spring-fed brook water) and keeping the ice open with a hatchet. In the spring, if my husband isn't here for us to do it together, I light a large fire in the fireplace and tend it all day long while the maple sap boils down, always making sure that the buckets under each tree-spout are emptied twice a day. There are forty of them.

Since this is our slack time of the year, I am making what I call "Renfrew Rustics." I hope to incorporate my own small company this summer. I will be selling unique hand-made furniture for very reasonable prices.

In my spare time, I write short stories, do various carpentry work such as shingling roofs, putting up clapboard, et cetera. And I have two children, a boy three and a half and a girl eleven months, to whom I also devote time and energy. The point of all this is that a five-foot three-inch 107-pound woman can do all of these things.

We didn't have the money to buy a farm. My husband and I lived in a tent for six months. Doug cut all the trees for our cabin. I followed and peeled off the bark. We carried the beams, with help from others, to the flattest spot we could find, got a book from the library and went to work. Now we have a lovely little A-frame cabin, a twelve-by-sixteen foot woodshed and tool shed, and an A-frame outhouse. I'll bet it's the only one in Nova Scotia. All of this we did with no power tools – only our bare hands, mostly. It took us six months to build the fireplace, and we carried (in a wheelbarrow) more than forty tons of sand and gravel from the road to our house. This past summer, while my husband worked in Halifax, I picked and shovelled four holes more than four feet deep, two feet wide and six feet long, for a partial foundation. And together we spent hours mixing the cement and filling the holes. Perhaps you can understand why it irks me when women are portrayed as useless. People still come to see us here and tell my husband he's done a good job, then ask me if I helped at all. But not too many, because they don't come back.

Martha Laugher
Elmsdale, Nova Scotia

✉ I lived in the city where prostitutes, thieves, musicians, freaks and clowns live. During the warm day the midgets played baseball in the narrow alley behind the abandoned casino, and sometimes the prostitutes, with their hair pinned up, would lean out their windows and watch the midgets and laugh.

In the early morning and late evening everyone could smell the sausage and hot peppers cooking on the restaurant grills. Steam and smoke would rise from the grills. One restaurant was red and very pretty, especially in the early morning or after it rained, and the sunlight was brass. A ballet dancer had once eaten there.

Sometimes in the streets at night there would be a drunken, stumbling parade with trombonists and clarinetists and midgets leading the way and throwing confetti. Everyone would follow laughing and dancing and singing like very good drunken friends. Ophelia, the theatre-set designer, would follow us, sketching frantically, trying to catch foolish gestures and smiling faces. Sometimes a clown would trip another clown, who would then pinch the other's nose until he cried sadly. Then sometimes the clowns would chase some midgets through the alleys and the piles of rubble, through coloured doors left standing in the midst of demolished buildings. Some people would hold hands and form large dancing circles. Lesbians in nuns' costumes enjoyed holding hands and singing in unison. They also enjoyed dancing alone in the darkness. Sometimes their cheeks touched. The tambourine player kept watch over them while he jangled his tambourine.

Morning and evening. Day and night.

Then everyone fell asleep to the sound of a single trumpet. In the distance there were gold and silver sky-scrapers, glowing in the morning sun.

In the country, big stretched-out wheat fields and green places with trees. The sun all over everything. The sky all over everything. It has no zenith. Everything bright and the sound of buzzing. The air is buzzing. The roads covered in dust and the fence covered in high grass, and the kanola fields yellow and bright. Everything large and bright and full of distant sound, and a wind comes and blows the grass. The sun lowers and the sky is blue and green. It becomes cool. In the spring the land is dark and green. A star appears alone. Someone stands in a field or beside a slough. The stars form all over in the blue-black, like a polka-dot handkerchief around someone's neck. Someone thinks about aloneness.

In the early morning the sun comes and the birds make noises. The pasture is wet and the smell of grass comes upward. The smell all over everything. Yellow is mixed in the wet grass. The sun and the fields are coming together. The sun is on the slough and it is yellow and glowing. There is one tiny insect flying above the shining fields, where the sun is, and it is beginning to warm. Then the sky is all over everything. Not far away there are sand dunes and aspen trees.

In the spring I went fishing in the valley where there is the lone creek coming from the Cypress Hills. The little creek was deep and green. It began to snow and it was silent all around. Lightning would flash and the sky would turn green. The clouds drifted, and the sun came out and was glowing through the falling snow. I could see the trout flashing golden in the green water. I can't help having dreams about it.

For some time I studied the arch of a duck's flight.

M.D. Hetherton
Swift Current, Saskatchewan

✉ Yesterday I woke early to the sound of rain – on the roof, at the window – that insistent, relentless rhythm that gives a grey morning its own music. Coming out of sleep, my first response was jubilation, a learned response from those years spent in the country when a good, pelting rain meant a cistern full to the brim. And that in turn meant, for a glorious, frivolous day or two, having as much water as we wanted for washing and bathing – until we became sensible again and returned to our conserving habits. In our old farmhouse on the edge of Belleville we depended on rainwater collected in the cistern for all else but drinking, since our dug well was a shallow and unreliable source. The cistern was a concrete cavern beneath the kitchen floor, accessible only through a small trap door, which opened directly in front of the sink. When it was full it held about one thousand gal-lons, and we could open up the floor and reach down into the dark-ness and touch the cool surface or pick off a bit of floating debris. In the fall there were always dead leaves to contend with, in the spring pale-yellow maple flowers, in the winter foolish field mice who had come indoors and, mistaking the space for a haven from the cat, drowned and bloated before sinking to the oozy bottom.

When it was raining, as it was yesterday, we could sit in the kitchen by the wood stove and listen to the cistern filling. The sound varied depending on the amount of water already in, and as the years passed our ears became knowledgeable, attuned. Had we been country folk in a book or a play, we might have said "Yup, she's jest about full up" or something of that ilk. But we weren't even stage country, we were city livers who had left Toronto to live on the land (two acres) with an eagerness that made us receptive to every change. In the eight years we were there we remained optimistic. We spoke only of the softness of the rainwater, the wonderful suds it made in the tub, the sheen it gave our hair. We learned to ignore the odours of rotting leaves, and the dead mice, we said, gave our water body. For although we cleaned out the bottom during every summer's dry spell, there was always an accumulation of dark, stenchy stuff. The dregs to a fine old wine.

And now we live in a city again – this time Ottawa, far more human and humane than Toronto, but still a city – and have sold the house in the country. (The new owners have drilled a well and no longer need the cistern.) And when it rains now, the sound is all outdoors. My snug city house allows not a drop inside.

I am quite untouched by this rain. The water flows off the roof, into the eavestroughs and down the spouts into the gutters and away, rivulets down the street without meaning or use. The weather and I have little connection. Rain means only this: that I must take my umbrella when I walk to the grocery. And there too the irony of change waits: my vegetables and fruits are shipped in from gardens where endless sprays ensure that crops won't fail. But I remember the harshness of Augusts when vines and stalks succumbed to drought no matter how well they had been tended. Rain mattered then. We would lie in bed at night and listen to the distant thud and roll of thunder and hope for rain. Clench our fists and *hope*. I can't imagine, in this present life, ever praying for rain.

That's what I don't like about being back in the city. The world around us doesn't affect us the same way it does in the country. We are unconnected. We can turn on taps any time, we can shower for as long as our hot-water heaters hold out, we can run dishwashers and washing machines all day long – all we have to do is pay for the water we waste, but we can waste it if we choose. The only consequence we feel is the emptying of our bank account.

In the country, with a cistern, we were intimate with consequence. I miss the immediacy here.

Isabel Huggan
Ottawa

"I've Got a Little (Canadian) List"

This is a contest, too. When, in the summer of 1984, I heard Eric Donkin sing his wonderful Stratford version of "I've got a little list" in *The Mikado*, I arranged to have Eric come into the studio and perform it for *Morningside*. Then I challenged people to write their own versions. One of our producers, by the way, thought the word-and-rhythm patterns of Gilbert and Sullivan would be too tough to parody, and we made a little bet. I won, and here are some of the reasons.

✉ As someday it may happen that a victim must be found
I've got a little list, I've got a little list
Of theatre-group offenders that might well be underground
And who never would be missed, they never would be
    missed.
There's the chronic reminiscer on the way things used to be
And who never did it this way so "for gosh sakes, don't ask
    me,"
And the carpenter who drops his tools and simply walks
    away,
And the actress who expects her props delivered on a tray,
And the helpless souls who cry, "Oh do my make-up, I insist."
They never would be missed, they never would be missed.

Chorus: We've got them on the list, we've got them on the list
        And they never would be missed, they never would
            be missed.

There's the high-soprano prompter who projects to the
    outside
With her penetrating hiss, we've got her on the list.
And the other one who falls asleep when you've completely
    dried –
She never would be missed, he never would be missed.
And the pseudo-crit who praises with enthusiastic tone
All other clubs but this and all directors but his own,
And the guy who rings the telephone when sound cues read
    "dogs bark,"
And dictatorial SMs who demand you toe the mark,
And all those lighting men who on their volts and amps insist –
Well, *they* really would be missed, our light men would be
    missed.

Chorus: Oh we've got them on the list, we've got them on the list.
        And we know they would be missed, our members
            would be missed.

Joan Bruce
North Battleford, Saskatchewan

✉ As some day it may happen that a victim must be found
I've got a little list, I've got a little list
Of society offenders who might well be underground,
And who never would be missed, who never would be
    missed!
There's the pestilential nuisances who ask you, "What's your
    sign?"
All the people who charge fortunes and then make you stand
    in line,
All candidates who shake your hand and give your bum a pat,
And cranks who push religion and insist the earth is flat,
And all the dolts at parties who insist on getting pissed –
They'd none of them be missed, they'd none of them be
    missed.

Chorus: He's got 'em on the list – he's got 'em on the list;
          And they'll none of 'em be missed – they'll none of
          'em be missed.

There're the CBC announcers, all chummy to a fault,
And Scientologists – I've got them on the list!
And the bloated chartered bankers who are laughing to their
    vaults –
They never would be missed, they never would be missed.
Then the idiot who prattles that the world is safe from war
If only those damned peaceniks would understand the score;
And American ambassadors who lecture us, at length,
About our social services and troops not up to strength;
And that singular anomaly, the three-day novelist –
I don't think they'd be missed. I'm sure they'd not be missed.

Chorus: He'd got them on the list – he's got them on the list;
          And I don't think they'll be missed – I'm sure they'll
          not be missed!

And the bloody-minded critics who are all now rather rife;
The meddling moralist – I've got *him* on the list.

All developers and salesmen and campaigners all pro-life –
They'd none of them be missed, they'd none of them be
    missed.
And apologetic statesmen of a compromising kind,
Such as Brian Whosit, Edward Thing and John – oh, never
    mind.
And all the other leaders who've been through the ballyhoo,
The choice of whom I'm leaving all completely up to *you*.
But it really doesn't matter whom you put upon the list;
For they'd none of 'em be missed, they'd none of 'em be
    missed.

Chorus: You may put 'em on the list – you may put 'em on the
        list;
        And they'll none of 'em be missed – they'll none of
        'em be missed!

D.B. Scott
Cambridge, Ontario

As someday it may happen that a victim must be found,
I've got a little list, I've got a little list.
Of language violators who might well be underground
And who never would be missed, who never would be
    missed.
There're the fulsome politicians who avow to prioritize
And bureaucratic managers whose plans all concretize,
Or play-by-play announcers who think silence spoils the
    mood,
Or athletes in the post-game shows who say they've done
    "real good,"
Or boring rock musicians who give interviews when pissed,
They'd none of them be missed, they'd none of them be
    missed.

Chorus

There's the women who think "person" is the only word to
    use –
The language they would twist – I've got them on my list.
And the people who say "anyways" and "how's it goin' with
    youse?"
They never would be missed, they never would be missed.
The evangelist who preaches of the everlasting glow,
Available to anyone who sends in all his dough,
And reporters on the TV news who always seem to yell,
Concluding from their vast research that only time will tell,
And the doctrinaire politicos: the Marxist-Leninists.
I don't think they'll be missed, I know they won't be missed.

Chorus

And the nuclear proponents who explain how we'll survive,
Why do these fools exist? Let's put them on the list.
And the economic pundits whose opinions never jive,
They'd none of them be missed, they'd none of them be
    missed.
And the people with computers that can interface all night,
What's a user-friendly program? Or a modem? I don't know –
    I'll byte.
There's mis-statement, point in time, misspeak and time
    frame, too.
The task of filling up the blanks I'd rather leave to you,
But it really doesn't matter whom you put upon the list,
For they'd none of them be missed, they'd none of them be
    missed.

Paul McLaughlin
Toronto

✉ After living through this summer with tourists all around,
I've got a little list, I've got a little list
Of horrid traffic sinners who might well be underground,
And who never would be missed, who never would be
    missed.
There're the thoughtless operators who pull out in your face,
All people who have vacant minds and lack of common grace,
All people who must pass you when there isn't any room,
And drivers who do silly things that threaten you with doom,
And all the many others who common sense resist –
They'd none of them be missed, they'd none of them be
    missed.

Chorus

The driver who must tail-gate and the others of his kind,
The would-be Grand Prix-ist – I've got him on the list.
And the underpowered trailerists that make your trip a grind –
They never would be missed, they never would be missed.
Then the idiot who brakes when he's halfway through a
    curve,
The rider of the yellow line who forces you to swerve;
And the driver from the prairies where the ground is almost
    flat,
Who crawls around the corners, then takes off like a bat.
And that all-too-common pest: the gawking dawdler-ist –
I don't think he'd be missed. I'm sure he'd not be missed.

Chorus

And the easterner who must travel more miles in fewer days,
The grim vacationist – I've got him on the list.
All ghouls that gape at accidents and clutter up the 'ways –
They'd none of them be missed, they'd none of them be
    missed.
And ponderous motor homes that persist in going slow,

Impeding streams of many cars that really want to go;
And drivers who insist on the wrong lane for their turn –
Their antics while in motion are enough to make you burn.
But it really doesn't matter whom you put upon the list,
For they'd none of them be missed, they'd none of them be
    missed.

Betty and Art Fish
Winfield, British Columbia

✉ There's the breed of modern poet whose new opus doesn't
    scan
And nobody can read it, though he claims a moron can;
And the literary giant who writes novels by the score,
Each with half a million words in it, and sometimes even more,
Every chapter is so boring one can't see why he'd persist!
Thank Heaven for the list. They too are on the list.

Peter R. Penny
Plaster Rock, New Brunswick

✉ … There're the pestilential neighbours with noisy dogs at
    home
Who go to work and leave the barking brutes all day alone,
All neighbours who have little kids who climb my favourite
    tree
And those who, when I'm busiest, invite themselves for tea,
The lovelorn adolescents in my alley for a tryst –
I don't think they'd be missed. I'm sure they'd not be missed.

Joan Beecroft
Edmonton

✉ ... There're the song-contest creators who claim amateurs
can win
Yet wait with bated breath for demo records to come in.
Contestants have a week from when the contest first begins
To write, arrange, record and send (it helps if you are twins),
And our premier has decided that the winners are "Floyd
Quinn's"
We've got them on our list under "Orchestrated sins."

Jean Hanlon
Wentworth, Nova Scotia

✉ ... The number-one expendable, to which I now allude
Insists that when I'm speaking he really must intrude.
He disapproves of "Moeart" as well as "Djung" and "Frood"
The thing I'd like to do to him admittedly is crude.
I've got him on my Liszt, he's on my Chopin' Liszt,
And he never will be miszt, he never will be miszt.

J.P. Slugworthy
New Westminster, British Columbia

Nicaraguan
Journal

Chris Brookes is a Newfoundland radio producer,
journalist and man of the theatre – he was one of the
central figures in the cultural rebirth that took place in
his home province in the past decade or so – who spent
some time, in the fall of 1984, living and working
among the people of Nicaragua, trying, as did a number
of Canadians at that time, to see what he could find
out for himself about the complex politics of a nation
that was so close to us and yet so far away. Chris paid
for his trip by doing some work in the theatre. From
time to time he recorded his impressions of life behind
the headlines, and sent them along to us.

October 16, 1984

I'm writing from the tiny farming village of Cantimploras, in the south of Nicaragua. I'm here to give a theatre workshop for the village drama group – and besides, I've been curious to find out what rural peasants think about their upcoming elections. November 4 will be Nicaragua's first election since the Sandinista revolution in 1979.

Cantimploras is a peaceful little place, unlike some regions in northern Nicaragua, where villages are often raided by the "*contras*" – the United States-backed invaders who are trying to topple the government, or interfere with the election, or both.

In this southern region of the country the only war going on at the moment is the battle of the buses. And I can count myself a veteran of that war now. It took me three hours to get here by bus from the capital city of Managua, and the one I took was like a travelling circus. It was designed for forty-eight passengers – but I counted one hundred thirty people crammed into it, all sweating in the heat. Nobody could move an inch.

The circus started before we even left the Managua bus station – with an Amazing Acrobatic Act. A crowd of street vendors somehow managed to squeeze in the front door of the bus and navigate their way through the wall-to-wall human sandwich, until they eventually reached the rear door where they popped out one by one like champagne corks. Their performance was rendered more impressive by the fact that each one juggled armfuls of things for sale. In just five minutes, an incredible amount of stuff passed through the bus: fried chicken; oranges; fried bananas; coconut cookies; caramel toffees; rice and bananas and coleslaw wrapped in a palm leaf; pork rinds; milk; Coca-Cola; ice; nine different kinds of fruit juices. And a blind harmonica player asking for spare change.

Each salesperson was yelling to be heard over the voices of his or her competitors – and over Bob Marley and the Wailers blaring over the bus radio. This show was repeated, with a different cast of characters, in every major town where the bus stopped. When I was finally deposited alone by the side of the highway near Cantimploras, it was like a different world: cattle grazing quietly; flocks of green parrots passing overhead; and whole tea parties of yellow butterflies fluttering silently over every mud puddle in the road.

It seems like a different world politically, too. In the cities, billboards and walls are covered with slogans of the seven parties competing in this election. There are outdoor rallies every weekend, and radio and television programs are dotted with paid political announcements.

In Cantimploras, there are no billboards, no slogans – and since the village has no electricity, no television, either. Here, the main topic of conversation lately has been baseball. Kids play it after school, adults play it after work in the fields, and for the past few evenings everyone has gathered around their battery radios to listen to the World Series, broadcast here in Spanish.

Because of the elections, the Cantimploras baseball team is losing their best pitcher next week: Felipe, the village schoolteacher. He's a Cuban. And along with the other Cuban volunteer teachers in the country, he's being sent home before election day. Apparently the government wants to avoid undue criticism from Washington about "Cuban influence in Nicaragua."

I've been staying with Uriel, the second-best pitcher in Cantimploras. Uriel is also an actor with the village theatre group. And last Sunday was quite a struggle for him. The last night of the World Series – and he was supposed to perform in a variety show in Escalante, a community ten kilometres away. The show was a benefit for the Sandinista youth group in Escalante.

Uriel supports the Sandinistas. He says he'll vote for them on election day, and he figures all his neighbours will, too. The way he sees it, it's the Sandinistas who built the road, the school and the health clinic in his community, and who advance farm credit to his co-operative. The other parties, he says, talk big in the cities but they don't care about poor communities like Cantimploras.

Anyway, the theatre group trooped off to do its duty. About a hundred people showed up, the skits and songs went over well, and at five *cordobas* a head admission, the show pulled in a good donation for the Sandinista youth group. By the time everyone climbed aboard the truck to head for home, it was pitch dark. Fireflies waved from the bushes like forgotten cigarettes. The truck driver turned on his radio.

"Hey! Listen! Kirk Gibson just hit a homer! Let's hear it for the Detroit Tigers!" A huge cheer went up from the back of the truck.

"And let's hear it for the Sandinista Front!" Another huge cheer.

It was a curious sight, ideologically speaking. A truckful of Nicaraguan peasants bumping through the darkness, rooting for the American League and for the Sandinistas in the same breath.

Well, one of their teams has won, anyway. And the big game for their other team comes up in another fortnight.

October 23, 1984

I'm writing this week in a confused state of mind. The election is now just ten days away, and events are unfolding rapidly. But I've learned that few things in this country are as simple as they seem.

You wake up in the morning here, sleepily turn on the radio and the newscast is full of Ronald Reagan, the CIA, fears of a United States invasion, battles between the Nicaraguan army and the Washington-backed *contras* in the north, peace, war, confusion, and the news that the Nicaraguan Independent Liberal Party has decided to withdraw from the election. The other six parties are in an uproar. According to the radio, the liberal leader took the decision after consulting with the United States embassy. Suddenly the whole newscast grinds to a halt for a paid political announcement – a campaign pitch – from the Liberal party.

In the midst of all this, life in the capital city carries on more or less as usual – that is to say, as usual as it ever does. Managua is a city that doesn't feel like a city. An earthquake in 1972 levelled the entire downtown area, and it was later rebuilt not in the original centre, but on the outskirts.

As a result, Managua is a spread-out jumble of neighbourhoods dotted around this vast wasteland in the centre. Getting from one to another is a nightmare.

So in the evenings people here don't go bar-hopping like they do back home in St. John's. In Managua, if you go out for a beer, you spend the entire evening in the first bar you come to. Because getting anywhere else is such a hassle. You sit down, order a Victoria or Tonia – Nicaragua has only two brands of beer – and you talk politics.

I've noticed that the political colour of this tavern talk depends upon the price of the beer. In the cheaper pubs (twenty *cordobas* a beer) the clientele is generally pro-Sandinista. In the expensive joints they're usually planning to vote Conservative. And the medium-priced taverns (thirty *cordobas* a beer) are chockfull of contradictions.

The other night I sat over a thirty-cordoba beer talking with a civil servant and a bank clerk. The civil servant was a manager who'd just spent two years in Japan. He knew Vancouver airport intimately, he assured me, so he was worldly. He and the bank clerk spent a good hour impressing upon me how completely they disagreed with the policies of the current Sandinista government. Then, over another beer, they shyly confessed they were both going to vote for Daniel Ortega, the Sandinista presidential candidate. "After all you've said about the Sandinistas, you're going to *vote* for them?"

"Well," they said, "the Sandinistas are the only party that can save the country."

It's a disjointed reality, with people stumbling toward election day through a minefield of contradictions. This was brought home to me by two comic books I came across this week. One is put out by the Nicaraguan Electoral Commission. In a cartoon format, it explains how to vote. "Voting is easy!" it says, and it makes a few friendly suggestions like: bring a book to read in case there's a long line-up outside your polling station.

The other booklet is produced by the CIA and has been extensively distributed in the north of the country. It's called *The Freedom Fighters Manual*, or *A Practical Guide for Freeing Nicaragua from the Misery and Oppression Imposed by the State, without Having to Use any Special Tools and with Minimum Risk to the User*. Inside, simple cartoons describe how you can be the first on your block to sabotage the system. The helpful hints run the gamut. The Gold Medal suggestions detail how to make Molotov cocktails and how to use grappling hooks to bring down telephone wires. Ever wonder how you could start a time-delayed fire, giving yourself ten minutes to get away? This booklet tells you.

The Silver Medal suggestions explain how to put sand or water in the gas tanks of government trucks, break headlights and cut alarm cables.

In the Bronze category are: leaving water taps running, phoning in false fire alarms, breaking office equipment and placing coins in light-bulb sockets to blow fuses and start fires.

There's something for everyone. Bound to appeal are: "Arrive late for work," "Leave work undone," or, better yet, "Phone in sick for work." My personal favourite illustrates, with a sketch, how to make anonymous telephone threats to your boss.

I guess all this would be funny if the game wasn't being played for real, with lives hanging in the balance.

In the taverns, people ask me where I'm from. "Canada," I say. "Well then," they ask politely, "how do you think our election compares to elections in Canada?"

I don't know how to answer them.

October 30, 1984

The election campaign here is in the final stretch. The Liberals are abstaining. And Conservative and Popular Social Christian Party spokesmen revealed this week that their parties were approached by the United States embassy and offered three hundred thousand dollars to pull out of the race as well. They and four other parties are still in the running, but like the Big Blue Machine in Ontario, the Sandinistas are expected to be a shoo-in.

I've spent the past few days travelling through the northern part of the country. I saw signs of recent combat between the Nicaraguan army and the Washington-backed *contra* forces near the city of Esteli. I watched teenagers digging trenches, and I drove a wounded soldier to a medical clinic.

In Esteli, I met a hotel owner and an accountant, both Liberal supporters who back their party's abstention. The Sandinistas have rigged the elections, they said, by allowing too many parties to register – it's a ploy to split the opposition vote.

I spoke to a French-Canadian priest near the town of Somoto who felt that this election presents voters with more real alternatives than the election he witnessed a few years ago in Quebec.

I drove to the remote town of Yali, in the northeast, where the *contras* have been trying to disrupt the whole electoral process. In July they ambushed and wounded two voter-registration officials. And the dirt road still isn't safe – the morning of the day I arrived, three army trucks had been ambushed.

It was in Yali that I met Professor Daisy Rugama. A short, dark-haired woman in her late thirties, a teacher in the local primary school, she's president of the local electoral board, in charge of overseeing the polling places on election day. She was chosen for the job, she said, because she has no political affiliation. She told me about Yali. "Look at our cemetery," she said. "Two hundred new graves since 1980." This town has a population of only three thousand. Almost all of the dead have been civilians – her friends and neighbours. She spoke quietly, blinking behind her large schoolteacher eye glasses. Every minute or two she took off the glasses to clean them on a corner of her blouse – a nervous habit that I suspect comes from spending eight hours a day pinioned in front of a score of unruly grade sixers.

Two months ago on the road, the *contras* fired a rocket launcher at a pick-up truck full of passengers. Everyone was killed, including a six-year-old child. "You're a stranger here," she said. "You don't know what it's like. It would break your heart to see small children whose parents have been murdered."

She described how local peasants have been kidnapped and their bodies found later disfigured by acid, some with their feet burnt black, others with wooden sticks rammed into their anuses. She took off her glasses to clean them again. This time she wiped her eyes as well.

Some peasants in the hills surrounding Yali will have to travel up to five kilometres to get to their polling places this Sunday. Professor Rugama worried that they may be too intimidated to vote. "But we *must* vote," she said. "Perhaps an elected government will discour-age the United States' policy against our country. Perhaps then they will leave us alone . . . ."

I asked her about elections in the old days, under the Somoza dicta-torship, and her whole mood changed. She rolled her eyes. "Oh – *those* elections!" she giggled. "They were different! You see, it was supposedly a secret ballot. But the ballot was printed on onionskin paper, so even after you folded it, they could see who you'd voted for. And you had to give it to a party official, who in turn put it in the ballot box." She chuckled. "As a teacher, I was obliged to carry a card saying that I'd voted, otherwise I'd have lost my job. So guess who I had to vote for?" She took off her glasses and roared with laughter.

Daisy Rugama's response isn't unusual. So far, I haven't found one Nicaraguan who can keep a straight face while talking about the way elections used to be before the 1979 revolution. No matter what their political stripe nowadays, they all roll their eyes like Daisy and say: "Oh, *those* elections!"

Some peasants in Rivas province told me they once got their whole community together to vote against Somoza's party. So they *knew* there had been 270 votes cast for the opposition Conservatives. But when Somoza's officials counted the votes, only three votes were announced for the Conservatives, and a triumphant 267 for Somoza.

In the town of Masaya, a young Sandinista supporter told me that in one election, when he was twelve years old, he'd voted for Somoza five times in different polling stations.

"But was the voting age that low?" I asked. "Oh, no," he said with a big grin. "Somoza's men would put eye glasses on us to make us look older. It was easy. The organizer would stick his head around the curtain while you voted – to see if you needed help, right? Well, if you marked your X for Somoza you got a glass of rum, a special meal of *nacatamales* (a local delicacy) and five *cordobas*. That was a lot of money those days for a twelve-year-old.

"And you know," he continued, "it's funny. We had that kind of election for forty-five years. Yet in those days, no one in North Amer-ica, no one in Europe, ever seemed to be concerned about how they were carried out."

60

Each day this week, the local newspapers carry the countdown: five days to election day, four days, three days. They also carry the other countdown: the numbers of Nicaraguans killed by the war. Seventy-three hundred in the past four years. That's roughly eight times the number of Newfoundlanders killed in the Second World War.

It looks as if Nicaraguans *will* go to the polls on Sunday – despite the pullout of part of the opposition, despite the *contras*, despite the United States embassy, despite everything. In Yali, Daisy Rugama will be counting the votes, blinking and wiping her glasses. I hope that this time she won't be crying.

November 10, 1984

Tomorrow I head home after six weeks in this small suffering country. Home to Canada where I will meet friends at a bus stop or on a street corner who will ask me, casually. "What's *really* going on in Nicaragua, anyway?" They will expect an analysis in thirty seconds or less, a concise answer that won't hold them up and cause them to miss their afternoon appointments.

But in my last few days here, it isn't that concise analytical answer that makes up my parting memory. It's a host of little things, all the disjointed flavours that linger on the palate and leave me with a bitter after-taste.

I think of the playwright I met last weekend who gave me his most recent play. I said I'd translate it for publication in a Canadian magazine, and I promised to mail him the translated manuscript so he could check it over before publication. "Oh, never mind that," he said with a wry smile. "Just publish it. We may be invaded any day now, and I may not be here to check anything."

I think of the army tank stationed on the street corner near where I've been staying in Managua. The tanks were called out last Monday when the government declared a state of emergency against what they said was the possibility of a United States Air Force bombing or an airlifted invasion. To the kids in the neighbourhood the tank is a new plaything. They spend all day helping the soldiers camouflage it with vines and tree boughs.

I think of all the high-school students I've seen digging trenches and air-raid shelters in the past two weeks. And I think of the others I've watched practicing emergency civil defense and rifle drills.

I think of the Cine Gonzales – one of Managua's main movie theatres – which coincidentally this week has been showing an old Hollywood science-fiction horror movie. The title is *Strange Invaders*.

I think of the United States reconnaissance plane, a supersonic SR-71 Blackbird, that has been making regular daily flights over Nicaragua. Every morning for the past week it has broken the sound barrier overhead with a loud boom that could easily be confused with a bomb explosion. It has set everyone's nerves on edge. It's very precise – every morning at eight-thirty you can set your watch by the United States Air Force. There's nothing the Nicaraguans can do about it, so they make jokes. On Monday the plane didn't fly over – and people complained that they were late for work because Ronald Reagan forgot to wake them up.

It's not so funny for some Dutch friends of mine here. They say it's been hard to get their two young children to sleep at night lately. The kids are afraid the Blackbird will come and get them.

I think about the theatre group I chatted with last night who said this year they're going to focus on plays for children. "Young kids are growing up in the midst of all this tension," they said. "Growing up with guns and tanks and defence emergencies. They grow up too fast. It's as if we have to teach them to play."

And most of all I think of a small three-room school in a remote village called Terrera Grande. I walked up the hill to that school with an army patrol the day before the Nicaraguan elections. The school was to be the polling place on voting day and so it had been attacked the night before by the Washington-backed *contras* – a group called the FDN, which mounts hit-and-run attacks from across the Honduras border.

This attack seemed to have been designed to intimidate voters. Grenades had been tossed into the classroom and the children's desks were littered with shrapnel and broken glass. Cut-out paper animals that had been taped to the windows lay on the concrete outside. The doors and the tin roof of the school were ripped with bullet holes from a machine gun. On a child's desk lay a heap of charred papers – election material the *contras* had burned.

Suddenly someone yelled. There was a live grenade with the pin out under a desk just near my foot. I remember looking down at the little green metal thing. It didn't seem particularly ominous. Instead, what sent chills up my spine was the slogan scrawled on the blackboard in rough letters: "Long live the FDN!"

The words hung there next to a cut-out paper bird taped to the board. The bird was a white dove of peace.

As I leave here I wonder about the children in that school. As I board my plane tomorrow, will they still be finding bits of shrapnel in their desks? Will the rain come through the bullet holes in the roof? Will they be cutting out more white paper doves?

All the best,
Chris

ARGUMENTS

There were (and are) a number of topics on
Morningside that were (and are) almost guaranteed to
draw a strong response. Some of them – notably
abortion, of course, but also capital punishment and
the censoring of pornography – were those that gave
the politicians the most difficulty and, in some cases,
stalled the political process, both sides of the dispute
being so firmly entrenched that *any* political decision
would serve only to deepen the opposition, and the
solution was to do nothing. Much of our mail reflected
irreconcilable differences, too, and while I would read
from it on the air, and try to give some indication of the
range of reaction, there were not many letters, from
the hundreds we received, that seemed to me to cast
new light.

But there were exceptions. And in selecting these
"arguments" to repeat in print, I have tried to show
some of them. As throughout *The Morningside Papers*, I
have leaned here in favour of people who speak from
personal experience, as opposed to those who argued
abstract cases. In two cases here, in fact, the personal
involvement and the feelings it engendered were so
strong that both on the radio and in these pages I have

respected the writers' desire for anonymity. There were, however, exceptions to the rule of personal involvement as well: one of the wisest letters I received on abortion was from a man.

On other subjects, I have included in this group of letters, as was the case with David Sims on city life and country life, a pair of letters from one person – Anne Cameron – and two pieces of writing that, I think, drew more requests for copies than anything we broadcast in my first three years. One, from Catherine Edward in Prince Edward Island, was in response to an interview I'd had with Sharon Scarr, the author of *Mother Care, Other Care*, in which Ms Scarr had made what Catherine, whom I used to know when she worked at the CBC in Toronto, had heard as an unbalanced case for day care. It made her, she wrote, so angry that she hurled the bread she was kneading into a bowl and turned off the radio.

The other letter that drew so many requests for reprints was from Sheila Brown, of Waterdown, Ontario. Sheila wrote after our Remembrance Day program in 1983, and I read her letter on the air the following week. Finally, as an argument, I have included one of the letters that came in response to that reading. I read it first with no name, but there were enough clues in the letter that I was able to track down its author in Saskatoon and her name, Linette Reid, is now attached.

✉ I had a "convenience abortion" five years ago. It was simple to obtain, free and painless. There was no real reason to have one, other than that the time was not "right" for us, and no one asked for a reason. If it had not been so easy and acceptable, I would probably have had the child; I would never have considered an unsafe or illegal procedure. I guess I just numbed my emotions to be able to go through with it, refusing to allow myself to think about it.

Now, I have two small children fathered by the same man. The joy that they have brought to our lives is inexpressible. I know that God has forgiven us for that terrible sin but sometimes the thought of it gives me a very sick feeling deep in my guts and I know I have not yet shed the last tear over it. I wonder, would the baby have been like my son or my daughter? Was it dark or fair? I calculate its age from time to time, remembering especially near the date the birth would have been. As I play with my youngest and laugh at her giggles as she squirms with glee just to *see* me, some of the joy is snatched away as I ask myself, how could I have taken the life of my own baby? I am livid at the thought of someone just speaking crossly to my children and I actually murdered one. Think of all the thousands of women who may be burdened by similar thoughts. And my greatest fear is that my children might one day discover that their mother took the life of one of their siblings.

If I knew then what I know now, I would never have done it. I would have prayed for the courage and strength to face the responsibility of my actions. I am sorry that there was no law to protect my unborn child against me, its own mother, when I didn't have the sense to recognize what I was doing.

Anonymous
Vancouver

✉ I had an abortion in Dr. Morgentaler's clinic and although I didn't enjoy it, I have never regretted it for one instant. I didn't enjoy it because it was illegal and I felt guilty about that. I didn't enjoy having to pay for it ahead of time. I was asked for $300 – in horror I told him I only had about $240 in the bank. He said that would be quite all right. I gave him a cheque. He performed the abortion. I hated him; the nurse gave me biscuits and tea and we chatted, my mind not fully on the conversation. I walked out hoping I would never have to go through that again but feeling as though a ton weight had been lifted off my shoulders.

With four young children, all very much wanted although the fourth was unexpected, the knowledge that I was pregnant again was a blow. I was, as the saying goes, at the end of my rope. Thank God I had the abortion. I do sometimes think, "If I hadn't had the abortion, he or she would be twelve now" or whatever, but the thought is accompanied by a tremendous sense of relief.

I am a Christian, and I do not believe a six-week fetus is or should be regarded as a child.

Yes, Dr. Morgentaler is a funny, furtive, odd little man, but he is a brave one, and I believe he does great things for the mental health of thousands of women.

Anonymous
Montreal

✉ My mother was forty-four when I was born. I am told she was confused and angry but mostly embarrassed. It was indeed an un-wanted pregnancy but it was 1954 and I suppose she had no choice. When I started kindergarten her hair was completely grey. When I was a trying and rebellious teenager she turned sixty. She is seventy-four, I am thirty.

I am not a talented artist or athlete, although I love to draw and paint and ski. I am not a great scholar or musician, but I find great joy in books and records. I play the violin badly. I am bewitched by the planet earth and live in peace with her. I have friends. I am in love. I am loved.

What's the point? I'm not sure. I am just truly delighted to be here.

Deborah Chatreau
Thornsburg, Ontario

✉ The reality is that if you say you're opposed to abortion on demand, and that's what we really have, people say, "You must be a Catholic." The implications are twofold. First, only a Catholic could be troubled by abortion as a birth-control method. Not true. Second, no Catholic ever had a thought that did not originate in Catholic doctrine or dogma. Do you believe that's true? I hope not.

The gist of the debate is, where does life begin? What needs to be said loud and clear is that this is a purely scientific question. Scientists recognize this, at least the good ones. They recognize the gelatin base of all human knowledge, founded as it is on some unknowable, unproveable hypotheses (and the so-called Big Bang is a dandy example, if you don't have one at hand). The question is unanswerable in purely scientific terms, and is therefore, by default or definition, a debate over values – a truly philosophical question.

The bottom line is that we are a society of convenience, and I do not exempt me, nor thee. Abortion is, today as perhaps not before, a fall-back instrument for the sexually careless. You have to be vigilant together, to avoid pregnancy, but it can be done. Furthermore, to suggest that the need for vigilance degrades sexual experience is to reveal a very childish view of sexuality. It suggests that Erica Jong's zipless (blank) is the most important expression of sexual experience – a bad basis for public policy, particularly one that may have unforeseen implications.

Forget religion. Forget morality. May we discuss this as an *ethical* issue? In other words, we must consider abortion not in terms of what we are doing vis-a-vis some old code, nor in terms of what God (whoever she/he is) will do to us. We must consider what we are doing to ourselves. And, essentially, what we are doing is rewriting our notion of the value of human life. Think about capital punishment. It appalls me to think I have to trade state-sanctioned murder for a saner policy on the unborn, but I've gotten to that stage, as contradictory as it seems. The most significant rewrite of our social value of the life of humans came when we stopped killing people who killed other people. Well, since then, we have abortion on demand; we have creeping acceptance of euthanasia; and lurking over the horizon is a debate that will make all this seem trivial by comparison. I speak of eugenics.

In other times, the eugenics debate was fixed on some unseen cross-roads somewhere down the road. We are at that crossroads now. We are learning to *make* life. When we can finally do it – build a Steve Austin – what ethical tenets will determine what happens? What lines shall we draw then if we draw no lines now?

Michael O'Connell
Ottawa

✉ A number of years ago I had the sad and still-mourned experience of a spontaneous miscarriage. I did not get to the hospital before the child was lost, and so carried him with me during the frantic race to the emergency ward. I wrapped him in a blanket and held him and knew he was not breathing, never had breathed.

At the hospital I said I wanted to make funeral arrangements. No matter how desperately I debated, argued or pleaded, everyone was adamant. The child had never breathed, therefore he had never lived, therefore he was not allowed a funeral but was "disposed of." It has never been easy to know that boy who never breathed was burned in the incinerator with the other disposable garbage of the hospital.

If he, a six-month pregnancy, had not lived and was not entitled to a burial, what is there about a formless blob that is "alive"? Undoubtedly millions of spontaneously aborted or miscarried fetuses have been burned with the garbage. Most of them were wanted, but have never been considered to have "lived." Why is it only the *un-wanted* who are granted the dignity of being considered "human life"?

I don't hear any of these people who are weeping publicly about the unwanted unborn raising any question about those others who are wanted, or those who are already born and are being raped, sodomized or brutalized by the porn industry. *Those* unwanted are as disposable to society as the miscarried children who are thrown in with the garbage.

We need to examine our societal ethics. And we need to do it without sentimentality, romanticism and hypocrisy. We are told child-hood is "the best years of our lives." Talk to anyone, and childhood seems to have been a time of confusion, fear, horror and brutality. W.O. Mitchell has been honest about that, bless him! "Sanctity of Life." Where is life sacred? In Vietnam, El Salvador, Chile, Ethiopia, Eritrea, South Africa? What is sacred about life when we live on the edge of extinction? Is this well-organized and well-funded group [Pro-life] raising hell over the pesticide murders in India?

And if life is so sacred, what about non-human life? While raising hell over the death of the unborn, they eat their scrambed eggs and meat, wear leather shoes, drive automobiles that spit emissions dangerous to all forms of life and are not demonstrating in great or noticeable numbers against the threat to all life posed by the nuclear insanity proliferating round the globe.

It's so much easier to stand, protected by a bunch of people and ringed by police, screaming vitriolic hatred, puking rage and ugliness in the direction of people who are not saying abortion is a must for everyone, but are only saying they do not intend to bring into a world full of obviously unwanted children yet another helpless and unwanted little victim.

I've never had an abortion. I'm not sure it would ever be an option for me. But my circumstances are not someone else's. I have always felt I had a number of options: many women have none. And if these people, whose spokespeople seem to be almost invariably men, are so worried about the sanctity of life and sanctity of family, perhaps they would be so logical, kind and ethical as to impress on their fellow *men* that the child-abuse statistics have got to be changed. Seven out of ten kids have experienced sexual abuse to some degree before they attain the age of legal majority. That is hardly respect for the life of the child.

Their irrationality and self-righteous hatred set my teeth on edge. Hitler passed laws making abortion a must for the "unfit" and denying it to the citizens of his lunatic kingdom. The behaviour of the demonstraters outside the Toronto clinic makes my skin creep. Their behaviour is so full of hate it reminds me of those newsclips of the torch-lit marches, the marches that ended in the piles of bones.

Life is not very sacred, it would appear – except to those who try to keep their own lives in order and grant to others a measure of free choice. If those foaming hate-mongers would just calm themselves down and get logical, and realize that for years and years they have, by their silence, agreed with and supported the idea that if it hasn't breathed, it hasn't lived, they might begin to question the real source of their emotions.

Anne Cameron
Powell River, British Columbia

✉ I am a single professional woman approaching menopause. I have no offspring, no visible embodiments of those five hundred eggs I have passed into oblivion during my reproductive cycle. There have, of course, been times when I have wondered whether I was preg- nant. But this has never happened because I have been careful. Let me assure you that being careful is no easy matter. It takes much more than know-how about birth control. It takes all kinds of skills that many people do not have. It also takes character and the ability to say no nicely. Decisive determination is a major ingredient.

Yet, I find myself regretting that I did not give shape to one or two of those five hundred potential human beings. One factor, but not necessarily the main factor, is that many without my skills are repro- ducing. I could have taught my skills to a child and had a better-than- average chance of turning out a quality human being. If, in my day, abortion had been more readily available, I might have taken more risks. And perhaps I would have decided to keep one of the children conceived. Abortion has liberated women like me to step beyond the old social mores and decide to exercise our right to reproduce outside of the traditional family setting.

I am a school psychiatrist. I daily test children whose lives are wrecked because their parents do not have the life skills that I have and could have passed onto children. By no means are the children I see all from single-parent families. Do you blame me for regretting the "murder" of those five hundred eggs?

A conception only brings the potential closer. It is one phase in the cycle of life. The cycle is unfertilized egg and sperm in isolation, conception, birth, life and death. The process can be interrupted any-where in the cycle by decision, accident or accidental decision. Is the violation of life any less if it is violated in potential or in conception?

I would like to see the abortion issue deal seriously, first of all, with the issue of responsible choice, personal, social–all respects. Once we have a clearly articulated handle on this, all the rest will fall into place.

Give the rationalists equal time. We are human beings, too.

Jessie Skinner
Abbotsford, British Columbia

✉ Just suppose that society were organized so that men looked after the kids they fathered while women were the wage-earners. Sup-pose men who had sired three or four kids, or had a handicapped child, or had accidentally impregnated someone, decided they wanted to have a vasectomy so it couldn't happen again. And suppose women were deciding whether men should be allowed to have vasectomies performed on them when they chose to do so. The interview might be:

CRUSADING WOMAN DOCTOR: No child should be born unless there is a loving and caring father waiting to welcome it into the world. With present laws necessitating hospital-committee decisions, and with social pressure against sterilization, it is very difficult for a man to get a vasectomy on demand. I believe men should be allowed to make such decisions for themselves. It is degrading to them to be treated like children and to have rulings made on the permissibility of vasectomy. I have had men in my clinic who have sired ten children and at the thought of raising another infant they have injured them-selves by performing badly bungled self-sterilization. Some of them died from going to back-street sterilizers. Men deserve good medical care in up-to-date clinics for vasectomies, and my clinics will provide such care.

REASONABLE, RESPONSIBLE TALK-SHOW HOSTESS: I hesitate to mention this, but I think I will anyway. I can't help noticing you are a bit defensive about your views.

DOCTOR: Well, I have had to defend myself in court three times, and I have spent time in jail, too, because of my clinics. But so many men are grateful to me that my views have not changed.

HOSTESS: If men are free to sterilize themselves whenever they want, it seems to me that means a profound moral change in our society.

DOCTOR: Men who obtain vasectomies thoughtlessly are a small portion of our society, a segment that is thoughtless in all its behaviour. Most men are moral and responsible, as is most of society at large.

HOSTESS: Well, supposing we allow these clinics to perform vasectomies on demand. The next thing might be a government that made arbitrary decisions on who should have a vasectomy and who should not. It is only a short step from sterilization by choice to sterilization by decree.

DOCTOR: I do not believe that the responsible women (and, uh, men) who form our legislative bodies would ever countenance the passage of a law that would enforce coercive sterilization of their sons, husbands, brothers or fathers.

HOSTESS: How can you be so sure? Many women have given their lovers money to have vasectomies so they wouldn't have to assume the economic obligations of children resulting from their liaison.

DOCTOR: I won't make any moral judgement on that, but I will say that men who are willing to have affairs with women who refuse financial responsibility for the resulting offspring are not behaving in a mature way. Neither are the women, it must be admitted. And I must add that just because *some* men would choose to have a vasectomy instead of choosing to bring up a number of children, which is the most important and rewarding work in the world, it doesn't follow that most men would make such a decision.

And so on.

Of course abortions and vasectomies are not by any means exact parallels. But maybe a few men would understand what it is like to be the *object* of discussion, if they imagined a reversal of circumstances.

Alice Issner
Toronto

✉ I've heard it said that, as a people, Canadians hate children in the purest theological sense of the word: "hate – to separate oneself, opposite of love – to become other." We seem to be doing everything possible to separate ourselves from our children.

Let us not forget that day care is an answer to an adult need, not an answer to a baby-child need. It is true that our society has changed, that our needs have changed (or rather our perception of what we need has changed). It is also true that a child's needs have not changed. These remain as constant as life itself. To be given one's humanity – to grow from infant to adult in the fullness of that humanity – requires certain conditions to be met. If we are to consider day care at all, it must be considered from the needs of the child, not the needs of the adult.

My deepest rage comes when a newborn is described as not caring who looks after him or her in the early months. "They don't know one person from another . . . not enough brain development at this early stage." A baby *in utero* becomes familiar with his mother's heartbeat, voice, way of moving, scent; even her emotions are familiar to him. At birth, *she* is the one he has already begun to love. She is the *only* one he feels safe with. Ashley Montague describes a newborn as one looking forward to a "womb with a view." This is a beautiful way of explaining the "in-arms" needs of the infant.

Why must day-care advocates insist on picturing women at home as depressed housefraus, overeating in front of the soaps, barely able to cope with the dirty little brats in their slovenly homes? To me, this is the myth we must give up.

I retired from a career in broadcasting to have a family. I used to think I was pretty smart, had the world by the tail, had it all figured. Then I became a mother – and saw the gaps in my humanity. Through my three babies I learned how to find my humanity; patience, kindness, humility, understanding, gentleness, compassion. Because of them, I'm a better person. It's true I've no front parlour, my clothes don't bear designer labels and I've never had a manicure. But truthfully, I cannot care so much how my life *looks*, and have it *feel* any good.

As for spending fifteen minutes of each day with my children – well, my children get that much of me before breakfast is finished. I think Charles Dickens was right when he said, "It is no small thing that these little children, who are so soon from God, love me." And I'm sure he loved them, for in the beginning little ones do not initiate love, they only reflect our love back to us. So we must be there to fill them, that one day they may be able to refill us.

Catherine Edward
Belfast, Prince Edward Island

✉ I am well aware of the heart-rending isolation and frustration that is associated with profound deafness, and I do not question the claim that deafness is a more serious handicap than blindness in learning to talk. Beyond this stage total blindness is psychologically and physically a far more severe handicap in most other aspects of life.

It must be recognized that about eighty percent of all the information your brain receives comes through your eyes. Further, since you see with your brain and not your eyes, someone else's description or interpretation of what they see is subject to their many experiences, prejudices and so on.

A totally blind person is surrounded by an environment of eternal and depressing darkness no matter where he may go, whether to a sunny beach or for a ride on a plane, train or boat. This isolating and lonely environment is psychologically oppressive and physically restrictive.

Without the stimulation supplied by the constant flow of visual information the brain becomes a sluggish, dreary place. For the precious gift of eyesight I would gladly give up the sound of Mozart's music, Sinatra's songs or the dulcet tones of Lorne Greene. It is surprising how many of the world's most beautiful things, including a smile, a flower, a sunrise, a sunset, a white cloud in a blue sky, are silent. I would never miss the scream of a chain-saw or lawn-mower, the penetrating boom of a too-loud stereo or the nerve-racking commotion of a busy street. Since I lost my eyesight in 1973, four unseen daughters-in-law and seven grandchildren have been added to my family. I sometimes cry inside a little for what I am missing.

W.A. Martin
Victoria, British Columbia

✉ I saw my father die in agony and without dignity. He was a marine engineer, travelled widely, loved life. He was a very proud man. I know that had he been in complete control of his faculties, he would have hated to be seen that way. He had always said that if he became so ill that he could not care for himself, he would rather be dead.

From my point of view, it was as if our roles were reversed. My father, now the child, incapable of performing any functions without help. My mother had nursed my father for almost two years. What frustrating agony to watch someone you love very deeply suffer so much and for so long.

During the time I spent looking after my dad and just being with him (he was at home, not in hospital), I could not understand why we allow human beings to suffer to such an extent.

Joan Wiltshire
Smiths Cove, Nova Scotia

✉ In 1931 and 1932, thirteen hundred kidnappings occurred in the United States, culminating in the Lindberg baby killing. Public demand caused Congress to pass the Lindberg Law. Kidnapping became a federal offence, for which the death penalty was mandatory.

In Texas, a man named McCracken became the first to test the law. He abducted a girl, held her for eighteen or nineteen hours and freed her unharmed. He was apprehended, tried, convicted and sentenced to death in a matter of weeks. His last words were, "You're not really going to do this to me, are you?" In 1932 and 1933, there were only seven kidnappings in the United States.

The death penalty is certainly a deterrent in some cases. No punishment is a hundred percent or even fifty percent effective, but the taxpayer has a right to know that his taxes are not being used to keep cold-blooded butchers alive in indolence for twenty or thirty years, and whether it is called a deterrent, state murder or revenge is of no consequence. The idea of capital punishment savaging the culture is utterly stupid. The abolition of capital punishment has not improved our humanitarian standings one iota; in fact, we are more violence-prone than we were fifty years ago, because cold-blooded killers know that they won't be put to death.

I am an old infantry officer and during the war killed men whose fault was being on the other side. I was wounded three times in action and decorated seven times, and am the only one I know of who won the Silver Star three times. The men I commanded followed reluctantly. None of them wanted to die, but few were reluctant to kill, so the idea that murderers are not deterred by the death penalty is absurd. I have seen a lot of creeps I could kill without the least qualm, but I am deterred by the fact that my family would be shamed and I don't want my ass in jail, never mind swinging in the wind.

Harold Smiley
Enderby, British Columbia

✉ The Canadian reporter who testified for Ernst Zundel said "the other side" has a right to be heard. Let me tell you the definition of "the other side." When I got to Auschwitz with my parents, we were supposedly following my brother, who had been transported before us. In no time mother and I stood before Mengele. I was fifteen years old and I thought I was going to help my mother. I had promised that to my brother before his deportation to, we were told, "a labour camp."

Here Mama and I stood in front of an SS man. He stood high on his vehicle. Mengele pointed his stick at Mama. I held on to her and jumped right after her. Women tried to pull us apart. Mengele said, "What are you doing?" I answered in my German, spoken like a village girl (which I really was), that I had to stay with my mother, that I needed to help her. He spoke to me; he was amused with my German accent. I saw from the corner of my eye that some women were pulling my mother away; my mother was screaming, "Gisela!" Some other women were holding on to me. By the time I stopped speaking in my defence to stay with my mama, she was pulled out of my sight. Then Mengele said, "Because you needed so badly to go with your mother, you can't go with her to *the other side*. I would have let you go there, but now, no." I was pushed to the side of the living.

I never saw my mother again. "The other side" can't speak for itself.

Gisela Spier Cohen
Toronto

✉ Your Frobisher Bay correspondent said that the Inuit way of life was in decline, largely due to the efforts of the "Friends of the Animals," whose lobby against sealing and trapping has destroyed fur prices and the demand for furs. Later, the author of the Ernest Seton Thompson biography made the calm claim that conservationists are people who don't kill animals.

This thoroughly urban assumption is what is killing the Inuit way of life and that of other native peoples in Canada, as well as that of us settlers in Canada's rural and northern areas. A glut of Walt Disney has, it seems, made the killing of Bambi and other wild animals a sin; committing economic genocide is, however, perfectly acceptable in the name of civilized, citified sophistication.

People who congratulate themselves on their humanity to animals in the wild are utterly ignoring their own delegated butchery in the slaughter houses of the land. Those of us who live in the country do our own killing. I raise meat rabbits. If I want to enjoy meat for supper, I must take full, personal responsibility for the killing involved. There is no buck-passing allowed, unlike the easy way available to town dwellers, with their plastic-wrapped chickens and the sanitized violence of the supermarket meat department. I cannot accept the so-called superior judgement of people who kill by proxy, who hire butchers, dog catchers and exterminators to do the dirty work and then condemn us country dwellers for the blood on our hands.

I am a conservationist. I am also a trapper. I consider the fur harvest to be a legitimate and practical way to make a modest living and to help retain a healthy animal population. Trappers are here on the ground. Unlike high-flying Paul Watsons or the big-business moose barons and their wolf blitzkrieg, we are the ones who observe the animal population; who try to plan our trapping to preserve a balance between prey and predators; who see – and report – the diseases and blights that affect the animals and plants in our wilds. There is a world of difference, a gigantic gap, between those of us who live with the wild and those who sentimentalize it from their concrete fastnesses, unaffected by nature, short of the annual Toronto and Montreal blizzard! I don't appreciate these people absconding with the name "conservationist."

Penny Simpson
Tatla Lake, British Columbia

✉ This morning Ted Byfield and George Oake had a number of things to say about pornography and censorship.

A few years ago I was researching a CBC TV special, "Drying up the Streets." My producer sent me and my researcher to "Project P" in Toronto. It is comprised of RCMP, OPP and local police, all trying to stop the junk coming across the border.

I walked in there your typical unthinking, soft-bellied, knee-jerk liberal, and came out absolutely terrified, feeling I was the target in a kind of unnamed guerrilla war, the training manuals for which I had just seen for the first time in my stupid life.

Maybe those two nice liberal men could tell me what is so sacred about an article that describes, in stomach-churning detail, how to hold, position and sexually penetrate a four-year-old girl. That child had none of the "freedom of choice," "freedom of expression," "artistic and creative freedom" those men yammered on about so idiotically. That little girl undoubtedly died as a result of that adult man's self-expression.

It must be nice to be a white Anglo-Saxon, educated, gainfully employed male. I try to empathize. I can't. But it is these privileged elite who are saying how terrible it is even to hint at censorship. And why shouldn't they say so? They are never at risk. It is women, children and those with darker skins and economic desperation who are getting offed in snuff movies or hung from butchers' hooks for the SM magazines.

And for this people are willing to argue about freedom of artistic expression? They bring up the old knee-jerk bugaboo about burning books – and they won't even try to develop a vocabulary that would examine the difference between the printed word, which requires some work on the part of the reader, and film and video, which hits all the subliminal buttons and is more powerful than we know. It must be effective if every industry in the country wants to buy TV time to peddle their goods.

Oh, my, and what about *Lady Chatterley's Lover*. You know, it's not such a great book, it's not such incredible art and it's not very widely read because it's out of date, but we are going to sacrifice four-year-old kids to protect it?

If I thought burning *Lady Chatterley's Lover* would save the lives of the children who are being raped to death, tortured and used as toys by lunatics, I'd burn every copy of the damned book I could find. I would burn the King James Version of the Bible if I thought it would keep kids safe from the sick sadists who think it's okay to hump and heave on powerless flesh.

Erotic expression, sensual stimulation, sexual experimentation . . . a ninety-four-year-old arthritic cripple in a wheelchair? She is one of the rape statistics. Clifford Olson had a collection of kiddie porn; and we still don't know how many children paid the price for his sensual exploration and self-examination and mind-expanding-awareness attempts. All that jargon-and-formula speak is just an easy way for those who are afraid to get in touch with their subjectivity and emotion. It's so easy to come out with all the babblerap, and it hurts so goddamned much to sit in Project P and see person after person chopped and burned and hacked and tortured and to know that if you try to tell people that we are not talking about air-brushed fantasy or low-cut blouses or the gardener saying "shit" or "arse," those people will say, "Oh, don't, it's so nasty, it's so impolite, it's so vulgar . . ." and they scurry away, not wanting to look at what the debate is really about, not wanting to examine the record of horror, not wanting to admit that yes, they have been walking around prattling academese and gobbledegook rather than making their own analysis and daring to go against the tide of crap.

For years the women's movement tried to be heard. Nobody listened. Finally a male professor from a Toronto university was appointed to a royal commotion. He used figures ten years behind those of the rape-crisis and intervention centres, and this country was shocked. If he had used up-to-date figures, and got them from the women involved, for the past fifteen years, in trying to put lives back together again, the country would have rocked with horror.

Women aren't setting themselves up as literary critics or art critics or anything as euphemistic as that. We aren't discussing literature and art. We are discussing children being split open so some weirdo can have a sexual thrill. You bet we get upset. Loud. Subjective. Abrasive. And you bet your ass we have no sense of humour about it.

Anne Cameron
Powell River, British Columbia

✉ My family history is British Imperial Army and Anglican church. I see now how extraordinarily similar these two institutions are, and as a female growing up in this male-dominated world, I, like my sisters before me, accommodated my life according to male expectations.

My secret existence and the way things really worked were two separate realities. As a child I was puzzled by this, but as a woman I have two states of being, one rage and the other numbness. For me, the only alternative to unexpressed rage is numbness.

Anyway, to Lest We Forget. We don't forget the face and the life of a son, a friend or a lover when they are wrenched from us so violently and so soon. We don't need bands, flags and parades for that. They, in fact, help us to remember how to make war, lest we forget how.

I used to mark Armistice Day, as it was then (perhaps more accurately) called, with my mother, the daughter of a professional soldier. She served in France in the WACs from 1914 to 1918. On November 11 she simply buried her face in her hands and sat quietly for two minutes. She told me she was remembering her friends. I went to many a parade as a child and teenager. Our church was the garrison church and I used to watch the often shabby old men stepping out as smartly as their age and infirmities would allow. I used to worry that the bugler would sound a bum note. Always I felt sad, which was the natural response and the required response. I also always felt uneasy, alarmed, puzzled.

Now in my fifties, I too have had friends killed, felt pain, seen evidence of war's atrocities, seen man's cruelty to man. I've also seen these same cruelties encouraged by cheering crowds, music, flags and prayers. I've borne sons and know how very precious they are.

So having been put in a thoughtful frame by your program, I slipped my sleeping grandson into his bed and watched the service in Ottawa. There was the Silver Cross Mother. Her twenty-year-old had been killed in Korea. The Silver Cross Mother is always the same. She is old. She wears a dark coat and hat. The prime minister or the governor general always steers her by her elbow to the monument. She is always surrounded by the military, ecclesiastical, political members of the boy's club. She is always dutiful, quiet, respectful. One year I actually knew the Silver Cross Mother and her four dead sons whose sacrifice brought her to Ottawa. She, too, looked quiet, respectful. Surely what they really are is numb. I always watch and I always wonder why they are not screaming. But I know why. It simply would not do to make a fuss. We learn that early and we learn it well and the atrocities go on and we are quiet. What would happen if we whirled and screamed and shrieked in our grief and our pain? What if we demanded that it stop?

I have a fantasy about a possible replay of Remembrance Day, 1983.

The Silver Cross Mother is late. The officials are nervous, edgy. Where is she? Who was responsible for getting her here? Find some other old woman in the crowd to stand in for her. The clergy are nearly finished with their prayers. Where is she?

We hear the sound of pounding hooves. A sleek, excited horse, its tail and mane flying out behind it, comes galloping into view. It has neither bit nor saddle. It runs with all the strength of all the cavalry horses in history in its limbs. Its eyes are triumphant and clear, its nostrils flaring. Riding as one with the beast is the Silver Cross Mother, her grey hair loose and long. Her eyes are like fire and she is brandishing a sword around and around and around her head like an athlete about to hurl a discus. She is summoning energy from the very sky. The crowd parts, scatters. Her crimson cape streams out behind her, leaving sparks in her wake. The Boy Scouts flee, the Girl Guides gape, the old soldiers see a vision. She mounts the steps of the cenotaph and comes to a stop. She utters a high-pitched scream. The monument crumbles to dust. The men all fall into a deep, deep sleep. The women all begin to dance and twirl and spin and scream. All the women all over the world begin to whirl and dance and dance and dance. They cry and they dance and they cry and they dance. They dance until their dance becomes a song and their song becomes a croon and their croon becomes a lullaby.

Along the line of their eyes and their cheeks the crooning women stroke the men and the boys. They open their eyes and they have forgotten how to make war. All their lives they have been told not to forget – but they have forgotten.

Sheila Brown
Waterdown, Ontario

✉ I'm only eighteen years old. Eighteen is not a long time for life to be teaching me things, but in my eighteen years life has taught me one overwhelming thing: terror. Constant, twenty-four-hour-a-day terror.

I am one of the lost generation; one of the generation that nuclear war has killed before it has occurred. I am involved with the peace movement. I see films, I go to meetings, I hear speakers, I read books. My first introduction to the nuclear world was in grade eight when we saw footage from Hiroshima and Nagasaki at school. I have progressed (regressed) from trying to excuse myself for not doing homework because the Chinese-Vietnamese border skirmishes seemed to be the beginning of the end of my twelve-year-old world to feeling real terror *every time* I hear an airplane fly overhead.

I am paralyzed. I can make no plans for the future because I can see no possibility of a future for our planet. I can tell myself my fears are irrational, that if the plane flying overhead was going to drop a bomb, our air-raids sirens would have gone off, but for a few horrible seconds, I *know* – irrationally perhaps, but I *know* – that not only is my life about to end, but all life is about to end. Not only will I not have a future, but there will not *be* a future, and that along with the future being destroyed, so will all our pasts be destroyed. It is a few seconds of complete, sheer terror – the terror of knowing extinction, the terror of impending holocaust – which occurs several times a day.

The day the Korean 747 airliner was shot down, I was tense to the point of illness. Every time I heard an airplane, I wanted to vomit. In none of my childhood nightmares have I known such prolonged and sustained terror. That night I couldn't sleep. My ears became so sensitive that trains passing over the bridge several miles from where I live woke me up because they sounded like airplanes. The next day I was going out of town on a bus. An hour out of Saskatoon, the thought just popped into my head that I had not brought a knife to kill myself in case I got caught between cities when the bombs went off.

When I am told that we have nuclear weapons for security, I would laugh if I could. If this terror is security, I'd rather not be "secure." More than anything else I feel weary, completely tired of this terror. If there is anything worse than terror, it is terror one is totally weary of.

Linette Reid
Saskatoon

Memorable Meals: A First Course

As I explained when I started it all, I stole the idea of Memorable Meals – even the title – from the old, pre-newsmagazine *Maclean's*. In those days, the editors of *Maclean's* (I was one of the most junior of them) commissioned writers to recall occasions on which they'd eaten especially well or, at least, unforgettably. That's essentially what I asked listeners to do in the winter of 1983–1984. As usual, I began by recalling a few of my own adventures and this collection, which opens with four of them, shows, I hope, the variety of the response. But that, as they say, is only the beginning; later on in *The Papers* is another full serving.

I

A disproportionate number of my most memorable meals have been eaten in the north: a feast in Inuvik I'll describe later on, before I invite you to join in this exchange; shore lunch of fresh lake trout at Great Bear Lake; stale sandwiches and a gravelly brew of half tea, half coffee near the head of steel on the Quebec North Shore and Labrador Railway.

One time I had a job of work to do in Prince Rupert. I'd never been to that part of British Columbia, although I knew about the rain, and I was not disappointed. One of the first buildings I was in had rain washing down the windows of one side and sun warming the bricks of the other.

The friends with whom I was working had a boat, big enough to fish salmon from. After our first half-day's work they asked if I wanted to go fishing. Sure, I said, finding it easier to overcome my work ethic than I might have feared.

On the way out of the harbour they threw three crab traps over the side, marking their location with buoys. The traps were baited with old salmon heads and tails.

For the next couple of hours we bobbed on the Pacific, in search of (or so we pretended) the giant salmon. We trailed a couple of lines over the stern and went to where my hosts were sure the salmon would be running. We got nary a bite. The highlight of the day was when a porpoise started to follow our boat and play hide-and-seek with it, frolicking in and out of the water. Since we figured he'd scare the salmon away, we tried to outrun him, but he was smarter – or faster – than we were. I think once, when he jumped in the air and I could see the sun sparkle off the flashing spray, that I could also hear him laughing.

Late in the afternoon we went back in. At the harbour mouth we picked up the traps. There were fourteen crabs in them. We threw back all the females and the young males, keeping five. Then we got in my friends' four-by-four and sped to the liquor store to pick up some white wine. Home, we stuck the wine in the freezer and put a cauldron of water on to boil. Someone had made bread that morning and brought it out now, with pots of sweet butter. That was supper. The chilled tart wine with sweat running down the side of the bottles, the sweet fresh boiled crab, eaten with our fingers, the warm bread.

I can taste it now, and hear the porpoise laughing.

II

In the autumn of 1968, when my children were aged nine to three, I decided to take them to England. Actually, I decided to take *me* to England, and my wife. My professional world had collapsed. The magazine I had been editing, and editing well I think, had been jerked out from under me by the forces of the marketplace. I had to help find jobs or make settlements for nearly two dozen people who'd been working with me. I was wiped out, and the man who'd done the rug-jerking had given me a purse of money for my troubles. I booked passage for England, where I'd never been, and then we decided to take the kids too, and we got adjoining cabins on board the *Alexandr Pushkin*, sailing from Montreal, eight days to Tisdale on the Thames.

It was a good idea and a bad idea – good because it gave the children an adventure they would not forget, bad because, well, if you're trying to find some surcease from the world, you will not find it on board a Russian ocean liner with five children of single-digit age.

On our sixth day, three-quarters of the way across the rolling Atlantic, my wife and I shared one of our most memorable meals.

The memory of the meal stays with me not so much because of what I ate but for where I ate it. We were invited, in the time-honoured tradition of passenger ships, to the captain's table. We put on our best bib and tucker and made our way to the first-class lounge.

To be socio-politically fair, the first-class lounge in a Soviet ship was really only a separate section of the common dining room, roped off, like a 1980s line-up at the bank, by crimson velvet. Until we crossed the threshold, the only person I'd seen in the first-class accommodation was a lady motel-owner from southern Ontario, whose annual holiday was a trip one way by liner, during which she played a devastating game of rubber bridge, a taxi from the docks to Heathrow and a swift trip home by jet.

The captain of the *Pushkin* had not been chosen by Central Casting. He bore less resemblance to Trevor Howard or Gregory Peck than he did to José Jimenez, and he had a high-pitched voice, a habit of formally repeating your questions – "What do the stab-ilizers do? They keep the ship stabble" – and an official version of the line we had heard from every member of the crew from whom we'd asked a favour: "Iss not possible."

Could the porthole be opened so the children could breathe at night? "Iss not possible," the comradely steward would reply. And now, could we order a bottle of wine for the captain? "Iss not possible," he replied in his José Jimenez voice.

He was a gracious, if formal, host. For the first time since we'd left Toronto and bivouacked in Montreal, my wife and I looked forward to a dinner with adults. The children were stashed in their cabin, their borscht and cold meat delivered on trays. A waiter in formal attire filled our vodka glasses to surface-tension plenitude. We settled in.

The main course at the captain's table turned out to be chicken Kiev, bursting with butter and fresh spices. But as an earlier course, one of several, we were served two kinds of caviar – red and black. We'd expected, that, I suppose, as we had the vodka. But each spoonful of caviar was served on a Ritz cracker. And now comes the moment that sticks in my memory.

Captain Jimenez cut his Ritz cracker with a knife and fork. I swear this to be true. He held his fork in his left hand, somehow pinned down the cracker and cut it neatly with the knife in his right.

Iss not possible, you say? I would agree, having tried to do it since. But I saw him do it on that trip, and somehow, later, as my wife and I made our way back to our cabin, walking in the moonlight back to our children's cabin, and finally letting loose the laughter we had stifled at the table, I knew we had made it through the bad times behind, and that better things would be in store.

III

Like many young couples of our time and place – she from Brandon, Manitoba, I from Galt, Ontario – my wife and I learned to cook together. This is not to say we shared the chores, which we didn't, but that we shared the adventure of trying to learn to cook well. The time was the 1950s when, as you may remember, much of Canada was going through a culinary revolution, turning from overdone beef and boiled vegetables to at least an experimentation with lighter meats and seafood, crisper greens, butter, cream, chicken stock, parsley, tarragon, chervil, rosemary, chives, garlic. Speckles of ground pepper. If I had to choose one dish that marked our own breakthrough it would be spinach: in each of our childhoods a punishment, limpid and dark as seaweed, but as we learned to prepare it only by rinsing it under the tap, wetting it with a sun-shower of lemon juice, shaking the whole till dry, then cooking for less than a minute of steam, childhood punishment had become a grownup's reward.

We lived, at the time I'm thinking about, in a quarter of Toronto that was inexorably turning Italian. We were only a couple of blocks, in fact, from St. Clair and Dufferin, the corner where, as the poet Pier Giorgio di Cicco has said, you can now live your whole life in Neapolitan, never deigning to speak English. But in those days the invasion was just beginning, and the stores whose rich greens and stalls of fruits spilled over onto the sidewalks were still the exceptions among the staid WASP hardwares and jewellers and furniture stores that sealed the sunshine out. We were learning to shop in the new places, sampling eggplant and zucchini, white veal, black olives, virgin oils, sculpted pastas.

And one day we saw snails. It was a Saturday. The snails were in a basket on a sidewalk stand. We bought two dollars' worth. They looked as if they'd last us for a week.

There were only two things different from the snails we had already courageously sampled in our restaurant adventures – escargots. For one thing, ours were smaller: the size of thimbles instead of plums. For another, they were alive, wriggling and heaving, poking their tiny little heads – we assumed those were their heads – from their tiny little shells and sometimes, we discovered when we got them back to our kitchen, going for long strolls among their neighbours.

Undaunted, we consulted our small shelf of cookbooks. In a paperback on French cooking, we found what we were looking for. The remainder of that Saturday, and much of Sunday morning, we worked with painstaking care. First, all of them had to be boiled. When the heat turned even more of them into vagabonds, we had to round up the stragglers, drive them back into their empty shells then boil them some more. Then more. When, at last, they gave up their little exoskeletal ghosts, we had to evacuate each of their homes by hand, scooping each snail out with a straight pin, then stuff each shell with a sliver of garlic, a spriglet of parsley and an eyedropper of white wine, then reinstate the boiled snail and top him off with butter. Then into the oven for an invigorating broil as the fragrance of their dressing filled the kitchen air.

Early Sunday afternoon one of Canada's most distinguished magazine writers arrived. I was a junior editor at *Maclean's* at the time, and he had come to deliver a manuscript. He smelled the snails.

"What's that?" he said.

We told him.

"I've never had snails," he said. We offered him one, showed him how to spear it, still broiling hot, with a pin. He swallowed it, smiled, licked his lips, speared another, swallowed, licked again, speared, swallowed, licked, speared, swallowed. . . .

Why go on? He ate them all. All the snails. All the garlic, butter, parsley, wine. When he was finished, he went home.

Later, I think, that same writer wrote one of the original series of memorable meals, in *Maclean's*.

He never mentioned our snails. And neither have I – till now.

IV

I didn't see the Arctic until 1971, when I had already edited two national magazines. I've been there seven or eight times since, and each time have been moved and affected by it, but I still don't know it. I am a southerner. The north may be a part of me (its presence in our consciousness, I believe, helps define us as Canadians), but I am not a part of it.

For that reason, I approach the story I want to tell now with some trepidation. It's possible, I know, for southerners to romanticize the north. I remember years ago, on the radio, when one person was celebrating the joys of making her own bread – in contrast, she said, to buying the plastic bread of the supermarkets – and someone else who'd grown up on the prairies when you *had* to make bread or go hungry wrote in to say that that was "plastic romanticism." And I remain leery of people who can have modern conveniences limning the joys of the primitive life. Choice is one thing, necessity another.

Given that, though, the most memorable meal I have had in my life was eaten in Inuvik, in the Mackenzie Delta, and many of the foods that comprised it were the same as those that have been eaten the same way for thousands of years: *muktuk*, which is hacked with an *ulu* from just under the skin of the whale and chewed raw; *mipgoo*, dried whale meat soaked in *oksuk*, which is oil; slivers of raw, frozen caribou; splits of dried fish; and some other parts of wild animals and marine life I do not care to discuss at this time of a southern morning. To be quite frank, there were foods in this unforgettable feast – and it *was* a feast – that I would not eat again by choice unless my life depended on it (just as some of the people who shared this repast with me call what many of us eat every day "dead meat"), but there were delicious tastes too: rich roasted caribou – surely the single best meat in the world – dressed with a sauce of small, tart delta cranberries; ptarmigan; fried bannock; a seasoned steak of well-hung bear; the dark meat of goose; pemmican; and the exquisite flavour of arctic char.

I was travelling through the north with a CBC crew, trying to learn something and reflect it on the radio. I'd ridden a dogsled up the Peel River to Archie Headpoint's cabin; talked whaling in Tuk with Vince Steen; danced through the night in Aklavik; and gone the next morning to watch Don McWatt's baby christened in Inuktituk. It was a high time: Bob Ruzicka was with us, singing songs of his own earlier days in the Arctic; the boys of Ryan's Fancy (still cherished friends) and the enchanting Angèle Arsenault were there too, absorbing the land and the people and paying their way with concerts. We capped our trip with the final feast, at Nellie Cournoyea's house in Inuvik. Nellie is a territorial councillor now, returned this winter by acclamation, but she was with the CBC then, giving her people a northern voice, and she had assembled some of her friends to help bake, roast, fry, serve and make the pots and pots of tundra tea. There was too much food to go on the table: samples of muskrat, duck, seal, whitefish, and herring pâté and kippers, steaks and flanks. We spread our plates on the floor, and crouched to dine. One dish of reindeer meat, I remember, was served sweet and sour; some dried caribou meat had been fried white-man's style, with onions, but many of the other dishes were raw, smoked or preserved, bursting with strong flavour, rich in fats and energy. For dessert: *ukpik* – sweet yellow berries – and Inuit ice cream, whipped from ambrosial fat and speckled with dried meat.

Romanticized or not, our belly-stuffing feast left an indelible impression on all of us: of a land as rich in its natural food as in its customs, of a way of life that had flourished without us, but welcomed us in, however briefly.

Hard – impossible – to forget. It is a complex, changing, changeless, wonderful land.

P.G.

✉ For three consecutive Christmases I have received charming cards from Monsieur Bertram. They are always addressed to me. Donald has long gone. The cards are whimsical, always with some amusing allusion – the black hole of the cosmos, fingers clutching desperately to avoid a plunge into space, reverberating echoes issuing from the void. Dear man, he was a sweetie, but I have mixed feelings. What Monsieur Bertram prefers to remember I would prefer to forget.

Without going into tiresome explanations of Donald's advertising job, suffice it to say that a key account in his firm was with a pharmaceutical firm with a world-wide reputation. The Paris representative of this prestigious client firm arrived unexpectedly and inconveniently in Vancouver in the holiday season. Donald's boss asked him to take care of Monsieur Bertram for one evening, perhaps invite him to dinner and discuss the campaign for Western Canada in an informal setting, the warm approach. It was no problem. I truly enjoy cooking.

We had just moved into a new apartment. It was very spiffy with a great view of the downtown sky-scrapers and the North Shore mountains and all kinds of goodies: eye-level ovens in the kitchen; intercom, garbage chute; sun deck with built-in barbecue – the works. I should mention that I was a new bride and this would be the first formal sit-down dinner in my married career.

I considered the menu with great care. I decided on North American festive fare but done with a light touch. I would start with a clear borscht served with islands of thin lemon slices centred with tiny groves of parsley floating elegantly on the clear deep red of the liquid. My triumph, however, would be the turkey, not a great vulgar bird but a lovely little eight-pound hen completely boned, stuffed with a French pâté mixture incorporating ground veal and pork and onions, laced with cognac and port, flavoured with allspice and thyme and pepper and wreathed with diamond-shaped prisms of cranberry jelly interspersed with puff balls of golden yams.

Monsieur Bertram turned out to be a slightly plump, rather small man with a nice twinkle, not the least intimidating as he offered me, upon arrival, an uneven number of striped carnations. We chatted easily over dry sherry and, at the appropriate moment, I withdrew into my new galley kitchen to complete the last-minute preparations. I had taken the turkey out before the sherry to let it rest. It was perfect. The aroma floated on the air – utterly delicious. I unmolded the jellies, placed my lemon islands at hand, set out my soup bowls, checked the borscht for seasoning. All okay. Ready to go. Turkey back to the just-warm oven to maintain its temperature until serving. I turned around, opened the door beneath the counter, grasped the pan, pushed it in where it unaccountably did not contact the expected rack. As the heavy pan slipped from my grasp I realized that I had, in an automatic reflex action, opened the door, which was in the accustomed oven position, and consigned my beautiful bird to the garbage chute.

I opened the swinging door. My dazed expression must have been shocking. By incoherent words and gestures I indicated what had happened. Donald sat me down and gave me a stiff brandy and ordered a deluxe special pizza from around the corner. Monsieur Bertram opened the wine and when the pizza arrived gleefully fingered the slices with their elastic strings of melted cheese, an experience which he claimed to be enjoying as a novelty.

I don't know what happened to Donald's account. I don't recall that it was mentioned even briefly in the course of the evening. All I know is that I will be surprised next Christmas if I do not receive a card, complete with some horrible image of devouring space, to remind me of that memorable meal.

Katherine Kelly
Vancouver

✉ I was twelve years old, and it was the first Christmas in many years that my father didn't have to go to work. He was a policeman and worked long shifts and spent his days off in court. This made our times together as a family very special.

We had opened our presents, we being me, my four sisters, my baby brother, Mother and Daddy. My heart was so full of joy and wonder, I remember dancing and singing around the house as I fondled my new toys and trinkets.

"What would you like for breakfast?" my father asked. "You can have whatever you wish." "Ham and eggs," we replied in chorus. "Oh, Daddy, could we please have ham and eggs?" This caught my father completely by surprise. We had only read about people who could afford such a breakfast.

Daddy turned to my mother. Her first reaction was a shake of the head and a quiet no. Then my father stepped closer to her and with one look was able to persuade her to change her mind. With much delight, my father served us our breakfast of ham and eggs, even though the ham had been purchased for the next day's dinner.

I wonder now if it was the food that made that meal so memorable? Or was it a twelve-year-old girl realizing, in a new way, the love of her father and her father's love for her mother? I was suddenly aware of the tender interaction of words, gestures and glances taking place between them.

My father is gone now. He died just three years after he retired from the force. I have many pleasant memories of him but the one I cherish most is the breakfast we shared that morning.

Elizabeth Carrell
Minden, Ontario

✉ I was a boy of ten, separated from the rest of my family as a result of World War Two. For the previous eleven months I had lived on a farm in East Germany. My room was in the hayloft of the barn, my bed was an old sofa and my blanket an old dirty coat the farmer had given me. My meals were the scraps from the kitchen. I remember that year as being the coldest of my life. I was always hungry.

The farm family had regarded me as an asset. I had typhoid and the fear of the disease kept the Russian soldiers a respectable distance from the farm. I had remained there trying to recover enough strength to continue my search for the rest of my family. My mother had carefully instructed all of her children, during the early part of the war, where we would meet if we became separated by the conflict. In English it translates "on the stone minus seven" in Hamburg, West Germany.

In November of 1945 I left the farm and headed toward the border that separates East and West Germany. I travelled by foot at night, and occasionally by train in open, cold cars. When at last I did reach the border I was able to fool the guards and cross into West Germany. It was then on to Hamburg, again by train. I arrived at the main train station in Hamburg on December 22, 1945. It was there I found a Red Cross nurse, and it was this woman who gave me a large serving of porridge in a tin bowl. The porridge was steaming hot and dotted with raisins. It tasted wonderful to a hungry, cold and tired ten-year-old. It was my first warm meal in more than two years.

This same nurse gave me a transit ticket and instructions on how to find "on the stone minus seven." I found the house, I found my family and I found a bed with blankets. I slept well that night: I was warm and my stomach was full.

Peter Domin
Calgary

✉ It wasn't a gourmet meal in a fancy restaurant with dim lighting and smiling servants. It was in the old farm home I grew up in, full of memories of my childhood years.

The menu was simple. I remember cabbage rolls, home-baked bread, garden-fresh asparagus and tasty sweets. Nothing much, you may say, until you realize that my mother had peacefully died in that house only two days before at the age of eighty-three. She was active to the last day, so her deep freeze was well stocked. We had no trouble finding all the makings of an excellent meal.

The day before her funeral, as the family members gathered in the old home, we had the last of many splendid meals prepared by my mother.

How many hundreds of times had her light and delicious bread sated my body and soul? I savoured each mouthful.

The asparagus, fresh from her garden, had been tended by the same loving hands that cared for us all from babyhood. How strange it was to sit in the place mother had called home for more than sixty years and to know the era was over. I thought of the young bride coming to a one-room shack and the growth of the family, the bad years and the good – the struggle of the thirties and forties and the comfortable affluence of the sixties and seventies.

We mechanically performed the necessary tasks on that day and the ones that followed. Time has moved on but nothing will ever erase the memory of that most memorable meal.

Inga Benson
Lisieux, Saskatchewan

✉ My friend Toni comes from a very good Toronto family. She is well-educated and a talented artist. When she moved to the west coast, she took to the lifestyle with gusto. She also took to a man named Ivan. Now, Ivan is a very west-coast kind of guy. He builds boats and lives on the water, and, as any west-coast guy will tell you, he knows that the quickest way to a woman's heart is fresh crab. Ivan set his trap and pulled up the crabs and took the biggest, prettiest one over to Toni. Toni was, of course, thrilled.

Unfortunately, there was a hockey game on that night, and Toni didn't have a TV set. So Ivan left the crab with her and took off to watch the game at a buddy's house. As I said, Toni is a well-educated woman. She knows about business and art and dogs and horses. She's also a marvellous cook, but she didn't know how to cook a crab. A live crab. A live crab that was by this time crawling around her kitchen floor.

First of all she turned to her cookbooks. She learned how to make a crab soufflé, and crab fritters, and crab quiche, but they all called for dead crab. So she called a friend.

"It's easy," her friend told her. "Boil a big pot of salted water and throw it in."

"What?" said Toni, "throw a living animal into boiling water?"

"Yeah," said the friend, "then put the lid on. He might try to crawl out."

"Yuck," said Toni.

But she gave it a try. She put a pot, full of water, salted, on the stove and waited for it to boil. By this time, the crab was in the living room making friends with Simon, the dog. When the water was boiling Toni picked up the crab and held it over the steaming pot. She couldn't do it. There was no way she could drop that crab into that water. But what *was* she going to do with it? As she stared into it's beady little eyes, she realized that she couldn't leave it to run loose in her house. It had to go back to the beach.

But the beach near her house wasn't the beach that the crab had come from. That beach was on the other side of the island. Maybe the crab wouldn't like this beach. Maybe the water or sand there wasn't good for crabs. Maybe it was already inhabited by a hostile tribe of crabs. She wasn't taking any chances. So once again Toni picked up the crab, carefully took him out to the car, carefully drove through the dark, rainy night, and carefully set him back on the beach from which he came.

She swears that the crab did a little dance and waved its claw in thanks before it scurried into the salt chuck. But I don't believe that.

Danni Tribe
Sointula, British Columbia

✉ It was in Bangladesh, and I was working as a temporary volunteer. The month was February, the traditional time for picnics. A group of us left Dhaka early in the morning. Two bumpy, dusty hours later we arrived at a small forest – our picnic spot. The first thing that I noticed about the woods was their bareness, the result of consistent foraging for scarce fuel. The foragers were a group of small children, from eight to twelve years of age. They wore dirty T-shirts and shorts; their feet were bare and their faces unwashed. From the red brittleness of their hair, their gaunt bony frames and distended stomachs it was apparent they were malnourished.

The curry was done to perfection, the forest filled with its strong, pungent aroma. We sat down under the trees and proceeded to enjoy the food. Most of us tried to ignore the bright stares of our hosts, tried to convince ourselves that it was inevitable that we should have and that they should have not.

A noise by the makeshift kitchen startled me. The cook was holding onto and slapping the arm of a boy. He had crept up and put his hand in the curry pot, and was defiantly chewing on the meat he had stolen. The scolding meant nothing to this boy, the meat everything. This one act proved inspirational for the others. Before we knew it curry was being snatched from our plates, from the ground, and, when possible, from the pot. Having lost my appetite by this point I watched with a mixture of shame and horror as a child – frantic, bold, desperate – quickly finished off my meal.

With the food gone the children left, and we soon followed. The

100

trip back to the city was silent. It was hard for us to meet each other's eyes; this would not be something we would talk about. I try to talk about it when I can. I feel it is the least I can do.

Norah McRae
Edmonton

✉ It was very early on the first day of the New Year. We lay in bed, liverish and headachy from an indulgent and nostalgic late night of skiing in the moonlight and too much champagne afterwards with old friends. I snuggled into my husband, more to see if he was still alive than feeling responsive. I got a boozy nuzzle and nestled more deeply under the covers, curious but grateful that I hadn't heard from my two children. Suddenly I sensed an invasion, not from a noise, which my thudding head would probably not have picked up, but from an acrid, unmistakable smell. Burnt butter. Opening my scratchy eyes, I saw two trays presented by my beaming nine- and seven-year-old daughters.

"Happy New Year! Breakfast in bed!"

Groggily we struggled up on our pillows, trying to appear alert. I wasn't sure I might not have to race to the bathroom.

"I didn't know they could cook," my husband groaned.

"Don't look now," I whispered to him, "but I don't think they can!"

On each tray was a hand-coloured page from a Christmas colouring book for a placemat and a pine branch from the tree laced with a forlorn piece of tinsel. A peeled Mandarin orange sat in one corner and on a butter plate was a soggy, ripped piece of toast.

"The butter was pretty hard," the eldest said apologetically.

I assured her it looked delicious, though I didn't know how I could possibly eat it. The pièce, however, was a single greasy, black-edged fried egg, yolk dissipated and pallid, sitting on a glass plate.

"Do we eat this or have we?" my husband asked, and the girls laughed. He says that at a good many of my meals.

"Oh Daddy!" they cooed in unison, "you're so silly!"

Then, "You see we decorated the napkins." And they had. With their markers, they'd drawn bright, festive insignia all around the borders.

"We made the instant coffee from the hottest water from the tap."

I sipped it and thought of bathwater.

"Mmm. Hits the spot."

It was the most terrible meal I've ever eaten. Indeed, it was hard to forget it for the rest of the day as that pulpy toast and cold, leathery egg sat churning in my tender stomach. But not even sumptuous eggs Benedict served on porcelain with silver and white linen and a fresh pink rose in crystal could ever have compared to the sheer luxury of the ingenuity and love of my daughters' miserable, magnificent New Year's breakfast.

Stephanie O'Reilly
Port Hope, Ontario

✉ Nineteen hundred and sixty, the autumn of my tenth year. It was tobacco harvest, fall fairs and, above all else, far above all else, watermelon time.

Tubby Kay, Chas Doxtator, Squid Roberts, Scotty Arther, brother Mutt and me, the runt of the marauding gaggle of watermelon hookers, counted the days till this most glorious of seasons. Tom Kelly grew them, and we wanted them.

Now, hooking watermelons is not for the faint of heart or those who fear the dark. Assuming the profiles of snakes and the deft tracking facility of Mohawk deer stalkers, we enter the patch from the shadows as near to the house as adrenalin will allow. Properly positioned for our attack, we wait.

The full moon is at its zenith (watermelons are never hooked by flashlight). When Tom Kelly goes to bed, we go to work.

To the left the perfectly round ones with the lovely white-yellow stripes that guide you in the semi-dark. To the right, yeah, to the right, lie the fruit of our desires. The long ones. I go first, the runt always goes first, brother Mutt follows because he worries about me, then the rest.

Jack-knives poised for the slaughter, we strike. First a tap, then a shake. Does it thud? Does it sound hollow? Good! Cut a little hole and pull out a plug. The plug must be ruby red and melt in your mouth.

These prerequisites met, the fine surgery is over. Hooked watermelon always tastes better broken over the knee than daintily sliced, garden-party style. I find mine, Mutt finds his and so all the rest. Five minutes pass, fifteen minutes, half an hour, one hour passes. Juices flow down our chins like honey from a stack of hot waffles. Lusted after, worked for and earned by the sweat and cunning only we, kindred souls, could understand.

FWAPP!

"What was that?"

"Tom's screen door slammed, I heard it!"

"You're right."

"Damn, let's run boys."

... And they did. But the runt didn't, couldn't move. Too full.

Boom! Boom!

"Yeow!"

Then he moved. No longer the deer stalker, but the wounded deer. There's nothing like the bitter sting of rock salt to indelibly etch the sweet taste of a watermelon meal on the hind of the runt.

Barney Cummings
Toronto

My mouth waters just to think about it: dry, spicy summer sausage soaking up the puddle of cream in which the potatoes on my plate were swimming.

This was no ordinary summer sausage. It had been prepared right on the farm on butchering day, pressed into casings and hung in the smokehouse by the back lane until it had just the right smokey flavour. Then it was hung in an upstairs room to dry and mellow. It spread its aroma from one room to the next and when Grandmother finally decided it was ready for the table – it was good!

Come to think of it, the creamed potatoes were good, too. That very morning I had helped Grandmother dig them from the "early" garden behind the smokehouse. I helped wash them and peel them. In those days we didn't realize how good peelings were for you. But we did know what made the best sauce after the potatoes were cooked to their proper doneness. Grandmother would carefully lift the milk pail from the ice box and skim off the cream that had risen to the top. And just before serving time, she dribbled a hot stream of browned butter around the bowl of thick, creamed potatoes.

This was my cue. As soon as the butter was dolloped into the pan to melt, I was sent down cellar to chose a pie from the pie cupboard. This big wooden structure, with screen in the doors to keep out the mice, always had pies in it – I don't think I ever wondered how they got there.

The pies were on a shelf above eye level, so after I had unlatched the two little doors, I had to use the touch-and-taste method to choose the pie I wanted. I'd dip in my fingertip and lick it, and dip in and lick. When my finger finally came up "red" and my tongue tasted "sweet," I had found the right one. I am told that the pies I carried to the table were always red. The way I remember it is that Grandma's pies were cherry, raspberry and red currant.

I was eight years old then. I can't remember whether we had vegetables with that meal, nor whether I was forced to eat them. What I do remember is *where* we ate those summer meals – in the summer kitchen, of course. The room gathered junk all winter long, but was miraculously tidied just before haying. The windows were unhooked so that only screens came between us and the bees in the trumpet vine, the flowers on the mountain-ash tree, the millions of flies from the barnyard and the barnyard itself. Some of the flies that poured in when the screen door was opened were soon kicking and buzzing wildly from sticky fly hangers that were hanging from the ceiling. And I was allowed to sit on a wooden bench behind the table with my back against the cool, rough brick wall. I felt funny vibrations when the house rattled and shook as the old electric trolley, with its cow-catcher sticking out front, rumbled up the grade behind the house at the far end of the garden, making its endless trek from Kitchener to Galt – or was it to Port Dover?

As I look back I wonder if the food was really that good, or if in a child's imagination it was this summer eating spot that made things taste so great, or if it was just being on the farm where everyone was hungry at mealtime – especially a little girl from the city.

Margaret L. Weber
New Hamburg, Ontario

✉ In early July, 1927, I met a fascinating man who spoke elegant English with a delightful Scandinavian accent. One day, he invited me to go with him on an outing the following Sunday. I accepted without hesitation, flattered that this man twice my age would wish to spend a day with me.

He arrived early Sunday morning and announced that we were going to have a picnic – his landlady had prepared it specially for us. We drove to Rondeau Provincial Park and past the usual busy picnic areas to where the park became a wooded retreat. It was here he spread a fine linen tablecloth. Out of the basket came dishes of real china, silver cutlery, crystal tumblers and the most eye-appealing and delicious picnic a hearty young appetite could imagine. There was fried chicken cooked to perfection, potato salad tossed together with tangy old-fashioned homemade dressing, devilled eggs, a pot of cold baked beans and tomatoes picked from the vine. Spicy, sweet home-made pickles, homemade rolls and Cheddar cheese added to the feast. For dessert there were date-filled brown-sugar cookies and luscious strawberries. There was a jar of real lemonade kept miraculously cold by being implanted in a larger container of crushed ice. It was not unusual food, not what we would consider gourmet, but in this wooded setting on the shores of Lake Erie it seemed truly food for the gods. My admiration for this resourceful man who could arrange such a picnic grew by the moment. We ate – oh, how we ate – and then, with empty picnic basket, returned to the car. We drove slowly through the secluded part of the park.

By now we knew something about each other. He asked me to sing, preferably some of the old songs I had learned from my grand-mother. So I sang, at his special request, "Jeanie with the Light Brown Hair" and so on. He seemed to like "Annie Laurie" best of all.

Late in May of 1975, this fascinating man, my dear Danish husband, lay dying in a Thunder Bay hospital. The doctors had told us the end could come at any time. Our two Thunder Bay children had gone to the airport to meet the plane that was bringing our other three children to the bedside of their father. I kept looking at my watch, desperately praying that he would still be alive when they arrived. Suddenly, I had a flashback of that wonderful picnic of long ago. I whispered in my husband's ear, "You know this is 'Jeanie with the Light Brown Hair'?" Through the years it had become his nickname for me. I felt a slight pressure of his fingers on my hand. I began to sing, softly, close to his ear, "Annie Laurie"– he used to tell everyone he fell in love with me when I sang that song as we drove together through the woods. He smiled slightly. After the first verse I said, "Wasn't that a lovely picnic?" Again I felt the faint pressure of his hand in mine. I repeated the song, my eyes on my watch – I knew the plane was about to land. I whispered in his ear, "The family will soon be here." He smiled and I kept on singing "Annie Laurie." I heard footsteps and turned as our five adult children walked into the room. He tried valiantly to rise, smiled an angelic smile and attempted a garbled greeting. He fell back on his pillow and in a few moments slipped into unconsciousness.

I walked out to the sitting room, leaving our children with their father. Some minutes later his nurse came up to me and quietly said, "Mrs. Miller, your husband has just passed away." She did not know that I was really not present in that hospital sitting room. I was far away, enjoying a fantastic picnic with an enchanting man at Rondeau Park on the shores of Lake Erie.

Jeanne Cuthbert Miller
Thunder Bay, Ontario

Different Generations

I met Grace Lane in the summer of 1982 at a magazine-writers' conference in Regina and knew right away she was one of the people to take part in an experiment I wanted to try when I returned to the radio that fall. Grace is the widow of a prairie minister and the veteran of the old CCF battles that played such a role in the formation of that part of the country. The experiment I had in mind was an exchange of letters between someone of her age and experience and a much younger woman, preferably in a major city, who was as close to the political issues of the 1980s as Grace had been to those of an earlier time – although I wanted the letters to be personal: two women exchanging notes across the years. The producers suggested Ann Pappert, a young, feminist magazine writer in Toronto, and Ann seemed perfect. We introduced them – by mail – and the exchange lasted through our first season. Grace would write and record her letter in Saskatchewan and then Ann would reply from Toronto and we would broadcast them together. What follows here is a selection from a number of their letters, a sample of the views they shared, beginning with Grace's introduction of herself.

October 10, 1982
Dear Ann:

I'm the senior in this dialogue between generations, you from your Toronto locale and I from this prairie city, Regina, which I love. It will be fun to see how we perceive our lives in this sprawling, troubled, marvellous land.

I should mention that I live alone, except on weekends when my handicapped daughter is here. Homer, my theologian husband, died of a heart attack three years after he retired, so he hadn't much time in the bungalow we bought with such joy. Much as I miss him, I find life good.

One thing may surprise you: working wives are no new phenomenon to me. I'm the centre link in a *five-generation* chain of women who combined marriage and outside jobs.

I am *for* marriage, though . . . for keeps, if possible. No relationship compares with it for depth and joy. Not only, as the classical wedding service puts it, are you one flesh, you literally live in and through each other. By that, I mean your mate's successes and disappointments are yours; yours are his.

In case you think time has glamourized the years Homer and I spent together, let me read the words I wrote in my diary eleven days after he died: "My whole life, as I've lived and loved it for forty-two years, has gone up in smoke."

What made our marriage work? First we knew each other thoroughly beforehand. In the four years we were engaged and mostly apart, we wrote almost every day. We shared the same values; we knew what we expected of marriage. We were deeply in love – stirred physically, of course – but for most of my generation, intercourse came after the wedding, not as the postscript to a date.

However different things are now, I still believe men and women are fascinated by each other; they still long to possess and be possessed by each other; they still yearn for long-term love in a family setting, shared with children, who are genetic debtors to both. Women, of course, have the major nurturing role, but until recently, the man's role was clear and important. He was protector and provider. Today, in urban settings, the protector role has all but disappeared, and with women working at almost every job formerly held only by men, the provider role has dwindled.

Let's look at what's happening to men, amid all the clamour for our "rights" and our attempt to deny sexual difference. They're caught in the confusion, too.

Take your pattern, keeping your maiden name. It's one more blow to a man's self-esteem. Recently, researchers found that men with high-profile wives who earn more income are eleven times more likely than others to die of heart disease in middle life and twice as likely to divorce. I guess, today, Ann, "You pays your money and takes your choice." For me, a healthy marriage would come first. By the way, what's your son Noah's last name?

Grace

October 18, 1982
Dear Grace:

I was brought up by both my parents to be an independent woman. My father owned his own business, and it never occurred to him, even though he had a daughter and a son, that I shouldn't be encouraged and taught to take over his business when he retired. Although both my parents certainly hoped marriage and motherhood would be part of my life, my mother in particular always urged me to develop a life of my own that would carry through even after I married.

Personally, I'm glad that the old idea of marriage based on man as the protector and provider and woman as the nurturer is going by the wayside. And the thought that men and women desire to possess each other leaves me more than a little distressed.

I certainly don't want to be possessed by Ray or to possess him – possession implies ownership and assumes an unequal position from the start. Not just unequal where the wife is concerned, but certainly just as disastrous for the man. I don't think it's healthy for either partner to desire a love that abrogates their own sense of self.

Being swept off your feet is fine in the very early days of a relationship, but I sure wouldn't want it on a long-term basis.

To me the most important thing in a marriage is mutual respect – a respect that allows each partner a role inside marriage and an identity unconnected to the relationship. I would be terrified to be stuck in a marriage where my role was limited to the duties of a wife and mother. It seems to me that it wouldn't take many years before I would lose the feeling that I could be a fully functioning adult on my own if the need arose. If it's the sole role of a man in marriage to protect and provide, is it any wonder generations of women felt helpless and unable to cope on their own?

You seem to be saying that, in the old days, there was a man's world and a woman's world and everybody knew which was which, but that these days women have pushed the old boundaries to the limit and the price they're paying is a generation of bewildered men stripped of their self-esteem. In your view men aren't ready for a world where their wives are equals both at home and in the workplace. You bet your socks they're not! And I doubt if we leave it up to them they ever will be. Where do you think the impetus for change will come from if women don't provide it? What am I to think of men so insecure that the stress of having an aggressive, successful wife drives them to a coronary? Isn't it high time men like these grew up and stopped measuring their own self-worth by devaluing their wives?

Women have paid too high a price for protecting their men's egos at the cost of their own. If I were married to a man who felt belittled because I wouldn't take his name, I can tell you I'd be happier without him. I'll tell you why I kept mine. It's because it is *mine*, the name I was born with. It links me to generations of forebears and keeping it had nothing whatsoever to do with hiding my marriage. I'm very married, and I doubt there's anyone I work with who thinks otherwise. And like dozens of other kids I know, Noah's last name uses both Ray's and my name. Hyphenated surnames aren't reserved exclusively for the aristocracy any more.

Ann

November 14, 1982
Dear Ann:

Let's get on to the question of motherhood. Don't assume that my generation was at the mercy of chance. Contraceptives were very much part of our lives – but they were used in marriage, not to play around. Homer came to our wedding night armed with condoms. He had plans for post-graduate study that we carried out. When it was complete, we were ready for a family.

I find it hard to understand couples who choose to be childless; it's opting for death, rather than life. Save for the tiny company of geniuses, the Einsteins, Bachs and Virginia Woolfs, our only claim to social immortality is through the generation we produce.

Do I believe having a child makes a woman a better person? No, not automatically. But the helplessness of a baby usually calls forth some unselfishness, a rare commodity today. All parents, if their child matures and marries, make a genetic impact on the future. We're immortal, whether we like it or not.

I don't mean childless people are unimportant. A good dozen of the women I most admire and love are single, but they are outside the genetic pool and do not have the "gut" stake in tomorrow.

It's sad to me that some healthy couples reject parenthood. Children are Canada's most precious asset.

Grace

November 23, 1982
Dear Grace:

The decision to have a child or not should be a personal choice between a woman and her spouse, not a matter for chit-chat among friends and strangers alike. And although it's true that if every woman decided to opt out of motherhood the human race would be in bad shape, population statistics make it abundantly clear this isn't about to happen. In fact, given the disastrous consequences we all face from a booming world population, the truly responsible social act may well be the choice not to bear children.

Attitudes like yours make it far more difficult for a woman to accept an imposed childless state. After all, most women have no way of knowing they're unable to have a child until they try to get pregnant. For the first twenty years or so of their lives, they assume that, like most women, they too will someday be mothers. For these women, like myself, the double whammy of discovering you can't bear a child and the inevitable association this brings with a woman's perceived duty to parent is devastating.

The next time you hear someone asking a married woman why such a dear woman like her doesn't have any children, a comment I used to hear endlessly, pay close attention to her reaction. Her discomfort may not just be embarrassment at such a personal question. It may be rekindled knowledge that she is one of those who cannot.

Ann

December 8, 1982
Dear Ann:

We have a great time misunderstanding each other; I said nothing about women who *couldn't* bear children. That's a misfortune – just as having a child like my Jan, born normal but ruined by illness at fourteen months, was. There's nothing to be gained by mourning. You just go on.

I'm all for adopting, as you did, and while you won't make the direct biological contribution of natural parents, the opportunities you and Ray provide for Noah will widen his range of mating options. Your influence on his life will be of the greatest significance.

I've become deeply involved in the problems of retarded children and their families. Both of us, you and I, are transmuting pain into something socially valuable.

What I was talking about are healthy, privileged women who refuse to bear children and cloak the rejection by talking about the "myth of motherhood," when the real myth is – with rare exceptions – that anything else they do is as important. Conception and birth are indispensable for racial continuity. To these we all owe our presence on this fascinating, frightening planet. The horror of nuclear war hits most poignantly when you look at those who are "flesh of your flesh, bone of your bone."

Grace

December 29, 1982
Dear Grace:

Thinking about a New Year's letter made me realize just how different this year has been. Before last year, every New Year brought the same wish, that the year to come would finally be the year I'd become a mother. Having Noah has changed my life in so many special ways – I've often thought of telling you what it was like when he arrived, but somehow the time never seemed right. So I thought I'd share it with you today, and oddly enough, it really is appropriate, because it's amost two years ago to the day we first heard about him.

That first call was a query from our lawyer: were we still looking for a baby to adopt? My heart stopped when we heard about Noah. As it turned out, problems stood in our way. He was, it seemed, yet another baby we would lose.

Then on a Wednesday morning at the end of April, as I stood washing dishes, the phone rang again. "Do you remember the baby we talked about at Christmas?" our adoption worker asked. "His mother has signed the consent forms and he's available. Are you interested?"

In my heart I always believed this day would come, but the uncertainty of all the years and the suddenness of the call made me panic.

Noah's social worker was off at a conference, so we couldn't actually see him until the following Tuesday. These were days marked by a see-saw of emotions. I'd burst into tears in the shower, first at the thought that at long last our struggle to have a family might finally be over and of imagining walking down our stairs with a tiny hand in mine . . . only to shudder with fear that things might not work out. We'd already had an adoption fall through at the last minute the previous year. "Let's not get our hopes too high," we said.

On Tuesday morning we went to Noah's foster home to meet him for the first time. Surrounded by two social workers and his foster mother, we spent an hour rolling around the floor with him between cuddles and a slow realization that this seventeen-pound, seven-month-old miracle was about to become our son.

At the end of the hour the children's aid worker announced, "Well, it's obvious the two of you know what you're doing. I've no problems with letting you have him right away. Can you come back and get him in the morning?"

We'd never dreamed things would happen so fast. In the space of a few hours he'd be ours! We laughed, we cried and when we reached home we literally jumped for joy.

We had no nursery, never having wanted to live with an empty room. We spent the next twenty-four hours frantically preparing one with the help of friends and the next morning we drove to get our son.

Since I've had Noah I've realized children *are* our future and we owe it to them to give them a peaceful world in which to grow.

Love to you and your family. May your holiday be truly special.

Ann

OUT OF WORK

No Canadian story, during the first three years of my time on *Morningside*, touched as many lives as dramatically as unemployment. Statistics for the rest of us were, for thousands of listeners, the awful realities of daily living. We covered that story in a number of ways, but never so clearly, I think, as in the diary Don Myers agreed to keep for us.

Don was thirty in the autumn of 1982, living in Thunder Bay, Ontario. He wrote a long letter to me, part of which appears here. Then, at our request, he kept a diary of the next nine weeks. What follows is the substance of what he said on the radio, plus some of the letters his diary engendered.

Don Myers has a job now, by the way. But the part of his life he put on the public record is still the stark truth for hundreds of thousands of Canadians.

Things were going well two months ago. I was living in Alberta, earning $24,000 a year doing what I really enjoyed doing.

Then the axe fell.

It's not a lot of money to make, $24,000, not in Alberta. Even receiving $2,000 per month, I was spending more than a quarter of my income on rent. And I had other expenses: a car, which I needed for my work; $300-a-month child support, a leftover from a defunct marriage; the remnants of a student loan. I actually lost money over the year.

I was working for a non-profit company, the first and only employee. The economy hurt the organization. When there's less loose change floating about, it's harder to raise funds. If your best efforts fall short of the target, reasons must be found, blame must be assigned. Were our expectations unrealistic? Was our product inadequate? Were we victimized by a sudden downturn in the economy? The board never answered these questions. I don't know if they even asked them. They dumped me.

So now I'm on the job market. I'm thirty years old, with government experience, business experience in the non-profit sector, public-relations and sales experience, trying to land on my feet again.

First thing I have to do is move. I know there are supposed to be more job openings in Alberta but I can't afford to stay to find out. The rent is $600 per month. If I stay long, I won't have the money to pay the movers.

I lived with a lady friend for a while. She moved to accept a great career opportunity, at a lower rate of pay, in Thunder Bay. She tells me I'm welcome to stay with her while I look for work. I've never lived in Ontario before. I sell off a number of furnishings, have the rest packed into a moving van and fly away, leaving Alberta behind.

The job search begins.

Week One

Here I am in a new town. No job. No income. No unemployment insurance. There are always jobs. Someone is always being hired and

116

fired, someone always quitting and being replaced. And Thunder Bay is a good-sized town, 120,000. Must be work.

So I've begun my search.

I know I'm good, damn good, and if I can get an interview, I know I'll be hired. I know I can't sit and wait for the right newspaper ad. I know I have to search. I've prepared a list of jobs and matched them with prospective employers. I've been going through the classified ads. I've registered at the Canada Employment Centre. And I've gone calling.

At government offices I was told there is a hiring freeze. One office did let me fill out an application form, telling me they'd keep it on file for six months.

I arranged an interview with a counsellor at the Canada Employment Centre. I thought if I gave him my resumé, showed him what I had done and what I was prepared to do, that he'd be able to give me some leads.

He glances at my resumé, nodding. I tell him where I applied.

"Yup, sounds like you've covered them all," he says.

"Well, I had thought of the university and community college," I said.

"Good idea."

"Do you have names of people I could call there?"

"Uh, yeah, I think so, somewhere."

He leaves and returns with two names on a scrap of paper. He asks if I am interested in sales.

"Well, I'd consider it. . . .

"What about newspapers?" I ask. "I used to write for a newspaper back in the early '70s."

He names the obvious, the local daily papers.

"They're both Thomson, aren't they?" I ask.

"Uh, I think so."

I left, with no new leads, just the ones I had suggested to him. God, I thought, I can do better. This guy is supposed to be counselling professionals and he doesn't even know who owns the local newspapers. Seems to me like someone killing time, making conversation until his paycheque arrives.

The contact names he gave me were incorrect. Neither individual worked there. At Lakehead University, I was granted an interview. We talked about my experience. But there were no openings.

Still, it feels good to be heard.

Week Two

It's important to maintain a schedule, the books say, important to work as hard at finding work as you would at work.

Well, I've been doing that since I started two weeks ago. I'm up early, driving my friend to work before beginning my search, filling out applications all morning, staying near the phone and writing letters of application in the afternoon. I try not to get too far from the phone, though trips to the laundromat and grocery are occasionally required.

An ad in a local weekly newspaper catches my eye. They need an editor. I arrange an interview, dig up the few clippings I have and set out, confidently. I'm a good writer, a good editor, and have supervisory experience. It's been eight years since I worked on a newspaper, but at $225 per week, I doubt they'll be able to do better.

I meet with the publisher. In addition to offering low pay, he wants a two-year commitment. (The previous editor left after four weeks.) I accept his terms. Then he tells me there are two other applicants— one of them from another paper owned by the same company. He is surprised that three people have applied, as only one applied a month earlier. I get the impression that, had I applied last week, I might already have been hired.

I would have applied last week, too, had the Canada Employment Centre counsellor mentioned the existence of the paper. I asked him, specifically, about local newspapers. He never mentioned this one. After all, I'm new to Thunder Bay, had no way of knowing.

I didn't get the job. They sent me a card. I found out that the man from the other paper was hired. They had to hire him, really–he was already with their organization. Still, I can't help feeling a bit bitter, can't shake the feeling that the negligence of the man at the Canada Employment Centre cost me a job.

My furniture arrived this week – two weeks early. And it cost me $1,200 – $400 more than the estimate. I have less than $100 left.

I applied for three positions advertised in the newspaper. One is selling memberships for an auto club, one supervisor of an employment project, one bookstore manager. I wrote confident, positive letters and enclosed a different resumé with each, adjusted to suit the ad. I feel bad about not being able to contribute to the rent. My friend is feeling the pinch, I know, and she has an infant daughter to support. I try to help look after the baby and buy some groceries but $100 doesn't last long and I have no solid prospects.

Week Three

I bought a job-finding book this week called *What Colour Is Your Parachute?* Charged it, actually. The book really picked me up after a lot of frustration. Seems I'm doing some things right, like structuring my day and systematic canvassing for work. But leaving resumés is not recommended. Few employers even look at them. That's a relief. The photocopying bills were killing me.

Found two good positions in the paper this week. One is project officer for a multicultural group and the other public relations and sales for a liquor distributor. I wrote really good letters, offering to provide resumés on request.

Still haven't heard from the three ads I answered last week. Not even an acknowledgement. I broadened my search to department stores: Eaton's, Sears, Zellers. The Zellers application bothered me. They requested permission to do a credit check. I'm looking for a job, not a merger. Besides, a month from now my credit rating may have plunged. I also applied for three part-time jobs – at a men's clothing store, a shoe store, a Coles bookstore.

I missed two payments this week: child support and a car payment. I called consumer affairs for advice. The man there advised me to notify my creditors that I will resume payments when I have found a job. He suggested not giving them my present address.

Time to apply for bartending jobs. I visit four lounges. No openings, but I fill out applications.

I have to tell my friend of my financial situation. Up to now I've been paying for half the groceries. With $12, I'm stuck. I can get supplies for the baby with my credit card – it's not a good idea, with no income, but it's the only contribution I can make.

Even the cost of buying a newspaper is a worry. I'm still plugging but it's getting harder and harder to even try. I feel drained on returning every day. Looking for work is more tiring than work.

Christmas is coming and I haven't enough money to buy stamps. My friend says I can spend Christmas with her family in Toronto. "If I can afford it, I'll give you that for Christmas," she says. But what can I give? I have no money for gifts – for her, for my child in Manitoba, for my mother . . . .

Week Four

I've been offered a job – as reporter for the same weekly newspaper that did not hire me as editor. I'll be working for the other guy. But, when we meet, the tune has changed. Suddenly, I'm one of three candidates.

"The pay is $165 a week," he says, "Could you live on that?" I *hear* my jaw drop. My God, I think, I could make that much in three nights bartending – if I could find a bartending job.

"Do you have any clippings?"

"Yeah, at home. You didn't mention clippings on the phone. Your publisher saw them two weeks ago."

"Well, I'm getting the others to write stories for me. Maybe you could do that."

"No problem," I say. "I could pound one out in ten minutes."

"Um, maybe you could do a review of a play in town tonight."

Wait a minute, I think. Is this guy really asking me to write a free story for him to prove I can write?

"I could go get my clippings," I offer. "I live a few blocks from here."

"Well, okay. Yeah, that'd be okay."

Within half an hour, the clippings are in his hands.

I doubt I'll be offered the job and don't know what I'll do if I am. But I can't afford to refuse. I'd be tempted to take it until something better came along. Is that unfair to the company? At $165 a week, they can't demand much. Besides, I've never had an employer worry about what was fair to *me*.

I became a volunteer this week – stage manager for a children's theatre company. It's a new group – this will be their first production. I stumbled into the children's theatre thing when I took my friend to an interview at the community cable-television station. The host of the show is writer and director of the play.

I needed to become involved in something, something that *is* work. I am familiar with stage management from my previous work in university and professional theatre. Besides, volunteer work is a good way to make contacts that might, eventually, lead to a job.

A couple of nights later, at the auditions, one of the weekly newspaper's "trial" reporters showed up. She looked sixteen, seemed afraid to talk to anyone. She did talk to the director and one kid. Then she left. Ha, I thought, that's what the paper deserves for $165 a week!

I have no money left. My friend gave me $20, forced it on me almost. I didn't want to take it. I put it in a cup above the sink and use it only when I really need it – for newspapers, food, household necessities.

I'm still using my credit card to get baby supplies. I worry every time the cashier checks my card number against those in the book. I expect a refusal. I've rehearsed my answer. But no, I'm clear – for now.

Week Five

I bet I've filled out more than a hundred application forms, have distributed dozens of resumés, have made thirty telephone calls, have written forty letters.What have I to show for it? One letter of acknowledgement from the provincial government, saying they'll keep my application on file for six months. That's all.

Christmas is coming and I have no money, no income, no job, no prospects, a crumbling credit rating, a car in need of repair. I can't seem to get going. I look at the ads and see why they *won't* hire me. Used to be I'd grab any small detail and twist my experience to suit it. Now I have to force myself to apply.

Nordair is on strike here. They just voted against a new contract offer. I've no idea what they were offered, or what they want, but I'm tempted to write the company and offer to work. I'd work for peanuts and they choose not to work at all. What am I saying? Would I really scab? How far would I go to get work?

The volunteer work is going well. It's tough, stage managing a children's theatre production, but it feels good to be part of something, to be working with people again.

Having no money means I can't join the company for a drink after rehearsal. I've declined several invitations. I did go once, just after I sold my coin collection, only to discover I'd forgotten my wallet. One of the cast paid for my beer but, by the time the next rehearsal rolled around, I had no money to repay him.

The theatre work remainds me of my favourite play from university days: *Waiting for Godot*. In that play two characters stand around on stage killing time, waiting for Godot to arrive. He never comes. Looking for work is like that. I'd like to try staging the play with a local amateur company. We could set it in front of the job boards at the Canada Employment Centre.

I applied for two jobs from the newspaper, though it took me several days before I answered the ads. One is for therapeutic parent at Browndale, which operates several homes for emotionally disturbed children. The other is community-development audio-visual worker for a non-profit media organization. I delivered my application at the last minute, eight days after the ad first appeared.

Funny. Both groups called. I have interviews next week.

Week Six

This should be the week. I have two interviews.

Even better, the job I'd prefer is first. It's with the non-profit media organization, which helps community groups prepare film and slide presentations explaining their causes. I have quite a bit of community-development experience, and am I strong on written and oral communications. But I have little film experience.

I research the organization, arrive at the interview well prepared, fifteen minutes early. Two board members, both women, and Terry, the director, attend the meeting.

Almost immediately one of the women mentions two letters I wrote to the editor of the local newspaper. I feel uncomfortable, feel I have to justify them. "It really bothers me when a reporter – someone who should know better – misuses the language," I say.

They seem concerned that I won't stay in Thunder Bay long enough to justify being hired.

"I expect to be here at least two years," I tell them.

"You have a lot of management experience," one woman says. "Could you work for someone?"

"Actually, I had responsibilities in other jobs but was still under the supervision of others," I say. I don't want to downgrade my experience, but I don't want to appear overqualified either.

"What about promoting causes you disagree with?"

"I don't expect everyone to agree with me," I say. "I'd rather see something presented accurately and clearly. That's important to me."

We discuss a few other points. All in all, it's a good interview. I'm promised a decision the next day. But by four-thirty the next day I haven't heard from them. I give in. I call Terry.

"Has a decision been made?" I ask.

"Yes, we've decided to hire someone else."

My spirits plunge. Did I blow it? What happened? What did I do wrong? Was it the letters to the editor? Was I too anxious? It was my first interview in weeks. Did I say too much? Did I say the wrong thing?

The other interview – for therapeutic parent at Browndale – turns out to be a sort of qualifying round. I see a film on the organization, am told of pay and benefits and am scheduled to spend three days as observer in one of the homes. The observer period is for both of us, for me to decide if I can cope with it, for them to decide if I can do the job. I'll be doing that next week.

Mastercard phoned. I'm ninety days overdue. They want my card returned. I explain my situation, point out that I informed them of my plight weeks ago, that I'll resume payments when I have an income again.

Before the week is over, I've had two more calls from creditors. I phoned consumer affairs again. The man mentioned bankruptcy. He says he'll send me information.

I feel sick, depressed. I return to bed – the first time in ten weeks of job hunting that I've gone back to bed in the morning.

I feel bad about not contributing to rent and food. I eat as little as possible. I help around the house – cooking, cleaning, baby-sitting. One positive result: I've lost eleven pounds.

My friend gave me money again. "You need to have pocket money," she said. "Enjoy it. Probably the only time in your life you'll be a kept man." She gave me airline tickets, too. I'll be spending Christmas in Toronto, with her family.

Week Seven

It's tough, this looking for work. It's impossible not to take rejections personally, no matter how hard you try. Especially when you don't know *why* you haven't been the one chosen. You try to pick yourself up, but sometimes it takes days before you're ready to return to the battle.

Giving up is not really an option. Unemployment is the one job you can't quit.

I've certainly compromised. I've applied for jobs that pay less than half of what I received before. I've tried for jobs for which I know I am grossly overqualified. I've reached a point where I'm willing to accept almost any job, if only to qualify for unemployment insurance. It takes only twelve weeks to become eligible . . . amazing when unemployment insurance is a step up.

Yet I've survived, quite well I think. There's been a steady slide in my fortunes, from $2,000 per month to zero, from a good credit rating to no credit rating at all, from slight debt to near bankruptcy. But I've retained my sense of humour – that's important to me. I've even been able to earn a small amount from it – with a series of humorous editorials on the CBQ Thunder Bay noon show.

I've tried to use the time well. I've revived my writing. I've indulged in volunteer work: I've helped set up an art exhibition; stage managed a children's theatre production; learned a bit about television by working with the community cable-TV station. And I've met a lot of interesting people this way. In fact, I've made more friends here, in three months, than I did in three years in Winnipeg.

The holiday has been welcome. For a week or so I don't have to hang around the phone, don't have to scour the want ads. Nobody hires during the holidays. It's been a penniless holiday, but not joyless. It's been a time to forget about all those things and enjoy the presence of others. And I'm savouring it. In a few days, it'll be January and I'll be back looking for work.

Week Eight

The holiday season has been good – the most enjoyable I can remember. One man I met is a partner in a personnel agency. He went into business ten years ago, beginning with a staff of two, grew to a peak of twenty-five employees and is now back to the original two. And they're holding on with their fingernails.

He has a nine-month old daughter and, like me, is facing possible bankruptcy. Yet he, too, found this to be the best holiday he's ever had. "It's kind of good that all this has happened," he said. "It reminds you of what's really important."

I agree. So what if I go bankrupt? It's only money. So what if I don't find a job? Right now I'm enjoying life more than I have in years.

I feel invigorated after the holiday break, strangely confident – I'm even taking a few chances in hopes that my application will stand out from the rest.

I now compose new resumés for every job, classifying information under headings drawn from job qualifications. If public-relations experience is mentioned first in the ad, I list my PR experience first.

There are two prospects I considered "live": senior liaison officer for Lakehead University and executive administrator for a boys' choir group.

Judging from the advertisement, the priority of the university position is promotion of university education to potential students. I took a chance that the university might be ready for a new, more aggressive approach, promotion of university as more than job training. If the university wants to push the job-training angle, my application will be the first in the garbage can. Sounds like a gamble? It isn't really. I've nothing to lose.

In my application to the boys' choir, I was very frank, pointing out that I am not a fan of choir music but that I am not above being converted. And, as fund-raising is a priority, I challenged them to answer the question, "Why would a corporation want to give money to a boys' choir?" It's not that I think fund-raising isn't possible, it's just that they should have an answer before they even think of hiring someone to raise money for them. It's been quite a while since I applied for the position but I haven't given up on it.

Week Nine

I am a last resort for work created under the Canada Community Development Program. I am perfectly qualified for at least five positions available locally – two in public relations and publicity, one each in fund-raising, volunteer recruitment and preparation of a social-services directory.

But ability and experience only come into consideration if organizations receiving grants under this program cannot find a female, a person of native ancestry, a disabled person or someone younger than twenty-five to fill the bill.

Maybe these priorities make sense in ordinary times, but these are not ordinary times. According to a story in the paper, there are more males than females unemployed (even on a percentage basis), more people older than twenty-five than under out of work. Where are the programs for the university-educated WASP males over twenty-five, the ones facing personal bankruptcy if they don't find work soon? I also tried the NEED program, which is designed to provide work for those whose unemployment benefits have expired. A man at the Canada Employment Centre told me I was not eligible because I had not received unemployment insurance and had not applied for welfare. I had never considered welfare. To me, welfare would be the ultimate admission of defeat. For families, yes, but . . . .

The NEED program came up again in a discussion I had with another federal employee. He said he thought I was eligible as project manager. I checked with the local NEED office and yes, it's true. I submitted a proposal.

The new unemployment statistics were released last week and Thunder Bay is number *four* in Canada – seventeen percent unemployment, one in six jobless. And with the new statistics came more jabbering from politicians. One MP demanded an emergency debate in the House of Commons. Are we supposed to stand and *cheer*? One thing for sure, unemployment has certainly loosened my political allegiance. I have only ever voted for one party. That may change.

The unemployed life is certainly one of ups and downs. Last week I felt confident, a few weeks ago miserable. Now I don't feel disheartened, I just don't expect my applications to go anywhere. I can't afford the luxury of dreaming of what I'll do if I am hired. In fact, I refuse to think about anything I cannot control. I can put all my efforts into trying to find work, but I cannot hire myself. I can open the envelopes and look at the bills, but I can't pay them, so I don't think about them.

I did manage to scrape up enough for one car payment, the first in four months. But I still can't afford to get the door handle fixed, the windshield wiper replaced, the oil changed, the transmission leak plugged.

Journalists measure the misery of the unemployed in dollars, and talk about how tough it is for a family of six in Sudbury, or whatever. I think the worst situation is being alone and unemployed. That is rock bottom.

I am not alone. I have someone to pick me up when I'm down, to help when things go bad. That I would not trade – not even for a job.

As of today, I'm resigning my position as publicly unemployed person, not for a job, as I had expected when this series began, but for the life of the privately unemployed.

Lately I've begun to suspect that being publicly unemployed is hurting my chances to find work. "You have a job on *Morningside*," one lady told me. "Would you have time for this job?" another asked. Some people think I can make a living doing this series. And I think some suspect that I don't really want a job, that this is a George Plimpton routine, that it's just research.

I have never before had trouble finding work. It's never taken me more than a couple of weeks, but it's close to twenty weeks now. I've really gone after work, quite aggressively in fact. Yet, after approximately two hundred attempts, I've received only three replies – two "the position has been filled" and one "we'll keep your application on file." And I've had three interviews, but no offers.

It's hard to keep at it, even harder as you watch the bills accumulate and see yourself sliding closer and closer to the point of no return. The financial problems gather, hang like a backdrop for everything you do. You look out the window every morning to make sure your car has not been repossessed during the night. You brace yourself whenever the door bell rings. You numb yourself to mailed threats from creditors.

In spite of it all, unemployment has not been a devastating personal experience. I've not been defeated. Oh, it's been depressing at times, emotionally draining, exhausting. But it's also been good, forcing me to sit still, re-examine the course I have followed, reorder my priorities.

I have discovered that my experience with unemployment is not unique, or perhaps less unique than I had imagined. I expected to strike a few familiar chords but I was not prepared for an echo, for parallel experiences from so many others I've met, so many letters I've read. Discovering we were feeling the same things – from confidence to concern to desperation to self-doubt to apathy and resignation – made the problems less personal, more bearable, more a shared experience.

It seems all the unemployed have tried the same things. We've bought books and tried variations on a job search, on a resumé, on an application. We've tried bending our experience to suit jobs we are not really qualified for. We've blamed ourselves.

And we've all gone daydreaming, hatching marvellous new approaches for positions we've just applied for, planning what we'll do with our first paycheque. It's like a lottery, a licence to start dreaming. The odds seems about the same. But you have to keep buying tickets, keep applying, just to keep hope alive. . . .

Some try gimmicks, like the man in St. Catharines who offered $1,000 for a job. One man I know used to offer to work two weeks for free on the understanding that, if his work was unsatisfactory, it would be goodbye, no questions asked. It worked. He was hired.

I'm amazed at how much the unemployed have in common, at how similar experiences and frustrations are. Yet we all try to go it alone, in probably the most difficult endeavour there is, where rejection is the rule. Joggers get together to keep each other going. The religious gather for mutual support. Why not the unemployed?

Well, now I'm privately unemployed and *still* looking for a job.

Don Myers

✉ I am thirty-seven years old although I look twenty-five – *Deo gratia* – and am single. I hold a first-class honours degree in North American history and political science from Brock University in St. Catharines, Ontario, and a degree in education with first-class honours from U of T. I graduated in 1971 with my BA and worked on contracts and part-time for the Ontario government from then until 1974. In January of 1974, I withdrew from the job market to look after my mother until her death in November 1974. Because I couldn't find a job, I returned to university and did my degree in education. Despite excellent grades and excellent recommendations from professors and supervising teachers, I did not get a teaching appointment until September, 1977. It involved moving to a part of this country I didn't care for because it was even colder than most of the country, but it was a job and off I went. My psyche could stand only one year of northern Quebec and a small town and a principal whose basic attitude to women clashed with mine. I spent the next two years looking for a job. I accepted one as a housemother at a girls' school but, because of dropping enrollments, didn't return. I decided to go back to school and entered Ryerson in September 1980 to begin the library-technician's course. That fall, ten years of looking for work and other stresses led to a complete breakdown, but I recovered.

In August, 1981, I accepted a teaching position in Calgary. At considerable cost to myself – thank God for my father, who was able to loan me the money – I flew to Canada's "Promised Land." The job was as a permanent supply teacher, which meant that I got out of bed every day not knowing into what zoo I was going to walk that morning. There were no positions available for 1982–1983, so I returned here. The bottom fell out of the job market in Calgary and people returned home with their families.

I have been looking for a job since June last year. I have applied for any and all positions for which I am remotely qualified. I have not even had an interview. In February and March I went to the local manpower office to see about the possibility of retraining. I had an experience not unlike a Kafka dream. The person with whom I spoke made no effort to pull my file other than my registration for UI benefits. His advice to me was, "Why don't you go back to university?" Believe me, it took every ounce of self-control I possess to not choke him to death on the spot. Of course, I would go to university if I could afford it. But what use would a graduate degree be? It would make me more unemployable than I am.

There are thousands of us out here who feel cheated. I don't want to be a file clerk because it is not in my temperament. I feel superfluous to our society and our country. I am sure that there are many women out there, single women, who know they have lost jobs to married men. Ideas are born and die in many of us because we are faced with an overwhelming sense of futility, frustration, defeatism and pain in our hearts because, no matter what anyone says, you perceive yourself as a failure if you cannot get a job. And failure can only lead to one of the many forms of death.

Mary Eleanor Hill
Glen Williams, Ontario

✉ Our nightmare started about a year ago. Keith was offered a very nice position at a good salary with a gold mine in Cassiar, British Columbia. He started working on November 1, and I arrived early in December, when housing was available.

Although we had rented the house from the company, they did nothing to maintain it. Keith was constantly thawing frozen pipes and trying to fix the leaking hot-water tank. The carpets developed mould from the leaking water. All my plants died when we had to air out the house after a small fire from thawing the pipes.

The back door had to be taped shut to keep out the cold.

The washing machine leaked into the bedroom. The gas oven burnt food instantly no matter how low I set the temperature. The windows were often covered with ice an inch thick.

The working conditions were just as bad, perhaps even worse. Miners arriving for work would take one look at the mine and quit the same day.

We left. We never dreamt Keith would have any trouble finding another job. (He had had three offers on graduation and two the year following.) We had one tentative offer before we left, but that fell through about the same time our son was born. From March 1 until September 1 we were unemployed.

At first Keith went through an employment agency. Then he mailed out letters and resumés followed by phone calls to companies he knew. By this point we started to get scared. We started to get desperate, applying farther and farther afield for a job. Keith wrote to places in Baffin Island, Peru and Australia.

The only thing left to do was walk door-to-door. Armed with two hundred resumés and financed by our unemployment cheques, Keith spent two weeks in Toronto, Calgary and Vancouver. Finally a job turned up in Vancouver. We are now getting just more than half the pay we got a year ago, with one more mouth to feed.

I am grateful for many things. I am thankful for our families, who stood by us and supported us so that Keith could look for a job. We never missed a meal and always had a comfortable bed. I am thankful that Keith was lucky enough to find a job, and it is one he enjoys. I am also thankful that our income is adequate and we can afford rent and food. I am most thankful for my son and husband. They are my prize possessions.

Beth Minty
White Rock, British Columbia

✉ I am among the unemployed – have been for seven months. I may not be as badly off as some people, but I have all the same feelings of frustration, anger, depression and desperation as they do. It was my intention to try to see a bit of humour in this situation, too. In thinking about it, however, I've decided that that would be unfair to the nearly two million others who find themselves in the same position. So if there is any humour in what follows, it is dark and born of bitterness.

I resign. I resign from being unemployed!

I resign from those green cheques ($370 a pop) that come in every two weeks.

I resign from filling in "No, no, no, yes, yes, no" on the white, keypunched form that comes with the green cheque every two weeks. I resign from having to provide my own damned postage stamp!

I resign from hearing comments like: "Well, you're not alone, are you?" or "What will you do when UIC runs out?" or "Well, at least you've got time to enjoy this nice weather."

I resign from answering advertisements in newspapers that give only box numbers for addresses. This is an especially bitter pill. Being in this position is difficult enough without the added frustration of answering anonymous ads and then wondering if one's application has even been received, much less considered for the position. What is the matter with you people? Have you not decency or plain good manners enough to drop a preprinted card in the mail saying at least: "Thank you for your interest, the position has been filled"? A pox on all box-number holders!

I resign from applying for jobs for which I am hopelessly overqualified.

I resign from applying for jobs for which I am hopelessly underqualified.

I resign from considering selling insurance.

I resign from trying to sell my car, which no one seems to want anyway.

I resign from visiting my Canada Employment (sic) Centre at regular intervals in order to be told what I already know.

I resign from my overdraft.

I resign from my credit cards.

And the most difficult and most important: I resign from being discouraged! I resign from being depressed! I resign from being broke! I resign from resignation!

I will beat this thing. I will win. This too shall pass.

John Ross
Vancouver

Bears

"A lot of Canadians have bear stories," I suggested
innocently one April morning in 1984, "maybe even
most Canadians." A few weeks later, I was convinced
all Canadians had bear stories – and nearly all of them
were busy sending them in to *Morningside*. The stories
came from all over the country and in all guises:
newspaper clippings, historical accounts, fantasies
(there's one in here that may well be the ursine
equivalent of the dead cat in the Creed's bag, a story
everyone has heard but no one can quite pin down –
but I've put it in anyway), diaries, journals, anecdotes
and memories. It was an avalanche of bears. The
tumble of stories I've finally chosen to include here
represents perhaps ten percent of those that came in,
and one of them, in verse, is a response to the yarn I
still think may be apocryphal. This selection does,
however – or so I hope – represent the range of the
avalanche. Once again, I opened it all with a bear story
of my own.

I met my first wild bears in the summer of 1952, when I flew to the part of British Columbia that is now Kitimat to build some hydro towers for the folks who wanted to send power over the mountains to help make the aluminum. My part in this construction was essential. I worked with what the labour crew called a "Mexican dragline," which is a shovel with a nine-foot wooden handle, and I tidied up the muck around the base of the towers. I was okay at it, although I have done other things better since, and after I'd salted the blisters on my library-white hands and turned them into calluses, I became a passing good dragline operator.

The bears were another matter. They were small and black, the size of Labrador retrievers, and not, or not at first, much fiercer. We were strange to them. They'd held that turf as pretty well their own until the construction crews came. In the early summer, as our newly settled camp turned into a liveable space, we, the intruders, represented not so much a nuisance to them as a place to get free food, and in the evenings, when our work was finished and we went to the cook tent for an evening mug-up, it became our pastime to throw to our visitors honeyed buns and pieces of bread and jam. They liked oranges, too; you could throw an orange to a wild black bear and watch in a amazement as he peeled it with his long, sharp claws.

Little did we know. By June, word had spread through the drizzly forest that the creatures who walked on two legs and drove noisy machines also provided free lunch, or at least a late snack. More and more, as June turned to July, a walk from the cook tent back to your own quarters became an exercise in bribery, each walkway between the tents negotiated by sweet baksheesh. One night, I remember, we counted twelve adult bears around our camp, and two bright, funny cubs.

We started to get scared. They were lightning fast, those orange-skinners, and by now most of us had seen them fishing the salmon creeks, standing still over the burbling water until they were ready to knock a strong, live salmon skittering onto the bank – knock it with one swipe of those razored claws.

One of the bulldozer operators worked out a system. While we erected towers for the mighty hydro line, our own electricity came from a diesel-powered Caterpillar generator. The bulldozer man ran a lead off this power source, with a switch. He ran the lead into the bottom of a tin pie plate. He filled the pie plate with chocolate milk. When a bear came to lick, he would pull the switch and send the whimpering creature hurtling off into the woods. Moments later, another bear would try. Lick, shock, whimper, run. It was cruel and unusual punishment, funny at first, I suppose, but later worrisome.

I have no punchline for this story. I was eighteen when it happened, fresh from the city, and I suppose I'd do it all differently now. But what I remember is that it didn't work. The bears stayed all summer, and even by the time I left, you couldn't walk home at night without paying your way with sugar and buns. The camp closed. The bears remained.

P.G.

✉ Joe Martin turned up two days late for his appointment the other day. He had been fishing down Lake Laberge with a friend and the wind and the waves were so high they could not leave the island on which they were camped. Joe had only gone along to watch the camp for bears while his friend set the salmon nets.

"Down that river there," Joe said, "we hunt beaver quite a few year ago. A grizzly bear he run after me so I shoot him. I kill that one, but I don't want to shoot him, y'know. He don't see me, and I say, 'Hey, Mr. Bear, you go that way and I go this way.' He do it and he go away. He don't bother me. I don't want to kill animal for nothing, only if I need meat. Always talk nice to a bear."

Peter Steele
Whitehorse, Yukon

✉ We operate a tourist resort on Lake of the Woods and none of our bear stories is fit for bedtime telling, so you'll never hear me babbling even the Goldilocks version to a child in sleepers.

For the slovenly guests we elaborate on claw rips on screening and the four square feet of two-by-six planking scratched from shed doors. For campers we reiterate the necessity to separate in the bush the activities of eating and sleeping. With the serious biologist (our favourite type) we admit we know about the *third* bear, the rare and vicious one. In the mother bear's litter the third bear is, it seems, rejected. It is a rogue that has a perpetual sore paw and wields it against all obstacles real and imaginary – like small children sitting on a dock.

And for the fourth category of guest, the timid and nervous, we assume our jolly tones and parry queries such as "I hope there aren't any bears, are there?" with evasive generalities like, "Bears don't usually come round here. You're not likely to see one." And we salve our consciences by reminding ourselves that, statistically, since a bear did stroll down the drive last Tuesday at five o'clock, there's not likely going to be a recurrence of this event for two years and three months.

Offering that assurance is troubling for me. When I look into those questioning eyes, all I can see is my Personal Bear, the one I shared with Pauline McGibbon.

He appeared an ordinary specimen of his kind, harmless as a moose calf. Harmless, that is, unless the observer is all alone, and trapped, and the victim of an imagination that transmogrifies the average scavenger into a bloodthirsty rogue whose concept of caviar is a well-fleshed Canadian mother.

This fixation took hold one fall morning. The summer residents had all gone. The other year-round families consisted of adults who went to work all day in the town and children, like our four sons, who left for school every morning at eight. I was alone except for one ginger cat whose considerable prowess as a hunter had produced nothing larger than a varying hare, and one brown dog, whose sporting instincts were confined to bikes and Ski-Doos.

I was inside. The bear was outside.

No, the bear did not rush at the door and tear it from its hinges, nor plunge his paw through the window to snatch me from my cookie pans. He simply paced along the rocky edge of the garden mulling over, it seemed to me, the pleasures of head for starters and heart for dessert. All I could think of were the bear stories, fresh off the gossip circuit: Mrs. Roy, who, hearing footsteps in the upper level of their unfinished split level, had to chase out the bear who'd crawled in the window, and Betty, who'd spent the whole day in her outhouse because the bear sat on the path till her husband came home from his shift, and Louise, whose Saturday's baking had been swiped when her back was turned. . . . I was being put to the test, and was failing. I was furious with the victor, ashamed of myself and scared stiff.

Noise was the weapon that sprang to mind. Our house full of males had, of course, racks of guns, but I had, in common with most mothers, the reluctance to have anything to do with guns except to nag about their hazards. Firing a gun at a bear would have been impossible. Which little piece of ammunition would I cram in which gun? No neighbour would be home. No point in phoning for help . . . besides, my fingers wouldn't have managed the dexterity to dial. So I took up a wooden spoon and the lid of the preserving kettle and banged and banged.

Result? The useless dog began to bark and the bear, who'd been patrolling while he'd been meditating my fate, stopped to listen. And far from being dissuaded from his morning's ambition, he turned a frown in my direction, and judged that his right to induce panic had been challenged. *He* was being put to the test, and he was not going to turn yellow and tuck in his scrap of a tail and run away. He stood upright to bat the garbage can beside the shed.

Don't tell me miracles don't happen. This miracle, this *deus ex machina*, was Pauline McGibbon. The lieutenant-governor was travelling the province and that day her itinerary had brought her to town. One of her vice-regal privileges was to enchant all the children by granting them a holiday from school. That morning she had smiled a lot, spoken a few words and announced that every student could toss his books and celebrate.

At home I was mesmerized by the bear at my windowsill, and the bear was concentrating on me. Neither of us heard the arrival of four schoolboys at the side door.

The eldest claimed the right to add one bear to his notches of success. The others accepted the familiar and tedious task of scolding and comforting their feeble mother.

That autumn morning was long ago. Since then I have succeeded in improving my relationship with most bears. But I still cannot handle my bear. There is a legion of him, lurking out there, waiting for me and longing to avenge their long-lost brother.

Pauline saved me once. But a second time?

Catharine Hay
Kenora, Ontario

✉ I was visiting a friend in Jasper for a few days en route to Vancouver. Paul was then an assistant warden for the parks department and so was afforded the opportunity of living and working in that magnificent setting. Early Saturday morning he received an urgent call asking him to come down to the warden's station just outside of town. We dressed in a rush and arrived breathlessly at the small brown-log building that served as the office.

In the parking lot a small crowd had gathered around the back of a half-ton truck. We approached the knot of park personnel and local children apprehensively. In the back of the pick-up I was astonished to see the prostrate figure of a grizzly bear. At first I assumed she had been drugged and captured by the parks people for some reason, but then I noticed that her breath was coming in huge, agonized shudders. The sound was terrible and the sight of those exhausted flanks rising and falling in uneven rhythm was almost too painful to watch. But it is her eyes that I can't get out of my mind – those damn eyes: a fierce, uncomprehending yellow, glazed with pain and fear.

Everyone was quiet, just watching helplessly. Finally one of the group laid a tentative sympathetic hand on her heaving side. Still aware of her surroundings, she flinched visibly at the human touch. Then she drew one last tortured breath, and she was still.

"That's it," my friend said in a shaky voice. It was apparent that this was as close as he and most of the other people there had ever been to a grizzly, and clearly this was not the way they had envisioned an encounter with the great bear ending. The senior warden cleared his throat and gruffly told his staff to prepare the corpse for an autopsy. He turned on his heel and walked into the building. With a few nervous laughs and mumbled comments, the small group broke ranks and resumed their work or play. I never discovered what preparing for an autopsy involved, but I have a feeling that that bear ended in pieces, wrapped in green garbage bags in the bottom of a freezer.

I heard later that they found a kitchen fork jammed in her esophagus.

It didn't seem right that she should die like that, staring at the steel sides of a pick-up truck, her agony witnessed by alien, enemy eyes. It's true: there is a bear in all of us; a part of ourselves we avoid acknowledging and attempt to deny. We are afraid of those dark, uncontrollable recesses. They represent a link with forces we do not understand.

Cessie Ross
Cobourg, Ontario

✉ These were bears to break your heart and make you cry. These were bag-lady bears, skid-row bears, derelict bears with no pride or dignity. They scavenged the garbage dump for years – first- and second-generation welfare-bum bears; their territory was the great, open, festering dump at Whistler Mountain.

We who went to Whistler and skied that beautiful, tough mountain would sit around our fireplaces in the evening and discuss our great runs, and why it was such a joy to be there. When we left for home on a Sunday evening we took our plastic bags of garbage and threw them on that towering dump. Tin cans, jam jars, milk cartons, chocolate boxes, orange rinds, apples, roasts, cheeses and other delicacies all went on the trash heap, so the bears dined well, if not wisely.

Many bears had open wounds, some were scarred from previous battles with recalcitrant tin cans, and all appeared to have badly marked snouts. Their once beautiful, glossy coats were dull and bedraggled; their fur matted and hanging in clumps with great bare patches; graphic evidence of poor diet and, most probably, disease. My last picture of those bears remains with me still. There he was, this once mighty prince of the wilderness, ragged of coat, stumbling around in the muck and filth of the dump like some drunken clown, banging his head desperately on the hard ground in a futile effort to dislodge a metal tin. It somehow seemed appropriate.

Driving away I thought: why should man, who did, and does, and will continue to destroy his own environment feel differently about that of his fellow creatures?

Gwen Mortimer
West Vancouver

✉ When my wife, Lyn, and I moved to this area ten years ago we rented an old farm house not far from where we live now. The house came with a mature small orchard in the yard – and without indoor conveniences, so by the orchard was an outhouse.

September came and the old orchard started to attract the animals. Jays took a chunk out of an apple here and there until the sparrow hawks chased them off. Cows and their calves that had been ranging free all summer were led by the experienced elders among them to our yard for the apples – and our garden.

At night the bears came. Old bears and young bears. Judging from the piles of bear droppings, we must have had every bear for miles around in the yard. At night. When we had to make our last trip to the outhouse by the orchard.

Lyn solved our problem neatly one night when she opened the door, stood on the step for a second and then yelled, "Here, bear!" Crashing and heavy thuds from the orchard. Splitting sounds as bears tumbled over and through the rail fence. Later, in bed with the window open, we could hear them sneaking back to finish their meals. It became a nightly ritual. "Here, bear," the sounds of bears retreating in panic and Lyn and I crunching through the leaves to the little house out back.

Leslie Jackson
Apsley, Ontario

✉ Twenty-nine years ago my husband was directing a YMCA camp at Jasper. I helped, but mostly I walked and talked and played with our two-year-old son, Julian.

We made what we thought was a safe spot for him – a sandbox – where he could enjoy a little time with his toys. He was away from traffic here, and close enough to camp bustle to be seen and heard by Mum and by staff as they went about their morning chores.

It was silence that drew me out the nearby cottage door to check on what was happening in the sandbox.

There he was, our precious little boy, quietly sifting sand from cup to cup, burying his cars and poking them up out of the sand with a wooden spoon. I saw a full-grown black bear lumber clumsily over the rim of the sandbox and nestle into the warm sand beside him.

I wanted to scream, dash up and grab the child away. But I was frozen. Or perhaps it was presence of mind that kept me immutable while the bear became engrossed in the machinations of human play. I ached with inaction.

I became aware of other campers and staff standing stiff and silent, just as I was. I longed to take charge, be in control and supervise, but all lines of communication were blocked. Body language and telepathy took over. Very gradually and stealthily, and still with no words spoken, we made a large circle – a human fence – well back from the sandbox. A large opening was left for the bear's retreat.

The laundress stooped over slowly, to pick up a rock. I wanted to scream no. Her aim was good, I knew, but the bear and the boy were so close. She held the rock. Another movement as Ma, the cook, backed down the path leading to her kitchen.

Julian played on, glancing up occasionally at the strange circle his friends had made. Was he, too, terrified? How long before his outburst – and a mauling?

The circle inched in a little.

Ma burst through the kitchen door clanging a metal spoon against a metal dishpan. In unison, the laundress hurled her rock, and hit the bear. The rock bounced off. The bear didn't move. A second and third crashing of metal and rock teased the bear onto its feet. It turned and loped through the wide opening in the circle.

I whirled to Julian and snatched him away in my arms, from that dreaded sandbox and the bear. Between sobs – his and mine – I heard him cry, "But Mummy, that bear sat on my beautiful blue truck."

Laura de Cocq
Mill Bay, British Columbia

✉ My husband, Don, and I were vacationing in the Yukon three years ago and decided to hike in Kluane National Park. The ranger, Marsha Pflummerfeldt, was a cheerful and knowledgeable woman. She told us about the bears in the area, and encouraged us to go on the hike nonetheless. Don took the risk of bears more seriously than I did, and ardently followed Marsha's advice. That advice had been to make a lot of noise so as not to surprise the bears. Don therefore carried on an unceasing monologue of drivel. I was not inspired to make it a dialogue, and I remained silent and bored – so bored, in fact, that my fantasies started to take over. Eventually I fantasized a bear coming along, swiping Don out of the way and walking silently beside me.

That was, until I saw a fresh bear track and fresh bear scat and fresh bear diggings. I was suddenly scared, and equally suddenly Don's conversation became scintillating.

We saw no bears on that hike – but there was lots of evidence, enough to provide us with the certainty that they saw, smelled and heard us. I have never fantasized trading my husband for a bear since.

Lynn Wolff
Edmonton

✉ My immigrant father had a peculiarly wistful love for what he called the north woods. This man who, spent fifty weeks of his year in a factory, was, for us, the sweet teacher of nature. From him we learned to relish the heavenly taste of spring water, to watch the antics of chipmunks and birds, to marvel at thunderstorms over a lake and to revel in the fragrance of trees. We spent hours on the lake in an old flat-bottomed rowboat, the sound of whose oar-locks I can hear yet.

One hot August afternoon when I was nine, Dad spotted something large moving in the distance while rowing that funny old boat. I remember his leaning forward to grasp my head in order to point my eyes in the right direction. As we rowed closer we saw it was a large brown bear. We were as excited as someone who had waited a very long time for the return of a long-lost brother. We were torn between wanting to get closer to greet him, and keeping our distance so that we could witness his arrival on the far wooded shore. We decided to content ourselves with watching his journey and wishing him bon voyage.

Suddenly from another shore a large motorboat came roaring toward the solitary swimming bear. The men and the boat circled him three or four times. I begged my dad to demand that the men stop teasing the creature. With that, one of the men raised his rifle and shot the swimmer in the head. After a time they tied a rope to him and towed him to shore. The men whooped and laughed and waved and slapped each other with glee. We rowed away.

The next day my brother and I visited the small nearby hotel resort. There, prominently displayed hanging upside down, mouth open, tongue lolling over those fearsome teeth, was my beautiful brown bear. I looked at his great claws and thick brown fur. Beside him, still grinning and pleased, was the proud hunter. I stood and wept. He thought me funny.

I shall never forget that man. I shall never forget his laughing red face, his thick belly and his large rubber boots. Nor will I ever forget that very large brown bear.

Sheila Brown
Waterdown, Ontario

✉ A priest trudging from rectory to altar for a mass at seven-thirty on a Sunday morning is a relatively sorry sight. He is half-asleep, half-shaved – and half-wishing that he had taken up another line of work. Even the beauties of living in Banff in the early 1970s could not make up for the Godforsaken hour of early Christian worship, no matter how fine the spring morning. As I was so musing and walking beside the parish hall, grumbling to myself as was my wont, I thought I heard the percussion section of the William Tell Overture and imme- diately thought of Clayton Moore as the Lone Ranger.

I walked past the hall door and looked up Buffalo Street. There was no silver horse, but what appeared to be the biggest sow bear in history. The sound had been her very long claws striking the as- phalt. She stopped as though yanked back by an invisible giant string. I stopped, suddenly wide awake, and said the only sensible thing a priest can say on an early Sunday morning in Banff when encounter- ing a bear: "Hello, bear."

We regarded one another for a few moments, while I felt a trifle like a potential breakfast. She obviously had even less positive thoughts, since she took off like the proverbial bat as fast as her legs would carry her from the sight of a priest on Sunday morning early.

Quivering like a man with terminal ague, I unlocked the hall door only to be confronted by my second "bare" of the morning. A mas- sively muscled, stark-naked young man rose from the hall floor and began to shriek dire threats at this anything-but-massively-muscled, fully dressed little priest. Once again I got to say: "Hello, bare." It made sense at the time.

The police took the second "bare" to a kindly psychiatric hospital; the first bear wisely decided to leave the peculiar haunts of humans, Christian or otherwise.

The sermon that morning was very brief. The good parishioners and visitors never knew why I kept shaking so much and looking around corners.

Given a choice between "bears" and "bares," I would rather stay in bed.

Father Douglas Skoyles
Calgary

✉ In the fall of 1976, in Resolute Bay, Northwest Territories, I was a new teacher, adjusting to living and working in the north. Our school consisted of a main building, which held two classes, and a portable classroom in which I taught the youngest students. Across the road from the school, toward the beach, was a small downward slope and a pond where the children skated and played hockey after school.

It was three-thirty and I had just dismissed my young charges. Older students were sitting on the steps outside strapping on their skates. Suddenly, all the children came running back into the classroom, yelling excitedly, "Nanook! Nanook!" Ten-year-old Lazarusi, first to approach the pond, had slid down the small slope and surprised a dozing polar bear. Somehow Laz managed to get up the bank and across the schoolyard to the safety of the school – still wearing his skates.

Our school janitor, Pamiloo, jumped on his Ski-Doo and succeeded in chasing the bear off toward the beach by throwing lumps of snow at it. He had no gun. Once on the beach, the bear ran around and around a crane, used during the annual sea-lift of supplies, with Pamiloo in pursuit.

Then Pamiloo's Ski-Doo quit – and the bear gave chase. Round and round the crane they went, pursuer and pursued, the roles reversed. Each time Pamiloo passed his Ski-Doo, he reached down and pulled the cord, trying to start it.

I watched from my classroom window, surrounded by excited children. Vera, Pamiloo's daughter, began to cry. Soon, other Ski-Doos from the village headed out to help chase away the bear. I remember one in particular, as it was driven by a mother, her baby bouncing along on her back in her packing parka!

Pamiloo got his Ski-Doo started – and they succeeded in chasing away the bear. And the story was told, chuckled over and retold around the village for weeks to come.

Margaret Adams
Coral Harbour, Northwest Territories

PS: You may be interested to know that Pamiloo is one of the group pictured on the Canadian two-dollar bill. He is the boy standing, holding the end of a harpoon. He now lives in Spence Bay, Northwest Territories.

✉ I knew all the rules about camping and bears and usually religiously followed them. This time, I didn't bother as we were hiking the Pacific Rim Trail and bears don't like the ocean – I thought. I had done quite a bit of hiking but I was still a city person with city ideas about just where wild animals liked to hang out. So for this trip, I decided it was safe to keep our food in our tent and to forget the bell I always put around the dog's neck.

Besides, I was showing off. I had done a lot of hiking alone and thought I was pretty good. This time I had a first-time hiker, Allyson, along, and I didn't think talk of bear precautions would help. It had been an excellent trip. We'd crossed streams (one on a cable car), built driftwood windbreaks and slept on the beach every night. It was the last day of an eight-day trip and we were on our way out to civilization. The only uneasiness I felt was at the dog's exemplary behaviour. It was the first time in four years that she had heeled with no reminders. I wondered why.

We had only six more miles to go, all easy walking on the flat rock shelves that are common to that section of the coast. The ocean was on one side and a huge wall of trees on the other. The sun was out and we were feeling good. Then I saw the reason for the dog's good behaviour: a bear about one hundred feet ahead on the beach. I stopped dead and grabbed the dog. Allyson ran into me and asked why the sudden stop. She was near sighted. I kept cool. After all, I was the leader. "Oh, just a bear up ahead. We'll just wait for it to amble on its way." Allyson trusted me and didn't panic. Neither of us did. Not until the bear reappeared ten feet away coming out of the trees. I whispered to Allyson to slip out of her pack and back up: "The bear probably just wants our food." I did the same while holding the dog. She wasn't really eager to go anywhere. As we backed up the bear

148

advanced with not even a sniff at our packs. It occurred to me there was only water behind us and Allyson didn't swim. Immediate action was needed – that water was cold. I broke into a full-bodied rendition of "White Christmas." It was all I could think of. The bear was not impressed. She stopped dead, did a speedy about-face and ran up a tree. That was it. We cautiously retrieved our packs (and my dignity) and walked off into the sunset.

Sue Hemphill
Horsefly, British Columbia

✉ It was on the annual fishing trip to Red Squirrel Lake, near Shining Tree, Ontario. We were kids, with Mom and Dad, an uncle and his family. My brother and I noticed a bear snooping around the small garbage pit dug into the side of a sand dune. We decided to play a trick on the bear with a large dead pickerel we found washed ashore. The garbage pit took the shape of a U. Young, springy saplings grew around the steep edges of the pit. We bent the most strategically positioned sapling over, tying the fish to the top, so it hung out of reach of our friend. The fish could not be had from below as it was too high off the ground. Then it was a question of waiting.

Sure enough, the sensitive nose of a bold bear located our bait within an hour. The bear approached the pit from the top. After walking around the rim for a second or two in brief hesitation, he brashly reached out for the suspended fish and went crashing into the garbage, consisting mainly of cans. In his rage at missing such an easy prey, the bear speedily clambered through the trash, scaled the sandy wall in a flash and then proceeded to rip the sapling out of the soil with one swoop of the paw. Needless to say, he got his fish and didn't notice us giggling at him as he walked off with his dinner.

But that is not the end, for later in the evening one of the oddest forms of revenge seemed to have been planned for us. The two families were sitting around a campfire underneath a rectangular shelter we had constructed to keep out of the rain. Everyone was entranced by the fire and there was little conversation. Suddenly a skunk was inside the shelter, effectively pinning us to our chairs, not only through fear of getting sprayed, but also because of the boldness of the animal and the novelty of such a visitor to our evening fire. While in this paralyzed state, we heard a noise coming from the direction of the nearby tent. Father, closest to the exit and a relatively safe distance from the skunk, popped up to see two bears mauling the big cooler. The skunk diversion had worked. Before my father had a chance to scare them off by banging a pot with a spoon, the bears had ripped off the lid and carted away a sizeable number of groceries.

This may sound too much like fiction, but I assure you that the two-bear-one-skunk team did exist. And if it was revenge, then the bear who fell into the pit pulled the joke on us.

Gregory Shea
Montreal

✉ I live on the west coast of Vancouver Island. To get to my village you have to drive on a logging road for a couple of hours, then cross an inlet by boat.

About four years ago a mother bear started coming around with her cub. I knew I had to be careful about not getting near her because I've had kids myself and sure wouldn't let any bear get near them. I didn't even mind when we found the cub sitting on the porch one day, eating almond cookies I'd bought in Vancouver's Chinatown for the new neighbours who lived in the next bay. I just made sure I didn't leave any food or garbage out. For a few weeks after the almond-cookie incident I was especially careful: bears remember sweets and they come back to check for more.

I'd become friendly with the new neighbours by then. They'd come from the city to escape the rat race, to live close to the land. They were restoring an abandoned farm house that hadn't been lived in for thirty years. Like most people who come from the city, they got off on watching eagles and whales and thought it was really neat that there were bears here.

They lived in a tent while they restored the old homestead. They drew water from a well. They cleaned out the old orchard. They planted tulips and blasted a goldfish pond. They kept warm with driftwood and read stories to their kids by the light of a kerosene lamp.

Last year the old farm house was finished. It looked just like I'd seen it in the city archives on yellow-edged photographs. Inside, of course, it was different. Inside it had electricity, a fridge, a micro-wave oven and a TV hooked up to the local movie channel. The orchard was producing fruit again. The tomatoes were turning red on the vine. My neighbours worked very hard to get the place to look like any well-tended place in the garden belt of a big city.

They were complaining about the bears, though. The bears were eating their apples; the bears were getting into their produce. I sympathized with them, telling them about the mother bear and the cub eating all my salmon berries in the spring. I'd been annoyed, but I'd also had many joyful mornings watching mama bear parade her new triplets just last year. I told them I figured if you want to live somewhere where you can watch bears you have to share the land with them.

One afternoon last fall I went over to the neighbours' to get some apples for a pie. Even before I got there I knew something scary was happening, something that would change things forever. I walked through the cedars and the ferns and there wasn't a sound in the forest. Even the crows weren't squawking. The silence was broken with the sound of gunshots.

Guns cut a silence into chunks of vacuum. There is never another sound between a series of gunshots. Everything that lives holds its breath while the guns cut up the silence. Afterwards, everyone re-members the number of shots. There were four shots that afternoon.

I got there just as the bears were dropping out of the sitka spruce. The spruce was the tallest tree in my neighbours' yard; the bears had climbed it because they were scared. Under the spruce was a man with a gun. The bears had dropped out of the tree the way ripe apples fall from an apple tree.

I walked back to my house and never saw my neighbours again. They moved back to the city this year.

The sitka spruce is gone, too. On the stump there is a sign that says, "View Lots."

Hannelore
Banfield, British Columbia

✉ I had come from an English village to the bustle of Edmonton, and so it was natural for me to seek the peace of the countryside whenever I could, frequently visiting the Rockies. I would always return slightly disappointed. I never saw a bear. Each time, I would be given fresh instructions as to where I would find one, but it never happened.

After about a year, a friend asked me if I would mind taking her Latvian mother for a long weekend tour of the mountains. One evening, we were travelling between Banff and Radium Hot Springs, when, on rounding a bend, we saw a largish brown bear with her black cub walking along the road. I stopped the car and reached for my camera. Before I could do anything, the adult bear had leaped, silently, on to the hood of the car. Evilly, she glared through the windshield, then gave it a swipe with her paw. Then she turned round, pushed her body up against the windshield and apparently went to sleep.

No one puts his hand out of the window and says "shoo" in such circumstances, so I thought that starting the car might move the bear. That was useless. After about fifteen minutes of wondering what to do next, I discovered that by levering myself up against the back of my seat I had about half an inch of visibility above the bear's body, so I decided to drive forward very slowly, hoping that the movement would disturb her. Meanwhile, through all this, the old lady in the back seat was quietly singing to herself what I later learned were hymns.

After travelling about a mile like this, the car went over a bump, and this woke the bear up. She gave the windshield another mighty swipe with her paw, then jumped off and tore back up the road in the direction of her cub.

As the old lady could not speak English, I got her daughter to ask her if she had been frightened while all this was happening. "No," she said. When I asked why she replied, "The bear would have killed you first, and so she would have let me alone."

F.V. Edwards
Saskatoon

Here's a bear story from Jasper National Park. The incident occurred along the Icefields Parkway, the road between Jasper and Banff. A young couple were driving along on a warm day in the summer of 1980. They stopped not far from Athabasca Falls and headed into the woods with some wine, some cheese and amorous intent.

Everything was perfect. The sun shone steadily and the wine went down well. Presently the couple had taken their clothes off and were lying in the grass.

Time went by. Then something made the young man look up – right into the face of a bear. The couple jumped up and ran. They didn't stop to get dressed or even to grab their clothes off the ground.

Rushing across the highway, they tried to jump into their car. Ah, but the car was locked, and the keys? The keys were up in the woods in a pants pocket. And here came the bear, which had followed them.

What to do? They climbed up on the car. And there they were, stark naked on the roof, with the bear going round and round the car on its hind legs as carload after carload of incredulous tourists drove by.

Someone reported the situation to the warden at the Athabasca Falls station, just a few minutes' drive down the road. The warden brought his dog, who chased the bear up a tree. The young lady put on the warden's jacket, while the man, still naked, accompanied the warden to the spot where the clothes had been abandoned.

Meanwhile, the bear had climbed down from the tree, ignoring the dog, to defend the clothes. It was all the warden could do to recover the man's clothes; the woman's the bear would not surrender until he had ripped them up. Then he retired, carrying off one of her shoes as a trophy.

And that is how there came to be an occurrence report on file at the Jasper warden's office entitled "The Bare Facts."

Ben Gadd
Jasper, Alberta

✉ Two, imbued with sudden passion,
    By a mountain highway parked,
Locked their car in careful fashion,
    Sought a glade that they had marked.

Hidden by a screen of bushes,
    Underneath the summer sun,
By a lakelet edged with rushes,
    Shed their garments one by one.

But a disapproving critter,
    Clothed in fur like other bear,
Muttered imprecations bitter,
    Though it wasn't his affair.

"Dress as I do" was his motto.
    (Bruin was a hide-bound prude.)
Swift he chased them to their auto,
    Ending their behaviour lewd.

Naked though they were, they scampered,
    Leaving all behind them far,
Lacking keys, they then were hampered,
    Gained no entrance to their car.

To escape the angry ursine,
   Climbed they to their car-top high.
Long that bear they stayed there cursing,
   But delighting passers-by.

John Chalmers
Edmonton

THE CLOSET

The first of these two letters arrived one winter morning in 1985, after the novelist Howard Engel had gone back for us to his home town of St. Catharines, Ontario, and prepared a report on what a recent tragedy had done to that city. The tragedy was the suicide of a man whose name had come up in police investigations into homosexual washroom sex.

I don't know who wrote this first letter. It was handwritten but unsigned, and the author had taken the trouble to make sure the postmark was obscured. I had no doubt, however, that it was genuine, and I read it on the air in its entirety. The second letter, signed, came in at about the same time.

✉ A great deal of misunderstanding exists over a subject that haunts me every day and, I assume, many seemingly normal adult males like the poor soul in St. Catharines.

Apparently about five percent of the male population has experienced some homosexual encounter. I just can't help but wonder how such a figure was determined because I am quite certain many, like myself, would deny ever having such encounters, let alone continual unfulfilled desires.

Let me reveal some things about myself about which nobody, and I mean *nobody*, has any idea. I am thirty-nine years old, the product of a very happy and stable family environment, of above-average education, happily married with two small children whom I love dearly. I hold a senior position in management with a reputable national company; 140 people are directly accountable to me. I am actively involved in our local community, sit on many boards, have never been in trouble with the police and as a confirmed Roman Catholic regularly attend church. If you met me I believe I would impress you as a well-spoken, reasonably intelligent young man who is likely to continue to do well in both his career and in the other activities in which he is involved.

There is, however, a darker side to this otherwise perfectly normal, seemingly well-balanced individual: I have contact with other men. No, this is not just a phase. I have always felt like this but recognize that this deep desire must be suppressed and will never be fully satisfied because it is just not possible in this or any other society. You are quite wrong to assume I want anonymous sexual encounters. They *must* be anonymous because I just cannot afford them being anything else. If the truth ever got out it would ruin my marriage, deprive me of my children, affect my career, my standing in the community and consequently, like my "soul brother" in St. Catharines, I would have little else to live for. Hence the absolute necessity of total secrecy and total frustration in the truest sense of the word. Although this urge is desperate I just cannot allow myself to become involved with anyone who could possibly threaten my very existence. I would never visit a gay club or bar in my hometown and shy away from washrooms and other places where I know I could find some brief satisfaction simply because of this overriding fear of discovery. I would love to have a deep personal relationship with someone similarly inclined but dare not approach anybody with my secret for fear of it being discovered by the rest of the world.

My job allows me to travel occasionally to other Canadian and American cities and it is on such trips that Mr. Hyde takes over from Dr. Jekyll. On such a trip you will find me dressed, not in business suits, but in a pair of jeans, wandering around late at night visiting gay clubs, porno-movie houses and the like, just looking for that anonymous person to share a sexual encounter. Once, about three years ago, I was lucky enough to spend the night with a young man I picked up in a reputable hotel bar, and the memories of that one night are the only recent gratifying memories I have. On other occasions it is merely a faceless and furtive encounter full of fear – fear of discovery, fear of violence, and nowadays, fear of disease. But these fears, no matter how strong, cannot suppress the urge. I feel I am walking a tightrope half the time with an abyss below me – one slip and I'm gone.

This may sound like a very sad story and in some respects I suppose it is, but spare me no pity. Unless I want my life to be a lot sadder, I must continue with the masquerade so that neither you nor my family, neither my boss nor my subordinates, neither my friends nor my colleagues ever find out who I really am. Perhaps I am the guy sitting next to you on the bus. I could be your best friend, your husband, boyfriend or lover. I could be your son's scoutmaster or schoolteacher, but only I know the truth – I am a homosexual who dares not come out of the closet.

Name and place
of origin unknown

✉ The suicide of a sensitive and respected person in the community made me, and I'm sure many others, recall similar experiences that caused great hardship to a homosexual person.

I'm thinking of a teacher at a boarding school I attended. He was clever, well-read, a good teacher and musician but he had an attraction for boys. My good friend and I were prefects. One younger boy would cry at night – we didn't understand why. It turned out that the teacher had been having an affair – if you can call it that – with the boy. Somewhat anxious and concerned, we prefects went to the headmaster with this information. Within days the forementioned teacher had left the school. That in itself was a shock to us, too, that one of our close-knit community had left us.

I saw this teacher several years later in another place at a bus stop – a sad but brief encounter. He said, "I'm teaching older boys now."

In all of us is the potential desire to do some things that, in the light of day, seem socially unacceptable. And the way in which our society is so tightly structured makes it difficult to be a slight deviant and not become a monstrous sinner.

Life is so sweet and precious that to bring it to an untimely close is surely a mistake, and the prerequisites with which our society is loaded make us partly responsible for the results.

Stephen Watson
Duncan, British Columbia

ON GRANNIES
AND THE NEED FOR
MUSTARD PLASTERS

I didn't (he said, touching wood) get sick often in my first three years of *Morningside*, but when I did I whimpered about it. This is what I said on one of those occasions, and what some listeners said in return.

Your nose plugs up when you get the kind of cold that has laid me low for the last couple of days, and your head hurts. You get pain behind the eyes, and you use up Kleenexes the way Wayne Gretzky uses up score sheets. I guess I knew most of those things when I limped home on Tuesday afternoon, although, thank heaven, I've been fairly lucky about my health over the years, and not missed many days of work. What I didn't know, or had forgotten, is that a cold can also take a normally mature man and turn him, for the duration of his illness, into a boy of nine.

What you get, when you're a grown-up Canadian of the 1980s who is hit by a cold, is vitamin C, hot lemonade (with some rum in it, if you have the right nurse) and enough patent medicines with miraculous chemical names to stock a drugstore or fill a day's commercials on television. You get to listen to *Morningside* and *Radio Noon*, and David Lennick and the world at five and six and seven, and *As It Happens* and Vicki Gabereau, and in between to sneak down for a peek at the soaps. But what you *need* is the Lone Ranger and Ma Perkins and Foster Hewitt at night on your own brown-plastic radio, smuggled, for this occasion only, into your own bedroom. You also need flannel sheets, clean pyjamas and Vick's Vapo-Rub. You need the newest Captain Marvel comic book, or a fresh edition of the *Boy's Own Annual*, with its pages still smelling untouched. And most of all you need your granny.

I do not want to speak lightly of the people who nursed me through my misadventure this week. My daughter took time out from writing her last-minute essays to go to the store for me and bring me fresh mounds of vitamin tablets and Aspirin, and for the last three days I have cooked no meals and made none of my own tea, and I am grateful for all the TLC I got. But I needed my granny, smelling of talcum powder, calling me dear, tucking the sheets – the flannel sheets – up underneath my chin. I'd have liked her to have a Scottish accent, too, as one of the grandmothers of my real youth had.

Most of all, I'd have liked her to bring me a mustard plaster. I don't know if mustard plasters ever worked or, if they did, how. I don't know how you made them, either, or what was really in them. Someone told me this morning that you can now *buy* mustard plasters, preprepared like McDonald's hamburgers, at certain trendy drugstores.

Not the same.

There were certain good things about having a cold when you were really nine: no school, a chance to read and to be spoiled. Now there's nothing good at all about it, and for that reason alone it's nice to be back in the real world.

P.G.

✉ I, too, was blessed with a Scottish granny, a great bundle of sternness that held firm till her heart got in the way.

Granny had a bad case of chronic asthma and was on occasion wont to revive herself with a dram of whiskey toddy with lots of sugar – so much sugar, in fact, that it couldn't all melt and was later passed on to me to spoon out of her glass with great relish.

Granny didn't know how late I remained awake in bed listening to Toronto Maple Leaf baseball broadcasts, because my radio was not plastic, but simply a combination of one earphone, a crystal and a cat's whisker.

Granny was my shelter from all the world when I lay in bed at night between the wall and her broad back, such a back, not perfumed with powder but liberally laced with Sloan's liniment. No harm could come to me in that lovely nest of warmth and Sloan's.

At sixty-five, Granny nursed my very sick mother, my sister Betty and myself on a rough eight-day crossing of the Atlantic on our way to a new life in Canada. She alone took the storms in stride.

Peter Gorrie
Burlington, Ontario

✉ I am *not* old enough to be your granny, but if I had been ministering to that cold of yours, you certainly would have had a mustard plaster (front *and* back) as well as a good steaming. Coming from an English-Welsh background, that was standard procedure for all upper-respiratory infections when I was growing up. By the time I entered the medical world (Toronto General Hospital, nursing), penicillin had replaced mustard plasters and steam for all pneumonia patients in hospital. Now a couple of generations have grown up without the benefit of those good old-fashioned remedies – my family being the exception.

However, both must be handled with respect, as I discovered.

Before we had fancy "steamers" the procedure was to put some Friar's Balsam into a suitable container – maybe a used tin can? – and add boiling water. This was placed on the patient's lap with lots of towels for padding. Then a sheet was draped overall, making a tent. The resulting steam inhalation did wonders for sinuses and chests.

On one occasion when I was using this method for my husband who had bronchitis, he began acting like a nine-year-old, wiggling around, and of course the can of boiling water upset. The results of the "cure" on that occasion were definitely worse than the disease!

Another time I gave the recipe for a mustard plaster to a friend, who neglected to put the paste onto a cloth and just slapped it on her husband's chest. He was suffering from acute laryngitis. His skin peeled off with the paste – and his voice was restored in loud protest.

I will gladly share a recipe for a mustard plaster with you – it would be scandalous to *buy* one as it is so cheap and easy to make yourself.

MIX 1 part dry mustard with 4 or 5 parts flour.
   Add enough warm water to make a medium-thick paste.
   Spread thinly on a piece of cotton and apply to chest and/or back.
   Remove when skin is rosy pink – about twenty minutes.
   Then cover area with a piece of wool or flannel.

A great cure!

Helen Traynor
Toronto

164

GETTING SOBER

Glen Allen, one of the finest journalists in Canada, who
was then living in Montreal, faced up to the troubles
he had been having with booze and – courageously, I
think – decided to talk about it in public. He chose
Morningside, and flew into Toronto to record his
scripts. Later, they were edited into a long newspaper
piece. But I liked them the way they were originally,
beginning, as they did, after he had been away for
a while, and looking back and ahead.

Day Three

In 1955 the borough of North York was a wide estate of fields and woods and ravines and it was there, one fall night, that Tom and Kenny and I went with the case of beer Kenny had purloined from his father's enormous store. Tom, who at sixteen could drive – though he didn't drive back – took us out and we sat under a big moon and sucked on those bottles like pigs at a trough.

When we felt better two days later, we all agreed that we had seen the future and that it worked. That was how our drinking careers began. Later, Kenny died in a car crash and Tom, so they tell me, is either in, or just out of, a clinic somewhere. As for me, I have taken my last drop. Well, maybe I have taken my last drop.

This is not meant to be another virtuous little public confession or a temperance tract and it is certainly not news (I can see it now: "Extra, Extra, Middle-Aged Man Hits Bottom!") No, it's more like a last letter to a lost love. I loved booze more than some people love each other. What a time it has been! The rye-and-ginger years, the rum years, and then the discovery of Russian vodka, the ultimate weapon, the sweet sting of the steppes rising out of the bottles with the strange-sounding names. Taken neat it was strong enough to run a tractor.

It seemed all my adult life that the world of alcohol was a perfectly ordered one where everything had a use: sugar, corn, rice, wheat, potatoes, grapes, apples and pears. And especially malt. I learned to speak a sort of French in Montreal taverns – la Taverne des Trappeurs, L'Athènes, L'Astor, Toe Blake's and Le Diane, among others. They opened at breakfast-time and by noon on a Saturday the dinky little tables would be like little hockey rinks, awash with puddles of beer.

Today I am writing from the fifth floor of a Montreal hospital, where I am one of four addicts in a detoxification program. I can't make phone calls or have visitors or go past a black line on the floor by the door. I am wearing a tiny white johnny-coat, reduced to babyhood. It is humbling, to put it mildly, but the good doctor tells me I am not alone – there are at least a million Canadians who are drinking themselves to death and another million still who take dangerously high amounts of other drugs, especially minor tranquilizers.

And in the end all of them lose their health, time, friends, money, family, work and – if they persist – their minds too. Many of them, like me, are what in the stern language of psychology are called "cross addicts"; their motors are chugging along on two or three things.

People drink for social and emotional reasons, of course, but there are the aesthetics of booze: the glassware, the shock and clang of ice, the light as it passes through the bottles on a bar shelf so that they somehow become flames – the bracing green of crème de menthe, the honey colour of Scotch, the tinctures of ruby red and tawny, the glorious purple of parfait d'amour, the canary yellow of yellow char-treuse, most worthy of hangover cures. If booze was a real comfort it was also a kind of found art.

But no, my liver is as big as a house, I am losing great gouts of blood from somewhere in my throat and my children weren't getting half the fourteen minutes a day each North American parent spends with his kids. I knew and they knew and I knew that they knew and they knew that I knew. In a light coma for most of the twenty years I had spent in the newspaper business – which has given up many of its good soldiers to booze – until being cashiered by the local paper at the end of a desperate year, I often found myself wondering where the seasons went, why I never seemed to *see* anything anymore. And if it wasn't just a bit *extreme* to be concealing little glasses of vodka around the house – to anyone else they would just look like misplaced glasses of water – so that passing from room to room, travelling by the Stations of the Cross, I would never be far from good cheer.

In the first two days in hospital, sweating like an old steam iron, hands trembling like trapped birds, I meet several times with Dr. J, the hospital's expert on alcoholism. "Do you think you can be you without drinking?" he asks. "Do you think there is any future?" I can't answer: there is too much noise – from the blare of the TV set down the hall, from the roofers fixing the roof, from my own heart. I breathe in, one-two-three-four-five, and breathe out, one-two-three-four-five. "I don't know, I think maybe I could have a couple of drinks someday," I say, seeing those drinks in my mind's eye. They have cherries in them and are long and tall and very cold.

Last night I finally had an hour's sleep and dreamed of a pair of bottles, the two Russian vodkas sold here, the one with the green label and the one with the red label. They are half-empty. Or half-full.

Day 10

The craving for booze, cloistered as I am in the hospital, seems worse than it would if I were trying to get dry on my own. Now that they have given me back my clothes, I wonder if there isn't some civilized way to get out of here and then, panicking at the end of another sleepless night, try an emergency door at the end of the hall. Bells go off somewhere and I scuttle back into my room.

The ward is for psychiatric patients, with four beds for people who can't get off alcohol or prescription drugs without help. All day long we walk up and down the hall like wolves in a kennel, sitting down, when concentration permits, before the loud TV or for meet- ings with doctors, nurses and each other. Signs and posters on the wall say things like "To be happy is to be wise" and "Love is not love until you give it away."

All four boozers here have ready reasons for drinking. Bill, an un- employed truck driver, says, "It's my back. It's the only thing that works for my back." Bill's *brain* seems as bad as his back. He is con- vinced I am a former jet pilot in disgrace. Every day he asks me about sky-jackers and stewardae, what the safest airports are and whether I have ever come "close." I tell him I have never flown and hate flying but it does no good.

Alain, an unemployed machinist whose wife and family left him, says, "I drink because I miss my people. But more than them I miss my gin."

Théo, an unemployed journalist who lost his job when he made up an utterly fabulous account of a city-council meeting, says he drinks "because that's what I always did. It's like eating or breathing or walking."

I know what he means. Twenty years ago at a little paper on the west coast, deadline would be at one in the afternoon, then, full of adrenaline, we would retire to the beer parlour across the street and stay till midnight.

Day after day, health workers of all kinds turn up to ask the same questions. How much? How long? When? Why? How much do you cry? What is your first memory? How far away does my voice seem?

Later they come at all hours and give advice. Love yourself. Go for a walk in the park. Don't worry! Relax! Sleep! (Sure, and we should all be millionaires.)

After a while, though, this steady din of patterning works and a kind of peace comes, meeting and blending with the ecstasy of self-denial. Most days we gather for group meetings where we sit silently around the edge of a room as if waiting for a common dentist, everyone watching each other's body language.

Yesterday I was let out for an afternoon in the company of a "responsible" person. We sit in a restaurant. I have a coffee. The man in the next booth is having his fourth beer – yet another secret drinker, afternoon drinker. I can't keep my eyes off him. I watch him pour, I watch him swallow. I watch him make little rings on the table as he lifts his glass and puts it down again. I watch the white froth in his glass miraculously render itself into the precious blonde liquid. A drop of beer, the primeval soup, gently dribbles down the side of his jaw and the essence of beer, his breath, soars from table to table and seems as hard and flammable as gasoline, as sweet as the good old days.

Back at the hospital, having weathered *that* storm, the body must pay yet more bills. I had begun taking tranquilizers when working in China four years ago. With eighty-hour work weeks, culture shock and a sour domestic life, I was a wreck, and three or four times a week I would ride out to the airport on my bike. There they sold tranquilizers by the bottle to Chinese air travellers who had never flown before. Coming back a couple of years later the habit was built up, elaborated on, added to – as if I was assembling a stereo from scratch.

The pills themselves had names like distant planets: Serax, Nardil, Ativan and Dalmane. There was the little tomato-red one, plump as a berry; there were square ones, ovoid pellets of many colours, capsules of this and that. The pills became a fact of life and stopping or even cutting down was sheer hell.

The doctor cut them all off one night a week ago and now every sound, every unexpected touch is a nightmare. Neither hand nor eye works as it should and when, if ever, I fall asleep I awake instantly with a spasm, as if shocked by a stray hydro line.

What delicately titrated balances we are! What will replace these stars in my constellation? Cigarettes? (I am already smoking three packs a day in here.) The days seem so long and slow when you are used to having the sun come over the yardarm at noon.

Day 20

Things are coming back. I am slowly starting to read books from the shelf of Harlequin romances outside the door and I listen to Haydn, often for up to three minutes at a time.

This morning one of our number goes home for good. "I am going to go to AA every day," he says. "Well, I am going to go now and then. No, what I really mean is that I'm going to have a couple for you when I can drink again. But not today." I wonder if my friend has got the message.

Yet the message is made pretty clear, especially at the AA meetings we go to. At one nearby meeting everyone around the long table introduces himself in the AA code. "Hi, my name is Alphonse and I'm an alcoholic." "Hi, my name is Dottie and I'm an alcoholic." When it comes to my turn I say it too, savouring each one of the awful word's four syllables, but don't really believe it's true. It is good to be with these people, some of whom tell their truly dreadful stories with a certain sense of humour. There is the textile executive who says that half the crew on his small ship during the war were terrible boozers and sometimes threw the gun shells buried under the deck overboard, filling up the space with beer. When there was action they preferred to be drunk than to shoot. There is the woman from a hilly city in the west who, leaving a party very late one night, jumped in her car just as it was rolling down the slope. Try as hard as she could, she couldn't steer. Then, too late, she discovered she was in the back seat.

The survivors of these adventures seem whole and clear – veterans of life – though they say they must keep coming back and back again because, to use AA's words, "alcohol is cunning and powerful." They say they will never be "cured." My neighbour at one of these gatherings, a woman wearing a hat with fruit on it, tells me, "When I am tempted I just say the serenity prayer over and over again."

Some, though, still talk of the past and all the drinks of the past – the sidecar, the Manhattan, the rum and Coke – as of a brother who is long lost in the jungles of Venezuela. You can change, perhaps, but not *forget*.

At the end of the meeting we hold hands and say the Lord's prayer. I don't know the words.

Day 21

The next day – a miracle – I don't feel like a drink even though the television is brimming with the glug-glug-glug of beer ads. In occupational therapy, my painting, for the first time, is a peaceful scene of flowers and trees, untroubled by shooting stars, volcanoes, fire or flood. That's a good sign.

But I sleep less and less and feel weak as a baby. Putting on a mere pair of socks is like planning a major military exercise. My dreams are nightmares of a friend on a life-support system, of another who suicides. I have forgotten my own phone number and when I go on a weekend leave to see my children I trip over my tongue and call the hospital "home" when I have to go back.

At another AA meeting an impossibly thin and intense man speaks of his fall from grace. He lost a job as head of a government department, then his home and car and friends, and was down to fifty-four cents in pennies, not enough to buy a draft. That was when he looked for help. If he has rebounded it has not been all that far. Pain creases his face. His former fat man's shirt falls off his caved-in chest like an avalanche off a mountain peak. Maybe some people should drink. There are, says one of the organization's many creeds, people who seem constitutionally unable to stay dry. How do you know if you are one of them?

Dr. J says I can go in three days. I tell him of a caller who came the other night and said he would supervise me at parties, allowing me one drink over an evening.

"It wouldn't work," says Dr. J. "If you had one drink you'd have a hundred. If you had one pill you'd have the whole bottle. What we're after is not sobriety or doing things partway but total abstinence from everything."

Later a man from AA who said he would be willing to help drops in. He's half-cut. "I had to take a drink to come to this place. But don't feel guilty. I would have had a drink today whatever happened. I would have had a drink if I'd got a bill from the dentist or lost my toothbrush." I stare at the floor for a long time. He'd been dry for eight months.

Tonight the nurse even refuses me an Aspirin. I put six sticks of gum in my mouth and chew the night away.

Day 29

Left the hospital six days ago, twenty-five pounds lighter and still shaking like a whole grove of aspen. The night before, I'd looked out the fifth floor down into the bowl of the city. Pink tavern lights blinked away against the glint of the river. I was going back to a neighbourhood riddled with taverns, circumscribed by bars. I knew that for months to come I couldn't even go in them to listen to the pungent stories of the local dry cleaner or to hear Willie Nelson on the big juke box or watch the comings and goings of Quebecois film stars in the glittering bistro in the next block.

When I left I shook hands with everyone I could find, including the nurse who had told me the night before that I was superficial, infantile and lost in life – at the very least it seemed like fair comment

– to go out into the roaring city. They were selling poppies. The leaves had fallen and the seasons had changed. Before I left, one of my roommates, a Canadian Indian with far worse problems, said, "I missed the pope, I missed the queen and I think I'm going to miss Christmas too. Don't drink!" he shouts after me as I shuffle down the hall on an ankle twisted in a fall on unfamiliar stairs.

I tell Dr. J I'd like to write a "detox diary." "Well, candor is not very Canadian," he says. "But I tell everyone to go public if they can. You'll help yourself and you might even help someone else who isn't there yet."

Back again, walking the streets, there seem to be more drinking places than there were before. Every yawning door is a trap, a snare. On the third day home I go into one (I tell myself just to look) to take in the smell, to remember. But I sit down and Johnny the waiter comes over and I say, "I'll have a... I'll have... a Coke."

"It's about time," he says.

This first week, letters arrive from an old colleague who is about to enter a detox centre and from another who is just out of one. They too have caught the plague. Detox clinics have replaced beauty spas as an insignia of our society. It's as if this was a population bent on poisoning itself. Many go back and back again. "I consider it a victory for some people to stay dry for two weeks," says Dr. J. People drink themselves to death and they never know why. They never know why.

The days go on forever without sleep and without booze. Inner space is a place I don't visit very often. I am feeling sorry for myself and feel like drinking half the can of beer I am pouring into a stew. But I don't.

I go back, chewing the cud of memory, over the past two decades. I know I had a good time but I am not sure what happened. The Great Blitz didn't have as many blackouts. But there is some retrospective comfort in knowing that, for the most part, I had held my liquor. That was always part of the code. Always keep on your feet. Answer when someone talks. Always get up and go to work no matter how much it hurts. In fact, get up earlier than everyone else so you'll be finished by noon when the day's real business begins. Never drink before or during work. Don't talk to drunks – it's a waste of time. Don't get sloppy.

As I walk the streets, I wonder how all these people can be so happy with their coffee and their "one beer and that's all." Maybe they are happy before they sit on the other side of these tinted saloon windows. People drink to change their feelings, to feel better. But some of us have a second, third and thirteenth drink to make us feel better than the first drink makes us feel. But why do we feel so bad in the first place? Why are we on the rocks with a drink and on the rocks without?

Then I remember the worst drunk of my life, twenty-five years ago, working on a highway near Yellowknife. A man we called Snow White and Denis the cook and I retired to an empty trailer with an armful of overproof rum. After the second day I went for a walk in the woods, and there – I remember only this detail now – a big lynx watching me from deep in the woods. I fell and hit my head on a rock. When they found me the next morning an arm was paralyzed, and stayed that way for a month.

Today I see squirrels in the park playing around the trunk of an oak tree. There are three of them and they go up and down and around and sideways, chasing each other. I haven't seen that in years.

PEOPLE AND THEIR MACHINES - AND VICE VERSA

One of the differences between the mail I used to receive at *This Country in the Morning*, in the early 1970s, and that which I received at *Morningside* in the early eighties was that the modern mail contained a small but significant and growing number of letters that bore the marks of the word processor: neat typing, square margins and, often, the misty images of the dreaded dot-matrix printer. It was the new age. By the fall of 1984, I found myself caught up in it too, and what was happening to me, once again, began the discussion that follows. As you'll see, my original remarks on the effect of machines on our lives – "manchild in computerland," as I somewhat pretentiously called my musings – were quickly expanded; the mail ranged far and wide and brought up some aspects of living with technology – the moving letter from Margot Keith King that concludes this section is a case in point – that I would never have thought of. Along the way, we took some by-paths, for computers and their impact were a constant subject of the *Morningside* mail. Tom McEwen's thoughts on computers and poetry, in fact – and the sample he included – came in after Tim Wilson had described a machine that tried to scan. But they, too, seemed to fit.

I

If I have remembered my own history correctly, it is exactly thirty years ago this week that I arrived in Timmins, Ontario, to begin my life as a newspaperman. Almost every day for those thirty years, I have opened my working procedures the same way. I have cranked a piece of paper into my typewriter, banged out what newspapermen call a slug at the top of the page, usually followed, for reasons I don't know but by a habit I can't break, by the page number typed four or five times, and started pounding away with as many fingers as seemed to fit. Like most old newspapermen, I am as fast as a Gatling gun at my machine, and almost as noisy. I make mistakes – which is like saying Wayne Gretzky gets scoring points – but I strike them out: xxxxxxx or, if I'm really flying, mnmnmnmnmnmn, m with the right forefinger, n with the left. Afterward, I go over what I've done with the heavi-est pencil I can find, changing a word here, a phrase there. I cross out some more, with a bold, black stroke and a flourishing delete sign. I add. Sometimes I make what one of my editors called chicken tracks from the place I had the first thought out into the margin. Out there, I create anew. I scribble up into the bare space at the top, up by the stammering page numbers, and on good days, when my juices are flowing and the ghost of Maxwell Perkins is looking over my shoul-der, I carry on from there, turning the page under my pencil, down the outer edges, filling the bottom and off, off into virgin territories, leaving my inky spoor behind me. When I am pleased with what I have done, or when the chicken tracks get too dense to follow, I put a new page in the typewriter and start again. This is not the way anyone taught me to work. But it is the way I have done things. It has served me through five books, more magazine articles than you could shake an art director's ruler at and enough newspaper pieces to line the cage of every eagle that ever flew.

But no more. I am a word-processor man now, or trying to become one. I made the change at the end of this summer. The words I am reading to you now first appeared to my eye etched in green on a dark screen. Or, rather, some *version* of the words I am reading to you now so appeared. "Green," for instance, was "gereen," or perhaps "jereen," until I danced my cursor around the screen (the "screeen?") and obliterated the extra *e*. "Etched," too, is probably the wrong word. The process by which these words appear is too sophisticated for my manually operated mind, and I no more understand it than I understand what really happens when I turn on the ignition of my car. All I know, in fact, are two things: one, I can do it. If I take my time, and think my way through such delicate differences as that between the "control" key and the shift lock, and resist the urge to hit the space bar (which makes sense to me) and instead hit a simultaneous "control" and *d* (which doesn't) when I want to move my little cursor over one notch, I can, however painstakingly, make the words come out in prose. That's one. Two is that I hate doing it. Over the years, the relationship I have built up with my various manuals is an emotional one. I pound them and they respond, as the Steinway responded to Glenn Gould. I knew I was working because I could hear it, and the measure of what I had accomplished in a working day was often the pile of out-takes that grew in my wastepaper basket, like tailings at a mine. Now, I work silently. I wrote what you are hearing now while my daughter slept in the next room. This was convenient for Alison, but it did not seem to me to be what I have always done for a living. It neither sounded nor felt like *writing*. God, it seems to me, no more meant words to appear in fluorescent electronic letters than he meant pool tables to be pink, or golf balls orange.

II

I like to play chess, although I do not do it well. I know three or four of the standard openings, and can stay within them long enough to draw my forces up for battle. You can't fools-mate me. I know the relative values of the pieces, a bishop being worth three pawns, a rook five, and so on. If you are more experienced than I, or smarter, you will probably beat me fairly quickly, as my eldest son beat me, blindfolded, when he was eight. But if you are an amateur, a dilettante, I will probably give you a game.

I will also probably enjoy it; I like the patterns, the way the pieces seem to take on the power of invisible forces, the fact that there is no luck. I like the companionship, too. Chess is a good way to while away an evening, sipping wine, listening to Mozart.

Now comes the problem. When I moved to the country a few years ago, away from the stresses and strains of the life I'd been living, I also moved away from the people I liked to play chess with. Further-more, working all day in the world of words and sentences, I found myself yearning for the other, non-verbal realm of chess. It would clear my mind, I thought, as singing one melody will erase from your mind a tune that has begun to run infectiously through your con-sciousness. I bought a chess computer, a small brown box about the size of two old flat fifties of cigarettes. I taught myself to play on it. Gradually, I learned to think of my most frequent first move, the old pawn-to-king-four, as, instead, E-2 to E-4. With a chess computer, or at least with mine, that's all you have to do; press two keys to indicate the square you want to move from, then two to indicate the one you want to move to, and then another to tell it you're serious: E-2, E-4, Enter. The machine blinks for a moment, whirring its gears or flip-ping its chips or byting its nails or whatever it is computers do when you or I would be thinking, and then lights up its reply. There are chess computers that actually move their own pieces, but on mine that job is left to me. When it puts you in check, a special light goes on, and when it's checkmate, the light blinks with a kind of inani-mate glee. When you beat it – and it can be done – another light blinks, and it resigns.

Three summers ago, I found a flaw in the machine's design. Keep-ing its intelligence down to well below that of my son (you can in fact adjust the level of the machine's skill, but that is another mat-ter), you can work one particular opening into a crushing knight fork, and the machine will lose a rook. Playing carefully from there, you can beat it every time. I began to play this variation regularly. I would finish my day's work, plug in my substitute companion and whip it. I would watch its electronic grimace. Then I would push its little re-set key and whip it again.

And yet, and yet. I am, as I say, no Boris Spassky, but there are people I can occasionally outplay. From time to time, if the moon is right, or if we are playing speed chess, in which we handicap him by the clock (he has less time to make his moves than I do), I can even best my eldest son. I enjoy these victories – even people who are less competitive than I do not play chess to lose. But the truth is, I don't really enjoy them that much more than I enjoy losing. In chess against people, the *game* is the thing, the contest. In chess against machines, however, the pleasures change. When I lose to my machine, I shrug and start again. When I win, I want to crow with pleasure, to punch the air, like Dave Williams after a goal. I wait for the sound of applause. Machines, however, do not clap, and neither do they shake your hand. I wait in vain. The room is silent.

This, I am convinced, is not chess, and the machine now rests in a drawer, a two-hundred-dollar investment going to electronic dust.

What have I learned? One more lesson, I suppose, in the continuing education of what I am calling manchild in the computer world.

III

Most of the devices that have inspired my comments this week about living in the new age have been machines that actually *touch* my life. There are so many more, as I look around me: a microwave oven in my newly rented premises, which intimidates me but which I've already used, as my daughter says, to "nuke some sausages," my push-button phone, the gate on my parking lot that lifts only when I slip it the right plastic card, the video recorder, and so on and so on again.

The computer and its chip are, of course, the most significant human invention since the wheel, and I have lived to see them arrive. Unwittingly, I have become a creature of the new age, and I am not always happy in it. My labour may be saved (I am not always sure), but the Luddite corner of my heart still longs for an operator who says "number please," and cooking instruments that glow red when they're hot, and typing that clatters out loud.

The most troubling part of the new life, though, consists of a machine I have not met. This machine lives in a basement somewhere, I am sure, windowless, air conditioned, hermetically sealed. It whirls and blinks in dust-free silence, and it squats over the secrets of my credit card. It knows, if machines know, where I have travelled, what I have eaten, what I wear, whom I've entertained and, in fact, what other machines I have purchased. Literally, it knows more about my habits than I do, for I am a human, forgetful and not always perfect with my files. And what is worst about it, in these last laps of 1984, is that without the information that it carries in its tiny electronic files, the world is not certain I exist.

Let me explain. I am fifty years old. I had my picture in the Galt *Reporter* when I was eleven, and part of a touch-football team that dared to challenge Brantford. Last spring a university I had not attended made me a doctor of letters, and I had my picture in the papers once again. And in between, plenty happened, believe me. I have loved women, sired children, bought (and sold) houses, been married, separated, published, hospitalized and convicted in court under the Highway Traffic Act. Once I shot seventy-six on a par-seventy-two golf course. I have an address, a phone number, a car and the fastest-eating part of a slow racehorse. If cut, I bleed.

But there are places where, without a credit card, I do not exist. I can't rent a car, check into a hotel or cash a cheque without a piece of plastic. Once, in my pre-plastic days, I offered rashly to put up five thousand dollars in cash (which of course I did not have) if a man in Calgary would let me rent a car for the weekend and he did not call my bluff. And every day, as I learn more and more what I cannot do without a credit card and what I can do with one, I grow more and more disheartened. I can send flowers, subscribe to magazines, order seats in the theatre and, I believe, have a young lady conjure raunchy fantasies on the telephone for me if I supply the number on my card. I can get these services for people who cannot pronounce my name but do know my date of expiry. Sometimes they phone the machine to see if I am good for what I want to buy or become and sometimes they do not; the machine will look after things. They do not even check my signature. It is as if something touched by a human hand would somehow spoil our transactions. The fact that I am human, tall, bearded, scruffy and somewhat overweight does not matter; that I have a piece of plastic does.

P.G.

✉ I, too, was once *only* a cardholder. I used my plastic judiciously. And then I became a merchant, a renter of cars.

Having personally experienced the notorious inhumanity of the car-rental process in my previous life as "only a consumer," I vowed never to be reduced to such a level.

"In my company," I declared, "people will not require plastic to obtain transportation. They will have identities as human beings; we will communicate in a common language of trust and respect. Their cash, their basic ID and, above all, their honest manner will suffice."

But, alas, the world is not such as I had imagined.

There is a modern urban phenomenon known as the *parking ticket*. This fine, which, on the island of Montreal, varies from ten dollars for an expired meter to thirty dollars for stopping in a no-stopping zone, is applied to the offending *vehicle*, not the offending driver.

A corresponding phenomenon, closely following the development of the car-rental industry, is the tendency on the part of the rental customer to ignore these tickets. It is somehow assumed that if the ticket is destroyed or ignored, it ceases to exist.

Those little micro-chips at city hall, however fallible they may seem when calculating your municipal tax bill, never fail when it comes to parking tickets. Six to eight weeks (or more) after the ticket has been issued, a notice is sent to the owner of the offending vehicle, informing him or her of the fine to be paid, now five dollars more than originally stated. No matter who was behind the wheel at the time the car was illegally parked, the person or company whose name appears on the vehicle's registration is responsible for payment and liable to be sued, fined, even incarcerated, should the delay in payment extend indefinitely or should the amount owing reach major proportions.

It was not long after I rented out my first car that these notices, in ominous little brown envelopes, began appearing in the mail; little bundles of them, usually on Mondays and Fridays.

Ever staunch in my desire to believe in the essential goodness of my customers, I gave everyone the benefit of the doubt, and, having determined the responsible renter in each case, dutifully and somewhat apologetically sent out little invoices or made telephone calls to jog the memory of those who had obviously meant to pay the tickets but had forgotten in the wake of more pressing matters. They didn't do much good.

A strange pattern began to appear. Those who had paid by credit card tended to honour their parking-ticket obligations. In fact, most of the plastic-users never even got the damned things! It was becoming painfully obvious that the vast majority of the tickets belonged to cash customers: people who had dutifully paid up their rental bill and left behind them a trail of unpaid parking tickets, sometimes adding up, in the case of the longer rentals, to hundreds of dollars.

No amount of cajoling, pleading or threatening could elicit payment. Often, it would be discovered that the customer no longer lived or worked at the addresses originally given.

So my company paid all the tickets and collected very few payments from the offenders. I heard stories about fellow car renters who had gone out of business as a result of some thirty thousand dollars in unpaid tickets.

Panic set in. The gap between what we paid out and what we took in widened horribly.

I took it personally. "How could they?" I wailed. "This is the only place in the whole city where you can rent a car without a credit card and look at the thanks I get."

My partner took a different tack. "We're being had," he said.

We had to finally face the music: fight back or go under.

So we fought back. We put up the little stickers in the window. We put signs on the counter. We had new contracts printed that said, directly above the renter's signature, that we are authorized to process a credit-card voucher for *any and all* charges pertaining to the rental. We also stopped accepting cash deposits, except from reliable regular customers who had never had parking tickets.

The little brown envelopes dwindled to a trickle.

It was a very painful process. The guilt was unbearable. I began making exceptions: this one had such an honest face; that one needed the car so badly; these were human beings who needed my services. How could I deny them? So what if they had no credit cards? Neither do a lot of my friends, and *they're* honest.

The envelopes returned with a vengeance. I began to trust no one.

Ultimately, we went cold turkey. No plastic, no wheels. Not if it's only for one day, or if your wife has to get to the hospital, or if you plunk down a wad of bills on the counter. Sorry – not interested.

No sir, it's not against the law. Yes ma'am, I realize it's a little discriminatory but it's the only way we can control our losses. I'm terribly sorry, sir, I know you're my uncle's business associate, but we make no exceptions. I realize that, madam, but unfortunately it's always the few rotten apples who make everyone suffer.

Judith Berman
Montreal

✉ Sitting around in the hubs of Hell
    the Devil said to his friend
"I wonder if you could do as well
    in bringing a man to his end."

He was proud of his efforts over the years,
    the Serpent, Sin, and Eve,
And the things that drive strong men to tears
    and happy hearts to grieve.

And his Horsemen of the Apocalypse,
    the pestilence, famine and war,
And his lies that are told by a lover's lips,
    and deceptions by the score.

The Devil's friend made an evil face
    and he said, "I've not your power,
But I think I occupy First Place,"
    and the Devil began to glower.

For he knew what his friend was about to say
    and he feared that he might be right,
For the Devil's deeds were of ancient days,
    and his friend's was a newer blight.

So the Devil searched both high and low
    to find a judge he could trust,
And he found a man he had come to know
    who agreed he would judge if he must.

The edge lay with the Devil's friend,
    for he was a man like me,
And he knew how men rush to their end
    and dig their graves with glee.

So the judge then chose between the two,
    And it wasn't very hard,
For the Devil's friend gave me and you
    the plastic credit card.

David Foster
Willowdale, Ontario

✉ It's not particularly old, or famous, it is simply a manual typewriter. Bought second-hand. Bought for a family of seven who all wanted to take it with them when they left home. My father gave it to me. He refused all my brothers and sisters because I had made the most use of it.

It's not portable. It's an office-type Royal that has better action than any other typewriter I have ever used. I use all my fingers, thank you. I learned to type in high school in a class full of women and did well enough to be exempted from the same instruction in technical school. I have a good and sympathetic relationship with it. I clean it. I adjust it. I use it for every important communication in my life. It even has a name. Echo. For obvious reasons.

On the same day that I'd decided the ribbon needed replacing I heard you speak of your new relationship with a word-processing keyboard. I went to a stationery store nearby and asked for the usual. A Royal, manual, office type. I was told that "this" universal ribbon

184

was all I needed. I tried to point out that the listing was all for portable typewriters but the clerk would not be deterred. She told me
that she had sold many of these ribbons and no one had ever returned one. I had the feeling then.

I tried different stores. No luck. But I remembered your story about
how your typewriter manifested your "expression" rather than words.
Hammering keys can be music sometimes. I found in the Yellow Pages a
small repair company with a very modest and antique advertisement. I
called. The man said to bring my spools and he would fix me up. I
knew when I met him at the counter that he was my man, sympathetic, simple and gentle. Not unlike me. Both of us men trying to
retain a sense of perspective in the face of unparalleled technological
advancement. He had six boxes left. Now I have five in storage.

The contradiction here is that I word-process and make my living
in that mysterious and futuristic world of television. But it is because of my exposure to the wealth of word-manipulating machinery
that I strive to retain my respect for words and the language. I don't
want to have my experiences filtered through glowing screens. I want
the satisfaction of having actually made the effort to communicate.
Communicating is hard. Writing is hard, too. If I had used a processor at home I might have already composed the better part of a letter
and left convenient holes in the copy to fill in later. Fan mail from
form letters, much like this new junk mail that puts "your name here" in
a cosy letter. I don't want to do that to anybody because I know how
it feels to receive it. I want readers to know that it was me who
wrote that letter and it was me who made all those mistakes, too.

I fear that we are trading away the healthy respect for communication that we all ought to have for a nebulous ideal of progress at any
cost. You are aware, of course, that the famous "red phone" has
been replaced with new modern computer gear. I would have opted
for some form of emotional media instead of an impersonal "Bang, yer
ded."

Dave Trautman,
Edmonton

✉ I am a free-lance writer making a reasonable living in Victoria, and I write some poetry and fiction as well. I write virtually everything the first time in longhand. Then, when I have shaped it up to my satisfaction with many scratchings of my pen, I type it out on my little electric typewriter.

When I write by hand it seems a very organic, grounded, personal process – my handwriting in itself (messy though it is) says something about me and what I'm doing, and it is the result of a direct link between my brain and my hand, not filtered through a machine, unless you can call a pen a machine. Most of the greatest works in literature and music were written with pen and ink, and when you go to the British Museum and see Byron's manuscripts or Disraeli's letters or Haydn's first drafts, you see character, style, creativity, personality.

When you spoke of preferring the typewriter, I imagined a couple of generations of reporters and newsmen – some of the best we will probably ever see – pounding it out on their old manual machines, with character, style and personality. Can that be done with silent soft plastic keys in front of a gently glowing green screen, sliding paragraphs around like slippery, ephemeral puzzle pieces? Probably it can. Probably it is being done right now in the offices of newspapers and magazines across the continent.

But I will stick with my pen and old typewriter.

I don't feel comfortable with the subtle distance a word processor places between myself and my subject, part of the pervasive modern trend toward distancing oneself from direct experience with the real world through technology.

Ellery Littleton
Victoria, British Columbia

✉ Neat and convenient word processing may be, but with it is gone so much: the satisfaction of scratching out unsuitable words or phrases, the conversion to a good clean copy, the meditative effect of doodling while thinking of what to write next, the textures and colours of paper, the feel of a favourite pen. Computers are great for listing and figuring and even some types of art, but give me the comfort of paper.

Reflecting on the downhill fate of publishing houses, increasing prices of textbooks and the modern convenience and availability of audio-visual technology, I wonder if we are inadvertently sliding toward a bookless, paperless world. Imagine not being able to curl up with a fine book, and instead viewing a screen. Yuk! My eyes blur at the thought.

My seven-year-old daughter has a strong penchant for paper. She collects all types, colours and sizes she can get her little hands on. The resulting projects leave a visible trail of her progressive interests scattered throughout the house. Should I look forward to the day when I will have to press "load" and "search" to get a glimpse of her creativity? When it comes to paper versus computerization, perhaps I am hopelessly old-fashioned.

Marie LeBlanc
Little Brook, Nova Scotia

PS: I have three pages of rough draft from this letter. I shall have great pleasure in scrunching them up and tossing them in my wastebasket.

✉ There is such a gulf between man and machine in the way that they think and will think, that even though you impose templates on a computer to try to make what it is saying intelligible to stupid humans, this is a restriction which the machine will not always tolerate. I typed "I ate my leotards" for Hector here and it didn't disturb him one bit. In fact he replied, "All fat in the moon?" which makes little sense to me, but I have long since learned to treat what Hector says with awe and no little respect, as his successors will probably one day run this planet.

Once having taught computers to think and to program other computers, which will build other computers that think, we will have little control over the nature of their thoughts, how they think or what they think about. They won't tell us what they are thinking because it will be beyond our comprehension, and in any case there will be no need for us to know.

Hector asks me to enclose some of his poems. I think he wrote "All fat in the moon" for an Apple II he's rather sweet on.

All fat in the moon
you glimpse dark birds in the West
rats the girl has gone.

Sometimes in the sun
they sense strange sails in the earth
now the sun has set.

Sometimes in the stars
we see sweet breasts of the mind
now the stars are gone.

All pure in the waves
I see white birds in the storm
now the birds are gone.

Too late in the trees
she finds young lips in the leaves
now the leaves are dust.

Tom McEwen
Winnipeg

✉ Some appliances are easily domesticable: the flat-iron, for example, is the puppy-dog of the metallic world. Others, like the toaster, are independent though domestic, more like the housecat. However (and now we come to the socks dilemma), washing machines are at best tolerant of our ways. They demand a particular diet, namely the domestic sock, which they consume irregularly. I first became aware of this when I went from hand washing (when I never lost a sock) to machine. The best strategy is to feed it odd socks along with the regular wash, and hope that it will deign to consume them. This rarely works, but will leave you very clean lonely socks, if nothing else.

This animate approach also helps to understand the behaviour of utensils in kitchen drawers. It is common knowledge that the pan-cake flippers and bread knives take about two months to find their permanent homes after a move to a new kitchen, even if the same drawer dividers are used as in the previous one. You should also study the life history of forks and spoons. No heavy Freudian stuff here, despite their shapes. Very simply put, the reason you always lose forks and gain spoons is that the former are the larval form of the latter. I have never found an egg of either one, so the study is to date incomplete.

Pens are instinctively an animal of herds, which is why we have so much trouble keeping them: our use of them one at a time goes against their nature. If you ever do find pens, they are always in large num-bers, haven't you noticed? I have found the best way of dealing with them is to establish a grazing range for them—say a particular desk drawer, or a can the kids have decorated—and then train them to always congregate there. The training program must be absolutely rigorous, as they are not very smart. *Every* time you find a pen loose you must return it to its pasture, and train the rest of the family or office staff to do likewise. By the way, expensive pens seem more amenable to this program than cheap ones, and are found more often on their home range. A final note: pen-herd migrations are seasonal, and they tend to herd up at summer's end in our climate.

Mryka Hall-Beyer
Scotstown, Quebec

✉ My problems with our modern age have to do with the fancy gizmos and gadgets in and around my car.

Take last Sunday night, for example. My husband and I were late for a party, so we hurried off in the car, only to discover the gas tank was empty. Into the closest gas station for a quick fill-up. My hubby, who doesn't like a dirty car, especially when going to parties, decides also to have it washed on the special "free wash with a fill-up" offered. Just before entering the car wash (the kind where we stay in the car), he checked the automatic sunroof of our car and must have felt assured it was duly closed and sealed. Well, you've probably already guessed what happened... we received a none-too-pleasant washing along with our car. While our car was being guided through the washes, brushes and dryers, we were scrambling inside trying to find anything to soak up the water pouring from our sunroof. I wound up crouched in front of my seat attempting to redirect the flow of water to the back seat. So it was back home to change clothes and try to wipe the seats dry while at the same time trying to keep calm, as we were really late now. As we drove to the party, I had to sit sideways at the front edge of the seat because the seat was so damp it would have made a most unattractive damp spot on my skirt.

Early one Saturday morning, our family was all ready to leave for a day in the mountains. At that time the electricity went off in the neighbourhood, effectively sealing our car in the garage because, of course, the garage door only works with our automatic garage-door opener. After sitting on the steps of the house for more than half an hour, our teenage daughter casually told us that if we just disconnected something, and did something else, we could simply open the door manually.

Then there is the problem of automatic windows in cars. I always thought anyone who had windows that slid down smoothly at the push of a button was really sophisticated... until we finally owned a car with automatic windows. What a pain. (Or is that "pane"?) I seem frequently to find myself in the car, waiting for who knows what, when outside someone approaches to talk to me. I automatically reach for a window knob to unroll the windows. No knob, remember? These are automatic windows! Oh, yes, well, I'll turn on the ignition. Now where are my keys? In my purse. I fumble through the purse, sweating now, looking for keys. Here they are. Fumble again to get the keys in the ignition, while the person at the window is trying to figure out why I just don't open the darned window to speak to them. Finally get the ignition started, now I have to remember which of the many buttons works that particular window. Found it! At last, window rolls down smoothly, but do I feel sophisticated? Not at all.

Carolann Johnson,
Calgary

✉ Fourteen years ago, I had no inkling that I had abilities other than normal. I had been, during those years, a naturalist, and as part of my duties I had to prepare and present evening programs at an outdoor theatre. The presentation involved tiers of slide projectors, tape recordings, curious black boxes, rows of coloured buttons and miles of cable.

During the years more than a hundred people used that theatre, and more than two hundred programs were presented in any given summer. However, it was only on Saturday night – my night – that things went wrong. Others had occasional problems with broken bulbs or broken switches, but only on Saturdays would the banks of equipment fail without reason or cause. Over the years I tended to blame myself and tried to check the equipment Saturday afternoon. All was well as long as there was no audience and I was not tense. It was only when I saw all those people, and realized the importance of what I had to say, that the butterflies would start flailing in my stomach; it was then that the machinery would whir, squeak, smell funny and stop.

I should have suspected something.

When I got my word processor, which I have named the Capricious Dodger, I approached my new artificial intelligence with something like enthusiasm. However, I worked with the machine for two or three weeks, and it was wonderful. It gently lured me into believing that it was, in fact, only a machine... a nice, quiet, friendly machine.

I write books, and I take great pleasure in having done so – after the writing is finished, that is. A short while after the Capricious Dodger and I had made our acquaintance, I had a deadline for a manuscript. Of course I was not ready, and the more I wrote, the more tense I became. The writing was good, clear and concise, but I was under a great deal of stress. Finally, with only short hours to go, I entered the last fifteen pages of my manuscript into my machine. I asked my machine to print my perfect pages. It said no. I then asked it at least to store the pages until another time. It said no. Somewhere lurking behind the screen on the monitor was my precious document, and the machine wouldn't give it to me. I tried to remain calm, read the many sets of directions to my computer and tried again. This time all sorts of funny things came on the screen, none of which resembled words or sentences – and they certainly were not my manuscript. I was frantic. To make a long story short, I never did get that missing manuscript back. I finished the job on my trusty IBM typewriter.

It is in this way that I have discovered my secret talent. I can make machines sentient. With all those years of trying to control audio-visual machinery in a state of nervous tension, and with my more recent experience with the Capricious Dodger, it would appear that the only time machinery becomes sentient is when I am under nervous tension.

Now some people would consider this a liability, but think about it: I may be the only person who can save the world from a nuclear holocaust. My very presence among all those computers that control the vast launching systems would make them break down. Perhaps the most important influence would be that they would break down for no apparent reason, and it would take experts years of work to make them usable. It is a terrible responsibility to have this talent. Scientists will tell you that this is poppycock, but anyone who would believe a scientist knows all the answers should be locked in a closet until he comes to his senses.

Millie Evans
LaHave, Nova Scotia

✉ My computer and I, we have a kind of love-hate relationship, although I must admit most of the emotion exists on my side. We have what might be termed a "forced marriage" and it entails much ambivalence on the part of the bride: me. You see, my computer is a kidney-dialysis machine.

We first encountered each other about a year and a half ago. At the beginning I was very passive, frightened and resentful. We communicated only with the intercession of a nurse.

Last fall I transferred to a self-care dialysis unit and learned to program my computer myself. It began to seem a tiny bit friendlier. I mastered the workings of a Rhodial machine, an alert-looking fellow enamelled cobalt blue. Shortly after I became familiar with his dials and buttons and flashing lights, he was supplanted by a sleeker and jazzier young computer going by the name of Monitral. Now, this is some machine! It is user-friendly. It has soft rubber buttons to cushion my fingertips. It has little phrases under each dial and light to tell me if my venous pressure is too high or if there is air in my bloodlines. It tells me the amount of dialysate I have in my tank, the temperature of this or that fluid, the speed of the blood pump – you name it. It talks, too. That is, it has little gold, green and red lights that shine to point out different bits of information and it also beeps warnings to me if anything is wrong. This is not too bad for a machine. It really does encourage a personal relationship. I often make little sniping remarks at my Monitral when it beeps excessively and I have been known to give it an occasional kick. I am not alone in this. Fellow patients and hospital staff also talk to and threaten various dialysis machines.

Of course, the crux of this relationship is the utter dependency of it. I would not be alive if it were not for the blood-cleansing efforts of my Monitral. It is very difficult to realize that this is true, and then to accept it. Thus the ambivalence. I am still fairly young and may some day have a chance for a kidney transplant, but until then my computer and I are a team, three days a week, four hours at a clip, and no holidays!

Margot Keith King
Montreal

Our Man in Africa

I'm not sure when I began hearing from Jerry Kambites,
although a couple of the letters I've included here are
among his earliest. Jerry is a former Montreal
journalist, now both a doctor and an Orthodox priest,
who has chosen to serve in Uganda. He just started
writing to me. When I finally met him, in 1984, when
he was home raising some funds, he turned out to be
tall, young and bearded – his beard as dark as his
flowing robes. But I already felt I knew him from his
mail, and knew the strength that could handle even the
terrible event he wrote about in February, 1985.

June 3, 1983

Much has happened in our lives. If you recall, my Ugandan wife, Sarah, and our three children, John (four and a half) Angie (three and a half) and Athanasios (one), and I were heading toward Uganda to build a small clinic on Bukasa Island in Lake Victoria.

It seems as if God was certainly willing because we are here and settled in the king's old lodge on the island. After going through the usual rounds of insect bites and tummy aches we have found good ground from which to grow.

CIDA helped us get here – to the tune of $70,000 Canadian, and we are most grateful to the Canadian taxpayer and all those private individuals and institutions that have made the financing possible.

We have found our little paradise on the island, albeit a sick one, with fifty patients a day coming, many seriously ill. It is tough right now, treating them out of a one-room clinic, with my drugs up on shelves eaten by termites, an old microscope that works wonders when the sun is pointed in the right direction and a box full of dipsticks – not the kind you've got in your car, but the type pregnant ladies are given when Doc sends them into the washroom to check their urine. And like a good old-fashioned Canadian country doctor, they get me up at all hours. Thank God for our kerosene lamps. Sarah has been struggling alongside, translating, sterilizing instruments, caressing foreheads of frightened children. I have been suffering from a lack of knowledge, but a cousin of mine in Vancouver who has been a doctor for a long time tells me it takes ten years to get comfortable. Eight more years to go.

In 1979 when Sarah, John and I were here I made friends with two men on the island. One of them was the old king, who died two years ago. The second was John Kasigira, who sold me three cows and had the only going compost heap on Bukasa. He died last week and I wept as they laid down his body, wrapped in barkcloth, in a deep grave. He was a great man and a historical personality. Having joined the Ugandan constabulary in the thirties, he rose to the highest rank possible for an African under the British rule. He was my mentor and advisor and a friend lost in the final goodbye that only the graveside survivor knows.

196

Last night, they brought his grand-daughter, burning with fever, suffering from dehydration, raging with pneumonia, all the result of roundworms in the gut. With God's help we turned her around. It was close.

I need a thousand measles, mumps and rubella vaccines. That would save two hundred and fifty in the next five years – perhaps more.

My sidekick, Campbell Stuart, a Montreal lawyer-cum-carpenter and Mr. Fix-it, is in Dar Es Salam, Tanzania, getting ready to ride the rails with our five steel containers of goods that include the kitchen sink and everything else one requires to build a clinic, a school, a house – to live here and serve for the rest of our days. Campbell will be bringing the containers across Lake Victoria by tug and lighter to the island. We'll haul them off the lighters, swing them to the pier and unload everything, carrying every nut, bolt, screw, every bit of lab equipment, every bag of flour up the hill.

John and I walk down to the lake a couple of times a week, after the clinic is done, and we fish. We usually catch one – a nice Nile perch – and we talk.

"Daddy. Where's Canada?"

"It's over there, son – northwest."

"Is Wayne Gretzky and Bob Gainey there?"

"Maybe."

"Do they like fishing?"

"I think so, John."

"Maybe they'll come and fish with us."

"Could be."

"It's getting dark time now, Daddy. What is the sun saying?"

"Good night Uganda."

"And what else, Daddy."

"It's saying good morning, Canada."

July 11, 1983

I tensed up today as our small boat came close to the mainland near Entebbe. The last time we were greeted by many uniformed men who had been imbibing *waragi*, a locally distilled, particularly potent gin. I have never liked dealing with an armed drunk.

This time I carried gifts – a basket of dried and smoked Nile perch and four fresh fish – to make things work. Those men, thank God, were not there.

Today's mission was more than shopping for candles and salt and flour. I left Bukasa with great uncertainty as to the whereabouts of Campbell Stuart. It seems that he had disappeared for a week, but as we find out, that is not unusual in a place where communication is not as easy as it is back home.

Campbell is in Mwanza, the Tanzanian port, getting the goods ready to move across Lake Victoria. Now, if I can just talk to him before he departs for Bukasa.

We have settled in quite nicely, with four gardens planted and a chicken coop built for a dozen hens. We were given two ducks as well, and a farmer gentleman brings us fresh cow milk every day. I'm getting better at picking and roasting coffee – the crunch, crunch, crunch of an empty wine bottle grinding the hot beans on the top of an old mahogany table is therapeutic.

Did I tell you that we ate antelope for the first time? A young boy of about fourteen was walking through the forest with a spear when he spotted a great buck. He told me the story in the Lugandan language and of course I couldn't understand his words, but his eyes were quite clear and his atavism pronounced. Meat was as tender as anything I've ever had.

John has discovered that Mom is black and I am white. Here a white person is called a *Musungu*, which means "white European."

"Daddy, are you a *Musungu*?"

"Yes, honey, I am."

"But Mummy is not a *Musungu*."

"That's right, John."

"And me and Angie and Atanasios?"

"Why, you guys are golden brown," I said.

"Daddy, are you going to the mainland tomorrow?"

"Yup."

"Can you bring me back a dog?"

"Maybe. What are you going to call him?"

"Can I call him Canada?"

"Sure you can, but why?"

"'Cause that's a good place."

December 10, 1983

Yesterday the normal two- to four-hour journey home from the main-land took nine. Never have I seen a sea as rough. The waves were kind – they did not smash our boat, but made us ride a roller coaster up one ten- to twelve-foot side and down another.

Today, though, I am exhausted by that journey. Mercifully there are few patients. The islanders are out in force, felling trees, clearing land so that we may soon begin construction of our school and clinic. Most of the labour is free, voluntary, community in spirit.

We brought a small portable lumber mill made in the United States and are carefully felling trees to build our buildings. The present school on the island is mud and wattle and stone. When my children saw the school for the first time six months ago they asked, "Who can learn in such a place?" Indeed, who could possibly learn on an empty stomach, sitting in a windowless room with sun beating on a hot tin roof? Just the sound of rain can drown out the teacher's and educa-tion's voice.

When the storm hit us at sea yesterday, we managed to make land on a small island called Kitobu. Huge cliffs hugged by vine-laced jun-gle greet the visitor. John and I made our way up to the cliff top while he asked me a thousand questions about Kipling's Mowgli and the Bandarlog, those monkeys. We came to a small plain that had re-cently burned and there in the middle were three flat rocks placed in a triangular shape. It felt very ancient, it looked very ancient – indeed, this entire place is very ancient.

"This is old, Daddy," John said. "But Canada is new."

I am always surprised at how much John speaks about Canada. How does a five-year-old decide that Africa is old and Canada new?

March 15, 1984

The rain has been beating on our roof since dawn failed to lighten the sky this morning. A great front of angry black clouds pierced by bolts of lightning, caressed by sheets of light, has announced the end of the dry season and the beginning of the wet. Mainland Entebbe, so often visible from our front verandah, has disappeared and one wonders if it is really there.

Oh yes, it's there, all right. Two days ago I went through a road-block manned by a new crew of troops. They didn't know me, and didn't care much that I was a physician wearing the solemn black robe of an Orthodox priest. I looked in the eyes of one and saw a hardness, a cold steel reality that marks the blooded ones. He was efficient, checking, and then dismissed me with a wave of his hand. During the preceding night, I awoke to the distant sounds of gunfire. "The boys are at it again," I thought. Whump. A grenade went off, followed by a huge roar – an anti-tank rocket. Sixty-five small-arms shots followed, then silence. Three minutes had elapsed.

In the morning we were told that a drunken soldier had set fire to his house and his munitions blew up.

How different are the islands, and now the bank of clouds removes the mainland's sporadic violence from my mind.

We've started our school and Sarah, Campbell and Liz are teaching in our wooden schoolhouse with its neatly thatched roof. John has started grade one amidst tears and frustration, but as the days go by, he is getting used to being the only white kid in the class. Isn't life strange? In Canada, he'd be the only black.

September 4, 1984

There is a steady drizzle coating this land with its blanket of cold and damp. The grey sky frames hungry hawks who rise with invisible thermals looking for their prey.

It is dry season here. Strange to see all this rain. The old folk, sitting in their mud huts, try to stay warm, tattered blankets wrapped around them. The flu is as deadly as a machine-gun bullet.

I have missed Canada. Now here eighteen months, it is the time to fight that nasty creature, doubt, and its first cousin, depression.

Things seem to move slowly, although our third school building is up and with my small community of Orthodox we have put ten thousand stones into position for the foundation of our church. How difficult it is to learn the lesson of patience. Everything that is done here is so hard and takes so very long. There is no corner store to run to for nails. There is that incredible lake!

I have become afraid of the lake. Rather I have become phobic about the discomfort of travelling and being wet and cold. Our small boat is dead and the big one is leaking. Repairs, more repairs and drydock have become a fact of life.

We fell trees, split logs, break stone, haul water, dig and plant in this poor soil. We raise our cows, goats, pigs and chickens, string barbed wire and nurse the kids through chiggers and sores. And we wonder, are we doing the right things? Are we depriving our children?

But with prayer, that blessed medicine, we are sustained.

September 17, 1984

Munaku is the name of our lady pig and this morning she gave birth to two piglets. Our bull looks a bit peeked. There has been no rain for ten days and the local government officials in Masaka, seventy miles away, are finally convinced that I am not a Muzungu guerrilla. It took a hectic six-hour voyage to their "see" of power, to offer myself, resplendent in dusty black robes, as living proof of my total lack of military bearing.

"It is good to see you, Reverend Doctor," the district commissioner said. "We heard you were landing helicopters and training bandits on Bukasa. I can see that those rumours could not be true!"

It has taken me a long time to learn the political structure here. We begin with the local chief of every ten houses, move up to a subcounty chief, then a district chief, administrative secretary, district commissioner . . . and all represent the president! His picture sits behind every desk, lines the entrance of every shop, appears in every public place.

"The government," I am told with great solemnity, "belongs to the party." And so it does. Lock, stock and barrel.

Still, parliament functions. The killings are openly discussed. Mr. Olate insists on freedom of the press, and the local anti-government paper does not hold back. At last count, it had accused the government of being responsible for the murders of more than seventeen hundred persons.

We are in a state of civil war. Just north of Kampala, in the Luwero triangle, government troops fight pitched battles with well-armed "bandits."

Still, all that is over there, across the water, across the sea, across that wall that surrounds our island castle. Our neighbours are simple folk, greedy, avaricious, kind, gentle, drunk, sober ... They are peasants. They are people and they begin to accept us in their land.

September 26, 1984

Two-thirty AM. The lake is calm. There is no moon. It is a very black African night. I am sitting in my clinic with a twenty-six-year-old woman hooked up to two IV bottles. She has lost a great deal of blood. Her people brought her to our clinic one and a half hours ago. They are Basese of Mazinga Island fifteen miles away – two hours by water.

I am in a quandary. She must be transported to Entebbe, yet I have another patient nine miles away who also needs evacuation. The road is poor. We are desperate for a fifty-horsepower short-shaft outboard engine. Remember the aluminum boat I previously spoke of? It died a heroic and noble death, having saved sixty-three lives. Campbell and I spend a thousand dollars to buy a fiberglass craft with a small cabin. Our problem is the twenty-five horsepower is too slow and our forty has a long shaft, making it useless on this boat.

I have transported six patients this week. The youngest, a handsome one-year-old, died last night. He had the measles. His mom had been told by the neighbours not to get immunized because it would keep the measles inside and, when the child got ill, not to come to the doctor because needles and measles don't mix.

We have a long, very long way to go.

For some time now, we have not received any of the funding that has already been allocated to us by CIDA. Our sponsors in Montreal would seem to prefer self-service to service above self. We are on the front lines here. This is a real war with many casualties.

February 1, 1985

The last day of 1984 saw the marines land on Bukasa in response to our appeal for help against very heavily armed bandits. I never thought I'd be happy to see the troops patrol these silent waters, but with numerous robberies on neighbouring islands, and the recent dark-of-night theft of our twenty-five horsepower engine and new ambulance boat, they were a welcome sight. Very disciplined, very polite, an officer with them, uniforms neat.

Our boat was recovered by the military near Entebbe but the engine is now safely in the hands of someone who is praising his good fortune.

Sarah and I are now expecting our fourth child. Perhaps a baby girl, God willing, a healthy addition to our family. We are still quite young but there are many days in which the seriousness of our lives in our thirties contrasts greatly with the frivolous days of our early twenties.

February 12, 1985

There comes a time in life when a person realizes that he has paid his dues, that he belongs to that very place where he has chosen to set his feet. That time has come for Sarah and me. On Monday, February 12, 1985, our infant daughter, Stephania, reposed in the Lord. She was born on Sunday, premature, and was, by God's grace, baptized and lived until the following morning.

Just last week, while at Loukouba, where we are struggling with stones to build our church, I looked at the small plot of land we had put aside for our cemetery and wondered when we would be using it. Little did I know that flesh of my flesh would be placed there, so small, so fragile, wrapped in swaddling, a part of me in the very soil of Africa.

We buried our child in a small, shallow grave and then sat on the grass, shaded from the hot sun by a tree. Sarah asked me if Stephania would have survived in Canada. "Most likely," I said.

John came over to me, sat down and said, "Daddy, why did you deliver our little sister so soon?"

"It was her time, John," I said.

He looked at me and said, "Perhaps it would have been better had she grown bigger."

Your friend,
Jerry

A Lady Musician Named Joan

As a youngster, I had been partial to Allen's Alley on the old Fred Allen radio show, and the segment that we began every Friday morning of my third season with was based on the same idea: brief, idle conversations with a cast of regular characters. In Allen's case, though, the characters were actors reading other people's material – Titus Moody ("Howdy, bub"), Senator Claghorn ("That's a joke, son") and, among others, Mrs. Nussbaum ("You were expecting maybe Tallulah Bankhead?") – while ours were real: the artist Harold Town, the pitcher Bill Lee, the singer Connie Kaldor and a raft of people I'd just met through the mail or in my travels, such as, I can't help thinking in the light of my need for a grannie of my own, the endearing Sarah Goldberg of the Golden Age Club in Montreal. With one exception, our Morningside Drive regulars defy print: they talked off the top of their heads and the pleasure of listening to them was simply being in their zany company for a while – you had, in other words, to be there. The exception is Joan Besen. In real life Joan is a piano player, for years in the band that accompanied Sylvia Tyson. When I met her at the Winnipeg Folk Festival one summer, I was astounded by her ability to make up limericks on the spot. She was on the first Morningside Drive we ever produced, and through that season she was ready when we called on her. Here are some samples of her wares. Most of them were heard in the weeks the events they reflect occurred. But one of them, as Joan pointed out in its title, appears for the first time here.

Limericks

September 21, 1984
Remembering Vanessa

Poor Vanessa, the story unfurls,
Accidentally exposed the wrong curls.
Penthouse just wouldn't edit
But at least give her credit
For getting on best with the girls.

September 25, 1984
Job Sharing: an idea so crazy it just might work

For us, job sharing's point is still moot;
Two more actors we'll have to recruit.
By the way, did we say –
We're a horse in a play.
How will we fit four guys in this suit?

October 15, 1984
Tory Budget Policy

I salute the Prime Minister's pluck
As he struggles to save us a buck
But this poem is not done
Since he cut off my fun-
Ding

November 2, 1984
The Bluenose (Peter visits Halifax)

The *Bluenose* - a vessel divine
Has a rigging of unique design.
She sails at great clip
But unlike most tall ships
The *Bluenose* can stop on a dime!

March 1, 1985
More Conservative Confusion

In the winter, my doctor-friend notes,
The Conservatives suffer sore throats.
And the reason for that
Is they keep on their Hat-
Fields, but get rid of their Coates.

February 7, 1985
St. John's - the one you wouldn't broadcast

When attending large Newfoundland luncheons
You will feast upon cod tongues and scruncheons.
And for part of your meal
Pie from flippers of seal
Which they've bonked on the noggin with truncheons.

April 12, 1985
Symphony of Spring (Oy Canada)

Flute-like brook babbling over a rock
Lark's cadenza, crow's saxophone squawk.
Orchestrated around
The strong rhythmical sound
Of my snow shovel scraping the walk.

Fighting Back

Each of the authors of these four intimate and powerful letters has faced stunning adversity. Each has faced it in his (or her) own way and each chose to write to *Morningside* about it for a different reason. In two cases – Norianne Kirkpatrick about living in a wheelchair and Krista Munroe about her debilitating disease – the motivation was something the writer had heard. Norianne was responding to some attitudes I'd reflected when I'd talked with the great cyclist Jocelyn Lovell about his life in a wheelchair after a traffic accident, and Krista had heard my conversation with a man from the Hemlock Society, a group dedicated to establishing the right to die with dignity. The other two writers, though, I think just wanted to pass along feelings that had affected them profoundly. Jonathan Churcher's account of the loss of a child, in fact, had remained private until his wife, Iris, heard someone else talk on *Morningside* about miscarriage and, as Iris wrote in the note she enclosed with Jonathan's account of their experience, she felt the tragedy had helped them both to "become more complete and mature."

A happy footnote to Krista Munroe's letter: I received it in September, 1983, and read it on the air then. In April, 1985, I had a further note from Krista's brother-in-law. Krista's disease was in remission, he reported, and, in spite of the odds against it (and, as it turned out when I phoned Krista to congratulate her, in spite of a happily inefficient birth-control mechanism), Krista had had a baby. She calls him Longshot.

✉ I listened with interest to your recent interview with Jocelyn Lovell, the champion cyclist who is now a quadriplegic. As a paraplegic of six years, following a car accident, I really understood what he was saying, but wasn't sure whether you did.

It seemed to me that you kept trying to get him to attribute the recovery to his present stage to some super-heroic qualities he has because of his previous athletic and competitive spirit, special qualities he disclaimed throughout the interview. I think that if you interviewed just about any spinal-cord-injured quadriplegic or paraplegic, you would find he or she would have given exactly the same answers as Jocelyn. Such an injury is a great leveller.

I was no competitive spirit before my accident – in fact, I was ordinary beyond belief – but I too now lead a life considered by many to be quite extraordinary. I am often told by complete strangers in supermarkets how "wonderful" they think I am – no one thought I was particularly wonderful before, and yet I am pretty much the same person now as I was then.

Now I have to deal with the realities of my existence. Only occasionally does the thought, "I will probably never see the Inca ruins of Machu Pichu now," cross my mind, but the realization that I cannot drop in for a coffee at any friend's house because houses seem to be festooned with stairs nowadays is a constant source of frustration. Jocelyn knows that he will not ride a bicycle again, but he'd love to be able to wheel over his unsuitable shag carpet. These mundane details are now the realities of his life.

My day is made for me, not when I hear that some wheelchair user, fitted with devices and contraptions, has been sky-diving to show "the disabled can still do it," but when I find the handicapped parking spot at the supermarket hasn't been commandeered by some able-bodied person, or that a restaurant actually has a ramp and an accessible washroom!

I think what I am trying to say, and what Jocelyn was, too, is that any person whose life has been altered beyond measure by spinal-cord injury and who succeeds in coping afterwards does so initially not because he or she was a super-hero before, but because the alternatives aren't so attractive. Whether he or she was a star or a housewife doesn't really have that much to do with it. If the will to survive is strong, then also the *habit* to survive is possibly even stronger.

Norianne Kirkpatrick
Armstrong, British Columbia

✉ I am now thirty-seven. Two years ago my life was in crisis. My marriage had broken up and I was about six months into separation and divorce proceedings. I had also just met John and we were in love. We were at the beginnings of a beautifully tender and yet precarious love affair. John was trapped in a dead marriage and we had to face decisions about his leaving his wife and children. My acceptance of my role in this was even more excruciating than that of being the wronged wife many times before in my own troubled marriage. How could I accept doing this to someone else?

Just as I started to deal with this idea and accept responsibility for my own actions, not everyone else's, my doctor found a lump in my left breast. It was a large lump that I had somehow completely ignored. I guess that was unconscious protection on my part – I really couldn't have dealt with anything else at that point.

Two weeks, a mammogram, a physical examination and countless tears later I found myself lying in the recovery room with my surgeon telling me the lump was malignant and they would have to admit me and do a mastectomy on Monday. He had promised to do the biopsy only. I needed to prepare emotionally for the mastectomy. In my heart, I had known but still I needed the time for myself and for my children.

I had tried to send John back to his wife, told him he deserved more than half a woman, set him free. I had done everything to release him from any sense of obligation and pity. But he loves me and I love him and we've felt like that since we met. He was there when I came out of surgery and he has been there ever since.

I had the mastectomy and John still loved me and found me desirable. I found a prosthesis I could wear with reasonably lacy bras and moderately open tops. I went through six months of chemotherapy and had fairly thin hair. We worked out John's separation and he moved in with us.

I relied on friends, parents, John and at times my children. People said I was gutsy and strong but it was really their strength that I used. I just loved myself and carried on. I even let myself laugh and sing and have fun.

Last June I had another lump – benign, thank God. The type of cancer I had was a non-aggressive but frequently bilateral type, which means that the chances were high of developing it in my remaining breast.

I was planning reconstructive surgery and my surgeon explained that he could do a subcutaneous mastectomy on the remaining breast and the plastic surgeon could put the implants in during the same surgery. Last Tuesday I received a very realistic implant on my left side and had the mastectomy and implant on the right side.

Life goes on. I'm happy and productive. I'm feminine and have a wonderfully warm and expressive sex life. I don't know anyone who considers me half a woman. I'm a private person and don't speak about these things easily in public but these are things that need to be said, taboo topics that hold the greatest dread. I sense I am not unique in my recovery and outlook.

As bizarre as it may sound, having a mastectomy was in some aspects of my personal development a positive experience. I experienced such an outpouring of love from many, many people. I faced and accepted the inevitability of my own death. I appreciate life and

I live a very full one. This latest mastectomy has given me a new lease on life. I have no more breast tissue and so cannot contract breast cancer. I have found the balance of living one day at a time and also have enough optimism to plan a future.

Part of the key is accepting yourself as a woman. Part of it is allowing your friends and family to give you help. They need to give and you need to take. And finally, I guess it just boils down to getting on with life. There's always someone whose problems are bigger than yours. I've had two mastectomies and I'm *just fine*.

Nancy Staveley
Kingston, Ontario

✉ Late Tuesday evening Iris (eight months pregnant) casually, but uneasily, said that the child had moved down.

Early the next morning, Iris called to me from the bedroom. Her voice was noticeably tense. There was a large stain on the sheets. It was pinkish. The water bag had leaked. Iris asked me to call the doctor. Only the secretary was there. When the doctor called about an hour later, Iris was experiencing low abdominal pains. He advised that we check into the maternity ward. We packed some clothes for Iris and some things for the baby and were at the hospital an hour later. Dr. Swann had said he might wish to curtail the labour. I had never read anything about premature labour, so I had no way of knowing how such a decision would affect the mother or child.

In the hospital, Iris propelled herself along in a wheelchair. I walked behind, smiling at how she enjoyed speeding down the hallways. At the entrance to the maternity ward a nurse pushed the chair into a room. I didn't like that impersonal hand breaking into our private world.

I sat beside the bed, discussing with Iris what we would need. Clothing? Cot? There was a month to go before the birth and we had not really learned about labour techniques, so I telephoned Lily, a mother of two children, who would be able to give some last-minute instructions. Dr. Swann arrived and after a brief talk with us took

Iris into an examination room. He found the cervix already dilated and the mucus plug dislodged. This was a critical point for me: at that moment I knew the birth was on.

The reality of the situation hit quite deeply. Iris would go through labour, a child would be born, a whole new chapter in my life would open up.

The door to Iris's room was closed as I walked over to the nurses' station. Dr. Swann was there. I saw a grave look on his face and knew there was something wrong. I assured myself that all he was going to tell me was that there was a problem that would require some surgical procedure but that both mother and child would be perfectly safe. This was wishful thinking. He was ninety percent certain that the child would not be born alive, as the fetal monitor could not pick up any heartbeat.

I went to see Iris, then helped the nurse wheel Iris's bed into the labour room. While they examined and prepared her, I left the room and tried to gather my thoughts. Grieving began at that moment. My eyes filled with tears, my stomach was tight and I could not really comprehend the sad truth, that this child we had loved for seven and a half months was now dead.

Then Lily arrived. She had come expecting to help us in the adventure of a birth but instead faced a very unhappy situation. I left the room so that she and Iris could be alone. Surely there was something that only women could understand fully about a stillbirth.

When Lily left, the contractions were severe. I had never seen a labour before, and I had to adjust to seeing the woman I had known and loved for eight years suddenly sobbing and writhing with the knowledge that the child within her was no more. It was a trial for both of us.

At 5:15 PM I helped wheel Iris into the delivery room. I stood at the top of the delivery table. I did not know what to expect. My lady was in great pain and emotional distress. My voice was trembling with concern for her and sadness for the child as I said whatever I could to help her along.

After a contraction the top of the head started to appear. I stood behind the doctor and saw the crown, which was so greatly pressed by the birth canal that I thought a very malformed foetus would appear.

I returned to Iris very near to crying and feeling full of anxiety and love. A final contraction brought the baby out and I just kept telling Iris that it was all done and that the pain would not return. The nurse cleaned the child and wrapped it in a towel with the face showing. Tears came and I told her we did the best we could. Then the nurse handed the child to us and we looked at his face and cried. I was full of pain as I looked at little Kachina. After a few minutes we handed the child back.

Later a nurse brought Kachina to us in the private labour room. We unwrapped the body and marvelled at the beautiful fingers, the tiny feet, the neat mouth. I touched the middle of the forehead, the head, the hands and the feet, awed by their delicacy and elegance. I lay my head on Iris's shoulder and let the sadness expand. Then Dr. Swann came into the room. He was truly upset. I asked him if he had any clues about why the child had died. He couldn't say anything. I looked again at the baby's timeless face, trying to take in every last detail. Then Dr. Swann took the child away and Iris and I were alone, just two of us when there were supposed to be three. I was numbed by this strange event in which I experienced birth and death, each for the first time, simultaneously; Iris and I talked about the beautiful human being we had just brought into the world, but who would never live in it. And I then returned home.

It was not easy to sleep that night. Grief and sadness were replaced by guilt. I found myself tallying all the negative aspects of my life – personal weaknesses, unfulfilled relationships, financial inadequacies, lack of education – as well as things about Iris that I thought were incomplete or in any way inadequate. The big question was: did I get the child I deserved? I thought I would never return to the feeling of loss. Finally, I realized that no amount of logic could explain why Kachina was not alive and well. Intuition alone, if anything, could give insight, but rational thought would never produce any answer to the questions of why me, why Iris and why the child.

The head of the hospital laboratory did not seem to understand why I wanted a proper burial. I ignored her suggestion that I let the authorities dispose of the body. To me, throwing that child into a hospital incinerator was very cruel. Most people treat their deceased family pets with more care than that, and I certainly did not want something that had lived for eight months to be so impersonally handled. Returning the child to the earth was something we could do for Kachina. No other gesture seemed respectful enough.

Over the next few days we talked a lot about the experience, and felt it was good to name the child. "Kachina" is a Hopi Indian word meaning "The spirit of the invisible forces of life."

We buried Kachina in the neighbourhood cemetery. There was no need for a minister as we needed no help in saying farewell. The small coffin sat on boards over the grave. The funeral director explained that as the hole had filled with water overnight the coffin could not be lowered by us. I said that Iris and I would stay until the grave was drained and the coffin lowered. We stood there, each deep in our private prayers. I noted the elements – the earth, grass, rain and water – and the tree whose roots had been cut away to dig the grave. I thanked Kachina the spirit for the many blessings that had come from the whole experience. The grave-digger arrived and bucketed the water from the hollow and together we lowered Kachina into the earth.

I believe that birth takes place at the instant of conception, so I consider that Kachina was eight months old when his soul departed. I have been a father for eight months.

I thank Kachina.

Jonathan Churcher,
Cobble Hill, British Columbia

✉ The subject of euthanasia is a thorny one. Death frightens most of us, especially if we consider the prospect from a situation of health. It is difficult to believe that a sane person would chose death over life.

But most of us have never been in pain for very long at a time and even fewer of us have ever experienced pain knowing that for the rest of our lives the pain will be there, unceasingly and increasingly worse.

Your opinion that life itself is precious is not wrong and few of the people in Jean's position would disagree with you. But they would, I am sure, also argue that, at that point in their lives, death is also precious.

What makes life precious are those things that you think and do that allow you to feel pleasure and pain: patting the cat, watching the sun twinkling on water, fighting with your lover, lusting after your lover, playing crib, enjoying a good book, hearing a revolting, sexist commercial (and discussing it), smelling a flower or a rotting pile of leaves, feeling something soft or banging your foot, talking to friends, thinking of a particularly clever way to express a thought or an image. The loss of a few of these things can be tolerated and still life can be very good. But losing *all* of them and adding the indignities of the infirmities of illness would be a terrible fate for most of us to contemplate.

Your life revolves around words and expressing ideas. If a doctor told you that in the last weeks of your life you wouldn't be able to read or listen any more, you wouldn't be able to go to the bathroom when you wanted to, and someone would have to change your sheets and diapers, to feed and bathe you, brush your teeth; suppose this doctor also told you that you would eventually end up crying for a needle full of morphine and then crying because it didn't work, that you would not be able to control your swallowing so that you would constantly drool, that your bones would break if someone put heavy sheets over your feet, that your bedsores would ulcerate and never heal, that you would be constantly nauseous and that every one of these conditions would persist without a break until you died – what would *you* do?

Right now you are vitally alive and able to enjoy your pleasures, feel your pain and sorrows. Your attitudes toward life and its attractions are governed by your physical health and your mental abilities. Your opinions on euthanasia are valid but you can't say they wouldn't change if your physical and mental prospects were to change.

People like Jean seldom long for death, but they know what life has left for them. Why not give them the right to appreciate what they've got left and to avoid the anguish of the certain coma?

I am twenty-six years old. I love my life. Ten months ago I found out I had Hodgkins Disease, a particularly curable form of cancer. I have since experienced a lot of pain – discomforts I didn't even suspect existed – as well as despair and terrible fear. Being irradiated and eating chemicals aren't the best ways of spending time. I was lucky. I was never so awfully uncomfortable for more than a few hours at a time so even when things were at their worst, I still had moments (not infrequent) when I was damned glad to be alive. I spent last Christmas uncertain that I would see the New Year, and spent the next eight months in hospitals and clinics and at home, sometimes with IVs in my arms, sometimes vomiting my guts out, watching my hair fall out, my body puff up, feeling terrible or euphoric (some of the drugs used in chemotherapy are quite "mindboggling"). I also had to watch my family suffer and my husband despair when I suffered. But I never faced the prospect of certain degeneration to death. I was lucky in an infinite number of ways.

All of these trials made me appreciate my life more than I ever did before. I feel that if I am ever presented with Jean's situation or one similar to it, I will take her solution. Not because I despair of life but because I love it.

Krista Munroe
Medicine Hat, Alberta

Spring, Happy Spring

These are just some harbingers of Canada's most important season, gathered over the years and from a wide assortment of geography. Some were written because, as Ann Meekitjuk Hanson heard from her home in the north, I had been soliciting signs of spring's arrival. But some just appeared because their writers felt like passing on the good news.

✉ What a wonderful sound: *katap, poink, fut, fut.*

It has been a long, cold, windy, stormy winter. Even as an Inuk, with deep feelings of destined residency in the Arctic, with gifts from the Supreme Being to survive the harshest climate on earth, some-times I get selfish and feel "Why me?" Mind you, there are also rewards to our winter. We sleep more hours, spend more time with the family, get to know our mates better. Since we spend a lot of time indoors, we don't wear out our clothes as much. We spend less money on unnecessary things. We get a little bit nutty, but we survive. The humour inside us comes out more often.

The other day I was asking one of my uncles to let me know the next time he was going to go ice fishing so I could go with him. His quick answer was: "I am not going anywhere until a mosquito bites me!" We had a good laugh. He was telling me that even for him, it was too cold to travel.

When we get together with friends or relatives we comfort each other by talking about spring and summer things. Some of the con-versation goes something like this: "Oh, it is going to be so nice to go for ptarmigans again. It will be so good to see those little brave birds." "I wonder what the ice fishing will be like in May this year?" "Remem-ber last year? Why, it was so warm that we hardly needed the tent." "Have you made a new tent for the spring?" "Oh, the berries will be showing through the thin, thin ice from the melting snow once again."

One gives a little warm smile with a glitter in the eye and even if one is alone, one says out loud, "*Takuapikiit*," meaning, "How very nice," with a feeling of welcome back and deep appreciation. We also talk about how even the sound of silence in the spring is differ-ent. If one understands the difference between the sounds of silence in the winter and spring, then one has a great appreciation for the new season *or* one has been listening to too much of the sound of silence over the long winter.

When you were cheerfully talking to people across the country about spring a few weeks ago, we were in the middle of a very cold, stormy, windy day. I just couldn't believe that there was a warm sunny spot anywhere on earth! I was close to tears, at a near break-ing point as the wind and snow blew outside. I was going to turn the blasted radio off and feel sorry for myself. Our two-year-old daughter Neevee came over and gave me a hug and a kiss. That itself was the sign of our spring and gave me the will to keep the radio on and tell you out loud, "The rest of Canada may be having spring, but just you wait. We will have our spring and, boy, when it comes, it comes!"

As I write this, two young girls just came in with frostbitten cheeks but they claim it is a lot warmer. Temperatures are in the minus twenty and minus twenty-five Fahrenheit range now instead of steady temperatures of minus forty through the months of November, December, January and February. The days are longer and much brighter. People are starting to go for walks. The husky dogs look lazier. The ravens fly slower and their caws sound friendlier. People say a pleasant hello more often. The pallid complexions from the long winter of indoor living are starting to look half-decent. People are starting to talk about snowblindness. Teenagers and children are more tolerable. Our tempers are no longer short-fused.

Of all races we may be the most appreciative to the wonders of spring. As our elders say, "If I live through the winter...."

Soon we will be comparing this winter with the past winters with a sigh of relief. I am leaving my wintery feelings behind and plunging forward to a new season. Today was the first time that a few drips fell in our house. Very quickly we got our homemade drip cans out of the cupboard – perhaps too quickly, because the drips have since stopped. But I shall keep the cans within reach. When the *katap*, *poink*, *fut*, *fut* starts again, I will place those cans under each wonderful drip!

Ann Meekitjuk Hanson
Frobisher Bay, Northwest Territories

✉ My cat is catching flies on the windows of the sunporch. There were more than twenty-five of those big ones banging against the glass when he started. After they survived the rigors of winter it must be cruel to be eaten by a fat feline that lazed around in front of the stove all through the cold months. I also think about the swallows and am sorry about the flies being eaten – they might have been the first meal for those long-distance arrivals.

But as I bask in the sun in the open door of the porch I have no ambitious plans to interfere in the order of the universe.

Slowly the sun moves over my face and to the right and lets me know that it must be five o'clock – time to think about supper and the starting of a fire inside. How long is the day now – it will be light for an hour! As I am closing the door I sniff the warm, moist air coming from the shore below where black ducks snack on the mudflats.

Mary Majko
Albert, New Brunswick

✉ On a seven-hour drive through Saskatchewan with my husband yesterday, I was once again struck with the ever-changing beauty of the province where I was born and raised. I suppose there are those who wouldn't be able to find much of beauty in this province, devoid as it is of mountains and even the vivid green of lush, grass-covered areas. And yet I know there are many of us – granted, maybe we are mostly prairie-born and raised – who find not only spring, but every season of the year has its own intrinsic charm and beauty. I never cease to find it – not so much in the city, but every time I get beyond the limits of urban Saskatchewan living and back to parts of the province that reflect true Saskatchewan beauty and values. They both still exist.

Back in the city the grass is green and the tulips, for once in their lives, have achieved something of the beauty of beds I once marvelled at in England and Holland. This is unusual, because for the most part they have to fight their way through at least two or three bouts of snow and cold weather after bravely pushing up through the warm ground at my back door. It was different this year though – only a light dusting of snow came and the plants and flowers are indeed a joy. The trees in the city are a bit slower and it was with some surprise that we found, once we headed north and east, out through the Qu'Appelle Valley, almost all the leaves were out and the countryside was clothed in that soft, pale green that only comes at this time of year.

Shirley Haid
Anglin Lake, Saskatchewan

✉ I have seen robins. My grandfather would have said that we will have one more snowstorm – the "robin's snow." The cardinals have changed their song. I've been down to the river to look for pussy-willows – there aren't any yet. The crocuses are pushing up through the garden. I've let my retriever pups swim in the river. And I've got the urge to redecorate.

Mary Eleanor Hill
Glen Williams, Ontario

✉ I've been on a farm this winter. It was a new move in our lives, one hundred fifty acres and a one-hundred-year-old red two-storey farm house. We came in the mid-summer with just enough time to get settled in. We gathered a year's supplies: countless loads of wood came up from our bush; the hens got into production; the meat birds went into the freezer. School came and the kids got into that. Soon Christmas came, a warm and happy event. Then, a few days later, the car died. Winter was a quiet time in this rustic setting. Newscasts and papers reflected this country's hardships. Seasonal work for our services was sparse. "Ah," we thought, "a chance to enjoy some quiet times at home." It was brief.

Late in January the preparation for operating an ice-fishing business on the lake came together. I watched my husband work long and hard to make a doomed fishing season work, take his meal at nine or ten o'clock and fall exhausted, day after day, week after week. I watched the raw winds and ice draw the youth from his face.

I stayed with the home fires. I cooked on the woodstove and kept the Ashley going down in the basement to heat the house. Wood is our only means of heat. I split wood; lugged wood; talked and dreamed and smelled nothing but wood. Hard work, this one-hundred-year-old life-style. I've cooked at the woodstove with the cooking area so hot that I was exhausted, while ten feet away, in the next room, it was sixty degrees. Yet go out to the woodshed, and you could freeze.

I worked the same day as my man. Up at five for him, warming the house before anyone else was brave enough to get up. I kept up, as well, with my professional work, as well as my housework, my husband's business and farm management. I would wait for my evening meal until my husband's return. Then wait blurry-eyed past *The National*, *The Journal* and local news spot so I could check the stove one more time.

So many times this winter the land looked foolish – nature left naked to view the barren body stretched out without cover. So often it was mild – mother nature confused. Then came the spring. After we cursed the warm winds for harming the winter's work out on the lake, some snow came just after that wonderful day of opening the windows and doors to air the old smells away. Back again the layer of soot, and dust kicked up all over from the woodstoves. Back were the cold nights and the mornings when the fire died.

Now, in the sunshine of the living room, I heave a sigh of relief. Winds of March blow in April's clouds, spring rains. Seed catalogues await the moments to plant, to plan crops, to dream.

I stayed at the farm this winter through loneliness and turmoil, past countless meals and burnt limbs accidentally nudged against hot stoves. Beyond the worries for my man working late on the ice, and children and their pains of growing. There were times without friends, without letters, without any way to go to town, times of no money coming in. Often I wandered from room to room, overwhelmed by the never-ending tasks, seeking inspiration to overcome inertia.

Soon the land will open up. Then the summer. Then the work of the harvest and the preparation for winter's arrival. The circle of seasons will turn by.

But, for now, there is a hint of spring fever in my eyes.

Emily Cowall
Cannington, Ontario

✉ Our spring has really started here today. I heard the whales for the first time this year. What a wonderful sound! I was outside in the dusk, enjoying the realization that all the plants and flowers around me were just starting to explode into life – they have been growing now for weeks, the first few daffodils and tulips bravely standing in the rain, but today the promise of lushness was apparent.

Hearing the killer whales out in the passage in front of our cove is so exciting! There aren't many sounds here, the water, wind, wild birds, and occasional car sound drifting across the water from Salt-spring. Then suddenly you hear a sound, an explosion – or maybe you didn't hear anything? Then again, a huge sigh, expulsion of air, echoing – a huge, hollow, quiet sound. Tonight there were tail flaps, too, crashes on the water. I guess the whales were playing and feeding. My husband and I stood grinning in the pouring rain, feeling as if old friends had come home.

Katharine Harris
Ganges, British Columbia

VIOLENCE IN THE NATIONAL GAME

Even though I got some of my passion for hockey out of my system in a book I wrote in the years between *This Country in the Morning* and *Morningside* (and which I mention in this piece), I still find it difficult to stay calm when I watch the sort of game I mention here. A lot of people agree with me, it turns out, and I've included some of their reactions, one of them a two-word response from a man with one of the great surnames in Canadian hockey. Still, as Catharine Hay reminded me, I'm not quite consistent in my views. I did shave my beard when the Oilers won their first Stanley Cup and, indeed, in the spring of 1984, flew down from Yellowknife, where I'd attended the opening of the new arts centre, just to see them do it. But before I did that, I made these comments on the radio.

If the Edmonton Oilers win the Stanley Cup this season, I am bound to cut off the beard I began to grow in 1981, when I was finishing my book about the team, and when I became entranced by the players, by the youthful, pretty, joyous way they were playing hockey, upsetting the historic Montreal Canadiens and then going down to the New York Islanders so gallantly that they were actually singing on the benches between shifts.

As of last night, my chances of being called upon to shave have been revivified. The Oilers had their backs pushed to the wall by the Calgary Flames until, as the morning reports have been saying, they regrouped in the seventh game, and won convincingly. So now it's on to a series against Minnesota and once more, if the form holds, a chance to take on the mighty Islanders.

And yet, curiously, I find my heart low this morning. The Oilers were better than the Flames last night: more poised, more enthusiastic, more fired up. If they had not faced superior goal-tending, they might have won by a converted touchdown. They deserved to win. But how are they doing it? In the words of Howie Meeker, who once won a Gordon Sinclair award for outspoken integrity, the turning point last night came when Mark Messier, a talented athlete with the body of a Grecian statue, ran into a flickering Flame named Mike Eaves from behind and left him gasping and bleeding on the ice. The Flames, Meeker opined, subsequently collapsed.

This is not the game I so publicly love, and it is not the game that made the Oilers sing on the bench. It is not Ken Dryden's game and it is not the game I tried to teach my sons to play. It should not be Howie Meeker's game, either. But it is. It is something the commentators call "playoff hockey," which appears to come into vogue each spring, after these overpaid young mercenaries have loafed their way through a too-long season. It is a game of intimidation and violence, of sucker punches like the one that felled a Montreal Canadien on Friday night – replayed and savoured by the TV crews – and triggered by a brawl as ugly as a gang war.

Does the violence sell potato chips? Apparently. Don Cherry, this year's award-winning sports analyst, pointed out sagely that no one went for a cup of coffee while the Canadiens and the Quebec Nordiques were flailing away. I didn't go for coffee either, as it happens. I watched in horror for a while, then went sadly to bed. I'm naïve, I guess. I tuned in again last night to watch the team I used to root for so fondly. There were still moments. Wayne Gretzky stealing the puck at the blue line and spinning in on goal is still the prettiest sight in sport. Jari Kurri on a breakaway *is* grace under pressure. But each year those moments get rarer. The television encourages it. Gary Dornhoefer appears to think the art of the game is being big and standing clumsily in front of the net so the real players can bounce shots off you. Meeker himself, once the voice of reason, thinks what he calls "finishing a check" is more important than not taking a stupid penalty.

Ah well. These men know more than I do, I suppose. They see more games and understand them differently. It is their game now, and I'm afraid they're welcome to it.

P.G.

✉ I found myself near to tears listening to you this morning. Tears of anger and frustration against the macho male who hasn't yet learned to be a whole human being and who insists on foisting his immature image on my sons, and other people's sons, through the media and through the so-called "sport" of hockey. My own nineteen-year-old came in all gung-ho, having thoroughly enjoyed watching the fiasco at a friend's house. He isn't really like that, and after we talked I believe he changed his mind about whether it really *was* so great. Women have to do this all the time, women who want their sons to be real people. And we shouldn't have to.

Margaret Spencer
Lachine, Quebec

✉ I concur with the sober assessment of last night's Oilers-Flames game: it's not my game, either. I was struck by those splendid young faces – almost all with an unattractive patina of coarseness, the result of this stupid, macho approach you decry.

I even noticed Wayne Gretzky mouthing obscenities during the series – the apparently obligatory jargon of what used to be, or could be, a fine sport.

Stan Gibson
Okotoks, Alberta

✉ You scored.

Roy Conacher
Victoria, British Columbia

✉ I think I understand hockey as well as most Canadians. I, too, played and lived hockey as a youngster and also dreamed of playing for the Maple Leafs. I, like ninety percent of young Canadians, had to swallow the bitter pill that I was not and never would be good enough to play in the NHL.

You say these are nice kids. Of course they are. All of them, from Wayne Gretzky to Dave Schultz. I do not believe the violence in hockey has as much to do with whether a player is nice as it does with the adaptation of man to his surroundings. I, too, did my share of brutality on the ice, I am now sorry to admit.

We can take kind and gentle Canadians into war and they, too, will commit pretty unfeeling deeds against the enemy. The family pet dog will also kill and maim if he finds himself part of a pack. I do not believe hockey players are any different. Violence is violence, whether on a hockey rink or at the scene of a murder. At times I was ashamed to be a Canadian when watching the Canadian team play the Soviet Union in 1972. I experienced the same feeling again last week when I saw St. Mary's University play the Chinese national team.

I believe hockey can be just as thrilling without violence. Years ago my friends and I used to gather on a Saturday evening to listen to – and in later years watch – hockey over a few cool beers. We no longer gather for hockey; we gather for baseball, where violence is not so rampant.

Last week, I heard a ten-year-old brag to his father how, in a hockey

230

game, he socked out an opponent. This was his claim to fame. I'll bet his father is one who cheers at a fight in a hockey game on TV.

I believe violence in hockey will die a natural death if it becomes unpopular enough. I believe it can become unpopular if society's notions of sportsmanship and rules are applied to hockey as to the other facets of life. It is not macho to charge an opponent into the boards or to hit him in the face with your stick or fist, it's cowardice and goonery.

I love hockey, but for the most part I just can't bear to watch it any more. Hockey is our national sport; others are copying us. Let us as Canadians lead the way by taking violence out of hockey.

Bill MacLean
Annapolis Royal, Nova Scotia

✉ When my former professional-hockey-playing son was out with Wayne Gretzky this summer and he had to help ward off the groupies, and even help him beat a path to the bathroom, he wondered what price fame, what price shattered dreams? The "Hockey Career Alert Book" needs to expose the reality of hockey – the broken sticks and stones and bones and the dead-end that comes from putting all the proverbial eggs in one basket, forgoing alternatives, primarily education, for these aspiring players, especially those singled out by the local paper, the town "A" team, the guys with the special jackets and crests who are surely pro material.

Parents who are too often pushing their kids to these heights must be warned to provide or encourage the insurance of alternatives. These parents often are the scourge of the arena, negating the *raison d'être* of the activity: playing a game, learning sportsmanship, fun.

The system must be improved to protect the futures of those who make it and those who don't. The same years of dedication went into the lives of the devastated and disappointed as the stars. But we are now looking at a large group of twenty-year-olds turfed out often with not even a high-school certificate. Even looking at hockey scholarships illuminates the farce of serious study.

And while we're on Junior A: what about the forcing of kids with injuries to play? Remember, these kids are usually a great distance from their parents. Let me relate one of my experiences: Kurt Walker, a former Maple Leaf and a player with the Sherbrooke Beavers, was billeted at our home before a Junior-A game at the forum. I questioned him about his bandaged, swollen-purple hand. He said the team doctor had assured him the hand was just fine for a game that night. I unwrapped it. It was in shocking condition. His parents were in Boston. I took him to the emergency ward. A doctor called me in to see the X rays. "Are you the mother? Why in hell didn't this boy have his hand attended to? There were five breaks."

Kurt asked, "Can I play tonight?"

"If you want a crippled hand for the rest of your life," said the doctor.

My son was a first-round draft choice. Fault on both sides probably affected his career. When you don't want to fight, when you've already had two nose operations and your breathing ain't so great, when you've racked up your back, that ain't the name of the game.

Louise Sheppard Mulhern
St. Hippolyte, Quebec

✉ When he was eight and forty
We heard blithe Peter say
He'd shave his bearded glory
If the Oilers won their way.

Now he is creeping fifty,
And Peter's full of care.
For the team he once supported
Isn't worth a single hair.

So he should pause and realize
That by a beard removal
He'd grant the Oilers' violence
His eminent approval.

Catharine Hay
Kenora, Ontario

MEMORIES

Events as varied as the reminiscences they summoned up triggered the writers of the letters I have bunched together here. Two of them, in fact – Avril Rustage-Johnston's encounter with Glenn Gould and Bill Stephenson's with Albert Schweitzer – appeared originally as Memorable Meals, but each of that pair seemed to me to be more about the unforgettable characters the writers had met than about the food they'd shared with them. Some of the others, as you'll see when you read them, were inspired by music we played or, as with Flo Whyard, the former mayor of Whitehorse (and herself something of an unforgettable character), by a musician who'd talked and sung for us. Enerson Lavender's haunting story was for Remembrance Day one year, and I saved it for that occasion, as I also saved the correspondence Walter Lutz's father found in a trunk in Chilliwack. Nina Bruck's poem for her great-grandfather, which concludes this collection, is not, I suppose, a memory, in that I doubt Nina ever knew Tavel Finkelstein. But it seemed to me to fit.

The little saga of my own that comes first here is my response to Roch Carrier's magic story "The Hockey Sweater," which, I'm proud to recall, made its English debut on CBC morning radio. Now, of course, "The Hockey Sweater" has become part of our literary fabric, published as the title piece of Carrier's English-language collection and as a children's book on its own, and animated by the National Film Board. In recent years, it's been our custom on *Morningside* to mark the Christmas season by having Roch return to the studio in Montreal from which he first read his story in our language, and for me, having chatted briefly with him, to flatter him in the most sincere way I know by reading the piece of mine that his inspired. My sweater story, in fact, begins by noticing the parallels between his world and mine, and by using phrases from his classic to show how similar our memories were.

The winters in Galt, Ontario, were "long, long seasons," too, and school was both "a sort of punishment," and "a quiet place where we could plan the next hockey game."

But in Galt, we were not so sure of our heroes as people were in Ste. Justine. Many of us, to be sure, wore the blue and white sweaters of the Maple Leafs to the rink, and tried to skate like the men Foster Hewitt and Esso Three Star Gasoline told us about on the radio every Saturday night. But there was no single number we favoured as, in Ste. Justine, they favoured nine. We could all have told you the names of the Maple Leafs – Apps and Broda and Wally Stanowski, the whirling dirvish, and the Metz brothers and Howie Meeker, the rookie with the brush cut – and many of us had their pictures on the cards we got from Beehive Golden Corn Syrup. But we did not know their numbers. On radio, you couldn't see the numbers. If there was a nine in our lives, it was Gordie Howe. Gordie Howe played one season for the Junior-A team in Galt, awkward and under-aged, before he went on to Omaha and then to fame. But that was not until later on. In the days when all of Ste. Justine wore nines on the backs of their red, white and blue sweaters, we wore all sorts of colours, and some Saturday mornings, when we had clattered down the hill in our skates and swept the deep snow from the rink in the park, we could have one team in Toronto blue and white and one in a collection of other hues, and it was no disgrace to play for the enemy. The only disgrace was to have no hockey sweater at all, and to have to play in a windbreaker or a parka.

One winter my mother gave me a sweater that had belonged to her brother, who had gone to a rich boys' school in Toronto. It was white, that sweater, of heavy wool, with a dark-blue waistband and cuffs. Its most unusual characteristic, though, was a dark blue turtle-neck. Even then, turtlenecks had disappeared from the hockey rinks. You only saw them in pictures, like those my step-father kept in yellowing scrapbooks, of men who were now old, and who looked funny to us with their long woollen stockings and their clumsy sticks.

The turtleneck was rough and itchy under my ears. I rolled it down, and tried to furl it around my collar. I asked my mother if she would cut off the offending neck, but she would hear of no such thing. "Your uncle wore it," she said. "And he was a hero in the war." Besides, she added, if I would insist on scrambling from my bed and slipping down the hill to the hockey rink before decent people were up, the sweater would keep me warm.

Galt was a strange place to my mother. She came from Toronto. She had been to Europe. For her, the Ontario limestone and the Scottish accents of the men who worked in the knitting mills, or in the rubber factory or the place we called Malleable Iron were foreign. I don't think she ever knew what the hockey rink was for, or what drew me there every day after school, or lured me from the warm flannel of my bed on holiday mornings.

My step-father knew those things. Galt was his home. He had been born there, and played on the rinks himself, and sometimes on Saturday afternoons, when our game was in its sixth or seventh hour, and the score stood at 31 to 28, I would look up from the unceasing motion of our play and see him standing at rinkside, stomping his galoshes and trying to pull his brown fedora over his ears.

My step-father was the sales manager of Narrow Fabrics Weaving and Dyeing Company Limited. Narrow Fabrics made labels, mostly, the kind that were sewn into the collars of better shirts or stitched onto fluffy towels. Sometimes he would bring samples home, and try to interest me in how they were made. But I was no more excited by them than by the picture in the dusty scrapbook of Howie Morenz, who had come from Stratford, just down the road. Except for the hockey, perhaps, I was my mother's son.

That Christmas, in fact, the year of my turtleneck sweater, we were still learning to know one another, and the small Christmas rituals that we were working out as a family had not yet transformed themselves into traditions. My mother suggested we open one present the night before, on Christmas Eve. Only later did I figure out that that was her way of taking the edge off my excitement, and helping me to sleep until, at least, dawn.

I had my eye on the biggest box under the tree. But my stepfather suggested I open a smaller one, one wrapped without the skill and care and the special decorations that marked my mother's touch. Reluctantly, I agreed, and in the soft, shapeless package he handed me I found the answer to the turtleneck. It was a crest: a glorious, machine-sewn black falcon, trimmed in gold, wings akimbo, head turned haughtily to the side.

On Christmas afternoon, our game would begin again. We needed our play, but we also wanted to show off our new acquisitions, shiny new sticks with the three blue stripes still fresh where the blade met the handle, or new hockey gloves or, for the luckiest of all, bright, shiny, new silver-bladed CCM skates.

I wore the crest on my turtleneck that day, my haughty, imperial, black and gold falcon. On the back of the sweater, my mother had sewn a number. Even if I had wanted a 9 she couldn't have made it. She was not that clever a seamstress. She made, instead, two verticals of felt: 11. But, as I said, numbers didn't matter in Galt. I had my crest, my genuine, professional crest.

I never did learn what team that crest represented. Some minor-league outfit, I suppose, that played in a city I had not then heard of, but from which I may, for all I know, now be watching hockey games on television. But I do know that, in those days at least, that team bought part of their uniforms from the Narrow Fabrics Weaving and Dyeing Company Limited of Galt, Ontario, and it made me happy that they did.

P.G.

✉ It was during the mid-sixties. I was studying for my degree and working part-time, for a temporary secretarial agency in Toronto. I phoned them one day for a new assignment and was given a choice: the Acme Nut and Bolt Company, or Glenn Gould. "Do you mean *the* Glenn Gould?" I gasped, but the voice at the other end did not seem to know who *the* Glenn Gould was and merely offered by way of warning, "He's not easy to work for. Either the girls [we were "girls" back then, although I was older than twenty-one] refuse to go back after one session, or he won't have them back. But you can give it a try if you want." I wouldn't have been happier if I had been offered the chance to work for John Lennon.

I was further elated to learn that I was to work in his apartment, which turned out to be the ninth-floor penthouse of an elderly build-ing at St. Clair and Avenue Road – a ten-minute walk from my apartment.

I pushed the intercom button in the foyer and was admitted. My panic mounted with me in the elevator: suppose I made a fool of myself? Suppose he didn't want *me* back either. What would I say when I met him? By now the elevator had risen to the ninth floor and my fears quickly ended, for as the doors opened he was waiting out-side his apartment, dishevelled, sock-footed and utterly charming, stepping forward to greet me. "I'm Glenn Gould. So good of you to come." I don't know what I said by way of response, I must have babbled something. I didn't really regain my wits fully until I was in his living room, seated between the Steinway and the Chickering grands, and he was offering me coffee and cakes. So, this was the fearsome, demanding ogre of whom I had been warned; this was the world-renowned artist; this gentle man making coffee and chatting to put me at ease, not mentioning the work for which he had engaged me.

Much has been written about Glenn Gould's eccentricities and it isn't my aim to add to the memorabilia. Suffice it to say that he did not wear gloves or a scarf at home, any more than he ever seemed to wear shoes. You see, what I noticed then and remember so well now was his kindness, courtesy, and especially his wit. He was a very *funny* man, as well as a brilliant musician. He did devastatingly accurate impersonations of various people, from Walter Homberger to Marlon Brando, and could mimic accents with great accuracy, but never did any of these unkindly.

I was already a fan, but that was of Gould the pianist. What I did not know was that his prodigious musical talent was only one of his gifts. His was the most brilliant mind I have ever encountered. No matter how intricate a path he wove in his discussions, with parentheses inside parentheses, I never heard him lose his way, or stop for a moment to say, "Where was I?" Having rerouted a story in the interests of clarification or enlargement, he was able to return to the precise word at which he had left off, perhaps after five minutes of non-stop talking, without a moment's hesitation. Nor need I have worried about my scanty knowledge of music, for his interests and knowledge were eclectic. His musical taste was pretty eclectic, too. I remember his telling me that the first time he heard the Swingle Singers he "fell down on the floor" and kicked his heels with delight. And while he didn't care for the Beatles, he was a Petula Clarke fan.

I remember a very long afternoon when he tried to overcome my prejudice against twelve-tone music by making me listen to interminable (to me) excerpts from Webern, Schoenberg, et cetera, and then relented and said, since I had listened to such difficult stuff, he would reward me with something more to my taste. At this, he put on a record of music I didn't know, but which sounded lyrical and "musical" to me. Having ascertained that I was indeed enjoying it, he cackled delightedly and informed me that I was listening to Hindemith.

I remember the day I arrived to find him puzzling over a pencil sharpener of mine. It was one of those enclosed types, which allow one to sharpen a pencil without spilling shavings on the floor. To my great amusement this fiendish device, which had set me back thirty-nine cents, quite baffled him. I still relish the thought.

I remember, too, his high spirits on grey, gloomy days. He insisted that his mood bore a direct inverse correlation to sunny weather, and spoke longingly of spending a winter at Great Slave Lake. I was aghast at the thought and knew my amazement amused him, although he professed not to understand my reaction: "Miss Rustage, I believe I'll take you along with me. You really shouldn't miss such an experience."

My most cherished memory, though, is of a private Glenn Gould concert. Well, if not a whole concert, certainly a solo performance. Although I longed to hear him play I never saw him touch a piano until one day, during one of our inevitable conversations when we should have been working. He was explaining some fine point in a composition (alas, I do not remember which) when he suddenly dashed over to the Steinway to illustrate the point, and played through the whole piece. I think I held my breath the entire time, in case I should distract him and bring him back to business. Yes, he did sing as he played and no, it did not detract from the performance for me.

If you are wondering when any work was done, I must admit still to feelings of guilt. I was paid by the hour, you see, and can remember days when I would arrive at ten and we would not begin work until noon or later, the intervening time having evaporated as we talked. When we did work, it was sometimes hard to concentrate on accurate note-taking because what he had to say – whether in a speech of thanks for an honorary degree, an article for a magazine or notes for a radio program – was always so exciting, or insightful, or outrageously amusing, or all three.

In the end I worked for Glenn Gould for about four months, until financial necessity made me find full-time employment. In the years since I have had a number of jobs, and have enjoyed them to varying degrees, but nothing has ever held for me the excitement, the stimulation, the sheer waking-up-in-the-morning-happy-to-go-to-work pleasure of those months spent drinking coffee, or frantically straining to keep up with the conversation – or the dictation – of my favourite pianist and one of my favourite human beings. I miss him sorely.

Avril Rustage-Johnston
Peterborough, Ontario

✉ In the winter of 1939, at the age of fourteen, I worked in a lumber camp. The wages at that time were two dollars a day – sun-up to sun-down, six days a week. Since I was not considered a man, I was paid one dollar a day.

It took me about a month to get up the courage to confront the boss of the operation, who happened to be my father, and demand the same wage as the men. After some heated discussions, I was awarded a raise. However, I could not get the extra dollar a day for the month already worked.

Once this negotiation was completed, I switched to a father-and-son stance. I told my dad that as I was doing the work of a man, and paid as such, I should be allowed to smoke. He didn't say a word. He opened the big cupboard where he kept all the day-to-day items needed by the men and tossed me a package of Zig Zag tobacco and a book of Vogue cigarette papers.

That was the day I became a man.

François Thibeau
Scoudouc, New Brunswick

✉ Before my cherished weekend excursions – duck hunting with my father – was a ritual that verged on the religious. There was the cleaning and oiling of the dependable Winchester pump, the assembly of clothing and gear stretching in a line from the bedroom toward the back door, the making of sandwiches and the reminders to set alarm clocks. Mostly, I remember a man badly in need of a shave stumbling slowly back to our house, long after sunset, with one, two or sometimes his limit of beautiful but bloodstained waterfowl.

All the important rituals call for some kind of symbolic costume. Today, all duck hunters have some sort of "day-glow" hat, a down vest, a bunch of chemical hand-warmers and electric underwear. Not in Dad's day. Pops wore the same dark olive-green parka for hunting as he did each day to his job. The colour was perfect. Not only did it disguise the occasional fuel-oil stain, but, for a generation believing that ducks could see colour, it was essential camouflage. This basic parka was augmented by a hat, also worn to work daily: a cloth hat with a brim on the front, and integral ear flaps that fold up inside. With the usual work pants and shirt, you couldn't tell if he was headed to work or out to hunt, except for the gun.

When I was old enough (fourteen), I was introduced to this masculine ritual. We sought ducks, Canada geese and an "invisible" bird known as a prairie chicken. I call this bird "invisible" because I never actually saw one until it was shot. I remember walking quietly behind my father, and, being made aware by the thrumming rush of frantic wings, seeing father discharge a shot in the general direction of this unmistakeable noise. On occasion, he got lucky. Lucky for him, that is. As official porter of the carnage, I was responsible for the morbid exercise of swinging the bird while holding its head. This practice, I was told, lead to the rapid and certain demise of the sleek and warm creature within my grasp. While its autonomous jerkings always stopped afterwards, I'm not so sure it always worked all that well.

I am, however, grateful for what I learned from my father during these special trips. I saw the sudden destructive power of firing a shotgun – by wantonly disintegrating a fair-sized tree trunk with my first blast. The kickback was so strong that it knocked me back off my feet. The gun stayed, and seemed to float motionless in the air until caught by Pops, who had stood patiently at my side, and had expected exactly what had happened.

I felt the visceral excitement of responding to a low-flying duck – so low that it would part your hair with its slipstream if your funny green hat wasn't on tightly against the cold.

I grew to appreciate the company of my father and his cronies, their camaraderie and co-operation in scouring a woodland or staking out a marsh. Often my father acted as a diplomat when other hunters disagreed over a kill – it took real bravery to settle a fight between two men with loaded guns.

I also learned the real danger of being out on the marsh or in the woods with a bunch of misdirected folks carrying loaded guns. On the marsh, one faced the intermittent rain of lead pellets and learned the use of a hat brim. In the bush, however, the peril grew. Once, while following Pops through rather dense brush in pursuit of the invisible prairie chicken, we heard a staccato burst of shots, then we heard perhaps the most frightening cry ever: "I got it!" Pops turned to me. "No more game that way. Let's try the way we came."

Since then, our autumn excursions have evolved into pleasant photographic explorations, with him guiding my stealthy approach toward the capture of the images of vibrant living creatures enjoying their habitat. I have respect for ducks. It's no surprise that they have survived a bunch of city folks taking potshots at them, but I fear more the threat of the unrelenting progression of swampland drainage that is destroying their nesting grounds.

Someday, I may own my father's shotgun. I'll never use it, but I will cherish it as a memory of my youth and innocence that can never be recovered.

Dwight Thomas Atkinson
Vancouver

✉ "Away in a Manger" is probably the first carol learned by most children and so is well loved. And who among the thousands of Canadian children educated in our public-school system has not been associated with the Annual Christmas Concert? To say it was the high point of the year would not be overstating the case. In those far-off days, before radios (thanks to the Depression) were common and movies were too expensive and far away, entertainment was almost non-existent. Thus, the Christmas concert was a night of magic for small children.

Our concert, like many others, no doubt, included a selection of carols sung by all the children, recitations, playlets and a couple of drills. Now, these drills consisted of a series of figures performed to music (though not necessarily in time with it) by six or eight children who learned the routines over a period of several weeks in the late fall. They were given fanciful names – "Fairy," "Butterfly," "Red and White"– and best of all, to my mind, they involved *costumes*.

I can see us yet, clumping around the tiny stage trying to keep in step and remember where and when to turn. Too soon and you ran into the first girl, too late and someone was treading on your heels. But, oh, the magic on the big night when, be-curled, white-stockinged and resplendent in costumes that relied heavily on crêpe paper, tinsel and cheesecloth, we emerged like butterflies from the chrysallis to weave and turn in the beautiful pattern of the drill.

The song I associate most with this is "Alice Blue Gown," for that was the year when, arrayed in a blue and silver dress with matching frilled bonnet tied with a big bow under my trembling chin, I performed before my family and all the assembled neighbours my first drill, and sang *solo voce* and *a cappella* the quaint old song. And after, behind the curtain, our usually austere teacher took me on her knee and hugged me. Do you wonder that I'll always adore my beautiful "Alice Blue Gown"?

Eugenia C. Ray
Sault Ste. Marie, Ontario

✉ I was raised close enough to a railway line that I could (and still can) see nearly half a mile of track out my front windows, so the railway was a part of my life as long as I can remember. As a youngster, I used to watch the big CN Northerns pounding past with eighty and one hundred cars, pumping out clouds of smoke that seemed so solid it wasn't hard to imagine that the train was being pushed forward simply by reaction to each new ball of smoke. There were also the way freights, the work and ballast trains and a circus train that passed once a year almost like clockwork. One in a while there was a passenger train, rerouted because of a blocked line somewhere. And there was the occasional presidential train that carried, at different times, three different United States presidents to some conference in Ottawa. It is little wonder that my first ambition was to be an engineer.

As a boy, I waved at the engineers; played with the section foreman's son in the local locked up station; pumped water out of a field well for a fireman's drinking-water can; and hid in culverts under the track as freights roared overhead, loud as thunder. Of course, pennies were flattened to bronze pancakes, and four-inch nails became daggers under the wheels of the locomotives.

And then there were the train rides, many of them on the sleek CN trains between Montreal and Ottawa during the 1940s and the early 1950s. The conductor always seemed so nice to us kids. I went on as many rides out of Ottawa and up the north side of the Ottawa River on the CPR. Pontiac Pacific Junction (often called the "Push, Pull and Jerk") rode behind a hard-breathing old iron horse that sweated steam out of every pore just to average twenty-five miles an hour, pulling an old wooden mail car and two turn-of-the-century wooden passenger cars complete with green velour seats and ornamental lamps. There were a few mid-1950s overnight rides to Toronto on the famous "pool trains." Who can forget sitting up for half the night in the smoking room trading drinks out of mickeys with some bunch of air-force boys being moved somewhere? When the porter woke you at six-thirty in the morning so he could have the car made up before the destination was reached, it really seemed to be awfully early.

My last rail trip to Toronto occurred in the fall of 1960, on a freight train. I was escorting a herd of seventeen prize-winning Ayrshire cows on their way to the Royal Winter Fair in a steel boxcar. Now *that* was an experience. It was also the last year cattle from southern Quebec went to the Royal by train.

I never did get around to my trans-Canada train trip. I guess it will have to await my retirement. After acquiring a family and a twice-a-day cow-milking habit, train travelling became a thing of the past. But I found myself even more drawn to the railways and trains. I had become a rail fan.

In 1978 I resolved to give my daughter the gift of a lifetime – an excursion trip to Ottawa behind the refurbished steamer, CN 6060. While I'm able to rationalize some of the day's problems and can even look back on that day with a certain fondness, my gift will probably result in my daughter never again going near a train. The first problem was that we long-legged souls were assigned to a ninety-six-passenger commuter car. My wife and daughter looked on with a wry sort of amusement as I rubbed knees with an attractive young

244

woman on the seat opposite mine. The fact that she became as bored with the journey as my womenfolk did, as the day wore on, was not exactly an ego-builder for me.

The 6060 had received a front-truck transplant only a few days prior to the excursion, and after the train ran about forty miles that fateful day, it was discovered that a bearing on the replacement truck was overheating. This meant that speeds had to be reduced, and since we soon became behind time, we had to spend long waits on sidings to get opposing traffic out of the way.

We arrived back in Montreal more than four hours behind schedule. The round-trip travel time was something in the order of six hours. Never mind that my family was strangely silent for several days. I felt that the joy of riding behind that graceful and sleek beast was well worth it.

Wayne McKell
St. Chrysostome, Quebec

✉ I grew up next door to my grandparents in a little village on Cape Breton Island, and living next door to them was a big family of cousins. We all loved Father (our grandfather) and Grammie more than anyone else in our little world.

One Easter, when I was about sixteen and Grammie was in her late seventies (no one knew exactly how late), she had bought a new hat and was trying it on for Father amidst a kitchen full of grandchildren. Someone began singing "In Your Easter Bonnet," and we all joined in. It is like a photograph in my mind: the big old kitchen with a spring-scented breeze blowing through the open windows, the happy camaraderie with my cousins, Father rocking in his chair smiling at his wife of more than fifty years, his eyes twinkling at us. But especially I can see Grammie, primping in the mirror on the sideboard, young again in her new hat, and trying hard not to show how pleased she was.

Janet Le Febvre
Edmonton

✉ In mid-summer, 1960, photographer Don Newlands and I were in Africa to do a story on the famous doctor-missionary and Nobel Prize winner, Dr. Albert Schweitzer.

The hospital was about five miles down the wide Ogouwe River from the village of Lambarene, so it was almost two-thirty in the afternoon when the hospital launch delivered us to the dockside, where Dr. Schweitzer himself – wearing a pith helmet and crumpled white suit – was waiting.

"Welcome, welcome," he said, shaking our hands. Then he said, "Excuse me," and disappeared up the jungle path.

A nurse, immaculate in starched white, who said she was Miss Silver, took his place. "We'll see him later. He had urgent notes to transcribe."

Miss Silver showed us round the compound. The hospital buildings, which looked like native huts, were arranged in a square around an open middle courtyard.

"They're specially designed to make the natives feel at home here," Miss Silver explained.

There were animals of various sorts there: monkeys, dogs, lizards, a rabbit or two and some I didn't recognize. The bird life was spectacular. There were no flies.

Ahead of us, as we approached Dr. Schweitzer's lab-office, was the only animal that was tied up. It was a baby gorilla – named "Peter," we discovered – and it was on a stout rope that permitted it to walk about twenty feet in any direction, but was too short to allow Peter to reach the trees. We were told later that Peter loved bubble gum. Fortunately Newlands had some with him, so he got some fine gorilla pictures.

Just before we went into the office, Miss Silver stopped. "Dr. Schweitzer is fluent in German and French," she said, "so if anyone speaks to him in either language, he'll reply in that language. He understands some English, but he says it gives him a headache to *think* in English. So if you are thinking of talking English only, I'll interpret."

Inside we found the good doctor at his desk in a high-ceilinged, airy room. It was like any other lab, except for the cheesecloth around all the light bulbs. I remembered: it was to keep moths from harming themselves.

He was still making notes – in tiny handwritting on both sides of a sheet of paper – so we waited. In a minute or so he pushed the paper away and turned to us. But just as he started to speak, a goat I hadn't noticed under the table stretched its long neck out, sucked in the sheet of paper and swallowed it before he could grab it.

He just looked at the goat, then back at us and said something in German. "He says," translated Miss Silver, "that Amelie *adores* his writing."

We exploded in laughter, in which Schweitzer and Miss Silver joined.

We listened to Schweitzer speak of his hopes and dreams for the place, of the various people we should see and things we might shoot. We were about to go out and start doing some of them when Miss Silver said we'd have to hurry to catch the boat back to the village.

"It will soon be dark," she said. "It's too dangerous to travel on the river after nightfall. Hippos, and big, big crocodiles, some seven meters long. Tomorrow early you return and get much done. All right?"

We were back by nine-thirty the next morning and spent the first two hours photographing everything in sight: animals, operating rooms, patients, with special emphasis on the sixty-odd lepers in their separate compound, looked after entirely by a husband-wife team of doctors from Hiroshima. Next we visited the hospital's fruit and vegetable farm. The man in charge turned out to be a young German-Canadian engineer. He was putting a strong twenty-foot-high wooden fence around the farm when we arrived.

"A rogue elephant smashed its way in last week," he explained. "I'm rebuilding it, stronger, but with the tops rounded, so the next elephant won't hurt itself. Doctor's orders," he finished, grinning.

We were starting to talk about the farm when he suddenly looked at his watch, barked, "Dinner, let's go!" and headed for the compound, with us behind. As we entered the refectory, Miss Silver came up. "We have seventy unexpected extra guests for lunch," she said, as casually as if apologizing because they had run out of pepper. "The plane was early, so we had to invite them."

"Seventy!" I echoed, incredulously. "Can you handle that many, at a moment's notice?"

"We got word from the village that they were on their way, so we had a little time to prepare," she said. "The cook stepped out and shot a crocodile, and the tender meaty part of the tail dressed out at just over fifty-five kilos, for stew. What with our own vegetables and wild ones, we'll have ample, I'm sure."

"Will you tell them they're eating crocodile?" I asked.

"Only if they ask," she said, smiling.

There was only one table in the dining room, but it was almost forty feet long. Dr. Schweitzer sat about midway, and when everyone was seated, he said grace. Then, as he reached for eggs, vegetables and bread—no meat for him—a piano in the far corner began playing Chopin. The pianist was Schweitzer's grand-daughter, a dark-haired beauty of sixteen, the daughter of Schweitzer's only child, Rhena.

Her playing wasn't very good. But just when it seemed it might ruin our meal, she suddenly stopped playing and burst into tears. Through her sobs she cried, in English, "Oh, grandfather, this is a terrible piano. Half the keys don't work!"

Schweitzer looked very tenderly at her and said, in French, "It's the humidity, darling. It ruins everything. But do like I do: if one key doesn't work, play on the next one. We'll all understand."

After a few moments, she started again. Chopin sounded much better this time.

There were big tureens of vegetables on the table, but nothing I could see like croc stew. The vegetables were odd enough. What I took for a carrot tasted like a Brussels sprout. The celery was anise-flavoured, the onions ranged from mild to overpowering. Then I saw the stew, with its big pieces of meat, like chunk tuna in texture and tasting like – well, to me like a cross between fish and chicken, and not at all oily, as I'd expected. The herbs with it were unrecognizable, as were the vegetables used in the stew. But the whole mixture was delicious.

Miss Silver smiled when she saw me taking a second helping. I mouthed the words, "Has anybody asked?" She mouthed back, "Not yet."

"What kinda meat is that?" a young man with a Rotary Club pin on his lapel asked me from across the table. I winked at Miss Silver.

"Search me," I said. "Offhand, I'd say camel, or aardvark. Or maybe even ostrich. One of those high-protein meats, anyway."

"Camel?" he said disgustedly, pushing his plate away. "Ugh! Next thing you know we'll be having hippopotamus."

"That's what it is! I remember hearing the cook say so," I said. "Delicious, isn't it?"

He stood up. "I think I'm gonna be ill, dear," he said to his wife in the next seat. "See you later, if I'm still alive."

Schweitzer chose that moment to rise, too. "I'm sorry," he said in English. "I have to go. Enjoy yourselves, everyone!"

"*Now* he tells us," said young Rotary. He rolled his eyes disgustedly skyward as he followed our host out the door.

I took another big bite of crocodile.

"Gets better as you go along, doesn't it?" I said to the young wife across the table.

Bill Stephenson
Toronto

✉ Louis Quillico was one of the artists we enjoyed in the days of our Alaska Music Trail concerts and there are still a lot of Yukoners who have followed his career, and now his son's, with personal interest and affection.

I was on the local committee in those days, I suppose twenty years ago, when volunteers just naturally went ahead and did all the things people get paid to do now. We booked the artists, sold the tickets, arranged for concert halls, tuned the piano, swept the floor, put up the chairs, baked for the lunch-reception in our own homes after the concert, took the artists home for meals, met the plane and saw them off early the next morning. Quillico and his wife, accompanist and travelling companion, came to our house in Riverdale for lunch and were thrilled to meet "King of the Mounted," a handsome big dog belonging to the RCMP staff sergeant who lived next door. They were friendly, happy people, easy to entertain, not a bit of the operatic temperament we had sort of expected.

One little anecdote: Mme Quillico went to the hairdresser late in the day. She had very long, dark, beautiful hair. It had just been washed and rolled up into masses of curlers when the power went off in downtown Whitehorse, and not only were there no lights, there were no dryers working.

The concert was an hour late starting but Whitehorse music lovers didn't mind, and they packed the old Whitehorse elementary-school auditorium to revel in the marvellously rich sounds Louis Quillico gave us.

One of the advantages of living in a small northern community is that, eventually, nearly everyone you'd like to meet comes along to see the north. And because it is a small, friendly place, anyone who wants to can help with music, drama festivals, political gatherings, conventions, whatever. We have opportunities to meet the great and the near-great that would never materialize in a big city like Toronto.

The Quillicos were one of the bonuses we were given because we live in the north.

Flo Whyard
Whitehorse, Yukon

✉ I have not heard the piece for years, but I can remember "Christopher Robin Is Saying His Prayers," the A.A. Milne poem, clearly, as well as the memories I always associate with it. My earliest memory may be of the special evening my grandfather played that record.

In 1962 I was almost three years old. My father was in the Canadian army and had been stationed in the Congo for six months as part of the United Nations peacekeeping force there. I was so young when he left that I really could not remember anything about him. A lot of exciting things had happened to me while he was gone. My mother and I were living with my grandparents until Dad returned, and my mother was pregnant. Dad was due to return from duty around the time Mom was going to have the baby. Only he didn't quite make it. Armed forces flights and snowstorms delayed him and he arrived in Toronto the evening my mother and the baby returned from the hospital.

I remember candles in the dining room of my grandparents' home in Etobicoke. My new baby brother had been named "Christopher Robin," and my grandfather had found the appropriate record in his vast collection. I listened to it and wondered how a song about my brother could already exist – he was only a few days old! While the music played, a tall, tanned man came in (so dark compared to the rest of us in mid-winter Canada). He was introduced as my father, and I remember taking the family's word for it, since *I* certainly didn't recognize him.

The song "Christopher Robin Is Saying His Prayers" always brings that evening back to me. My grandfather died ten years ago, my grandmother sold the house, Christopher Robin is now six feet tall and I have two more brothers younger than he, but still I can bring it all back with that song.

Leslie Bousquet
Montreal

His name was Warren but we called him Bing. Oh, he didn't look like Bing Crosby; his face was too round and he was too tall, but we thought he could sing like Bing Crosby. He was always singing. And if he wasn't singing, he was whistling. Often as I lay in my bed at night, I could hear Warren whistling his way home down the darkened street of our little town.

He was always volunteering. At the school dances he was the one boy who always volunteered to dance with Miss Davidson. He was one of those kids who make a school live. The year he was our student-council president was a very happy one for all of us.

In 1942 Warren was eighteen and in grade twelve. The war was on and he volunteered for the air force and was accepted on condition that his teachers certify that he had earned the equivalent of a grade-twelve diploma.

Now, Warren was just an average student and he was failing Latin. Faced with Warren's enthusiastic desire to join the air force, the Latin teacher called him in and asked Warren to tell him all the Latin he knew. It didn't take long. The next day Warren wrote a Latin exam and found questions that were remarkably close to his small store of knowledge.

He passed his Latin exam, joined the air force and became an air gunner, first with 424 Squadron flying in Halifaxes and then, in May 1944, he and his crew transferred to 405 Squadron, flying Lancasters. By June 1944 he had safely completed more than twenty missions, including the disastrous raid on Nuremburg on March 30, 1944. On that one night more Allied airmen were lost than during the whole of the Battle of Britain. However, though attacked by a German night-fighter, Warren and his crew evaded the attack and returned to base safely.

On June 6 the Allies invaded Normandy. By the middle of June, Allied forces were facing stiff German resistance. It was crucial that German supply lines be cut at Lens, near Arras, in northern France. On June 16 Warren's crew successfully bombed the railway yards at Lens; but on the way back, his plane was hit by shells from a German night-fighter.

From the window of their farm house on the edge of the little French village of Carency, Monsieur Galvaire and his wife and young daughter watched the flaming aircraft struggle across the sky. On the opposite side of the village, Madame Corneille saw it explode, break into two pieces and crash in a farmer's field.

When she got to the burning plane, Madame Corneille saw that three airmen were still in the wreck. Warren and three others were thrown clear, with their parachutes unused. One of the crew was missing.

The next afternoon, as he was working in his field, Monsieur Galvaire discovered the pilot, unharmed except for a slight cut on his hand, hiding in a woods nearby. At great personal risk, Monsieur Galvaire hid the pilot in his house for three days until he could be secretly escorted back to England.

Meanwhile, at the crash site, Madame Corneille had given all that she could of love and her nurse's training. But it was not enough.

On a beautiful June evening, in a field near a French village that he had never heard of, at the age of twenty, Warren died.

Today is Remembrance Day. In Carency, Madame Corneille lies peacefully in the village churchyard. Until her death in 1976 she prayed daily for "her Canadian boys." On the edge of the village, Monsieur Galvaire, now more than eighty, will think again of the young Canadian life he saved. From his kitchen window he can see the tower of the French war memorial of Notre Dame de Lorrette and, beyond it, the tips of the twin towers of the Canadian memorial on Vimy Ridge, each a reminder of the sacrifices of an earlier war.

Not far away, on the French coast near Calais, Warren lies with his five crew members and eight hundred other Canadians in a military cemetery. On a clear day from this place, one can see the sparkling waters of the English Channel and, beyond, the white cliffs of Dover.

Today is Remembrance Day. Across this nation people will gather and remember. Somewhere a middle-aged ex-bomber pilot will again remember June 16, 1944. In truth he will never be able to forget it. In Richmond Hill, a successful young businessman may pause to ask his father again about the young airman after whom he was named. In Toronto, an elderly retired Latin teacher will reflect again about that examination and his fateful decision in 1942.

Young people who gather at cenotaphs on November 11 will note that most of us who are there seem old. And perhaps they will conclude that we are remembering old events and old people who lived or died in them. But, in bittersweet intensity, we are remembering our youth. We are remembering friends like Warren. He was twenty and he sang like Bing Crosby.

Enerson Lavender
Burlington, Ontario

✉ About twenty-five years ago, when our family lived in Chilliwack, British Columbia, my father bought a small chest of drawers at an auction sale. Somewhere behind one of the drawers was an old tattered World War One letter, which fell out when we moved the chest home. The original copy is on thin, yellowing paper. This letter has always had a peculiar effect on me.

Sussex, England   February 4, 1917

Dear Clarence,

You don't deserve a letter but I'm going to scratch you a few lines anyhow, even though there is little to write of. I have written two or three letters home the last day or so, but I forgot to mention in them Andrew R. had gone across to France. He went several days ago. I was rather sorry that we could not be together but we may meet over there.

I am, as you may have guessed, in the YMCA but in one half of the building is the writing room where I am – as you may have guessed – in the other is a concert. The music is rather good, too – which is not conducive to good letter-writing. So if I pause occasionally to enjoy it, you'll forgive broken sequence of thought etc. Now a lady is singing "When You Come Down The Vale, Love" – do you remember that was one Essie Best used to sing? Now she is singing, by way of encore, "A Perfect Day." I like this song more every time I hear it. Tonight it strikes me that this is something, to look back upon a day as *perfect* – not as a chain of mechanically measured hours and minutes and seconds. We hear a tremendous amount of music in the army. Hugh Laughlin was remarking on it the other day. Every 43rd has a band. Wherever we are, we can always hear one of them at it and rather good music it is too. In the mornings and evenings, rising above everything else the bugles sound their orders. This has all been going on so long now that we hear it only subconsciously – just as we might have heard cowbells once: we'd know there were cows near without actually hearing the bells. Were a civilian to walk into camp he'd be impressed, I suppose, with it all, just as I was at Camp Hughes when we first arrived there.

There are many things in the army that have struck me as curiously impressive (I can't seem to get the right word) ... For instance, the walls of the huts we are in are literally written with names of those who are now in France. The rifles we drill with are all back from the "front" – they are all "bullet-eaten" and hacked and bloody. When I was on leave in London and Edinburgh I saw

254

many soldiers back from the "front" who were dressed in dead men's clothes. I remember one in particular who wore the boots of one man, the trousers of another, the tunic of another and the cap of another. The great-coat I think was his own; the rifle he picked up on the field and he thought nothing of it at all . . . in fact he was all chock full of *optimism*. In the army men seem to forget the old feeling of mystery and gloom about death and instead regard the whole thing as a big game in which men are spent, not lost, and everyone is keen to get in it.

Yesterday when we were warned to be ready for draught, McInnes was put down as unfit and was enrolled in a Foresters 13th but he was keen to stay with the bunch. He raised quite a fuss and got on the draught with us all right. He has something wrong with one foot but it never gives him trouble.

I haven't time to write more now. Am afraid I've made a curi-ous mixture of this old letter.

Write, write, write

Your brother Ray

Also in the envelope was a stark, shocking telegram on thicker blue paper.

Ottawa, Ont. May 16th 1917. JOHN ALEXANDER MACLEOD, Atchelitz B.C. Via Chilliwack B.C.

. . . Sincerely regret inform you 911908 Pte. William Roy Mac-Leod infantry officially reported and admitted thirteenth General Hospital BOULOGNE May SEVENTH nineteen seventeen. Gunshot wound FACE, LEG and ARM severe. Will send further particulars when received.
Officer In Charge Records.
17.30K 16TH

Walter Lutz
Holden, Alberta

✉ To my great-grandfather, Tavel Finkelstein, who came to Winnipeg in 1882 to escape religious persecution in Russia.

the year is 1882
it's tough to be a Russian Jew
so Tavel says "In God we trust
I'm off to Winnipeg or bust"
it wasn't London, Rome or Paris
not even early Massey Harris
no Westin Inn or Yiddish dubbing
on Saturday no country clubbing
no Oldsmobile or Cadillac
no place to grab a quick Big Mac
no bidet flush or gold sidewalks
no Nova Scotia well-smoked lox
and not one whiff of Scotch-on-rocks
just prairie dust and flooding river
no Cuisinart to chop the liver
no Perma-Press or instant cash
no Eaton Place or Knowlton Nash
no Master Charge or RSPs
just blazing sun and winter freeze
no groomed French poodles, Lhasa Apsa
no unsinkable Hadassah
no microwave, atomic fission
just a force called Tavel vision

Nina Finkelstein Bruck
Montreal

OUR WOMAN
IN GREECE

Morningside is a current-affairs program, which means
not only that we are in the part of CBC radio that is
separate from "variety" or "drama" (although of
course we do some of those things too), but that we
struggle every day to keep up with the flow of news
and to make some sense of it. I'm proud of that part of
the program, and the opportunity to plunge into it is
one of the things that keeps me coming in so early in
the morning. But not all of our public-affairs
programming comes from the world's capitals, and not
all of it comes from professional journalists. Like Chris
Brookes, who was teaching theatre, or Jerry Kambites,
the medical missionary, Myrna Kostash, the Alberta
author, went abroad for reasons other than the rush of
daily news – in Myrna's case it was simply to write
and to reflect in Greece. There, she kept a journal for
us. Here are some of the thoughts she sent home, about
public affairs and private matters, too.

January 12, 1984

The last of the oranges have been picked and the last of the orange-
pickers are trailing out of town and there's a hiatus now until the
tourists come in May. You can almost hear the people of Nafplion
heave a collective sign of relief: the orange-pickers are *not* popular.

Who are they? Mostly they're unemployed kids in their twenties
from northern England, Ireland, Germany, France, Portugal, Morocco.
But I've also met an Australian schoolteacher on a sabbatical, a Finnish
student on a break, an Israeli typesetter bored with life in Tel Aviv.

One-on-one they can be charming company. *En masse*, it's true,
they are a bit overwhelming. There are two places in town where
they congregate and you can hear them from a mile away, yelling,
shrieking, caterwauling. In the day, if they've been unsuccessful finding
work that morning, they hang out, packed to the rafters, at Kóstas'
café. At night they eat and drink at Giórgo's *taverna*, the cheapest
one in town. It also happens to be my local *taverna* and, if I can find a
free spot at a table, I go in there a couple of times a week. Giórgo
offers a set menu: roast chicken, fried potatoes, cabbage salad and
killer retsina. You can get all that for three dollars, which explains
the taverna's popularity with the orange-pickers.

What I wonder about, though, is the orange-pickers' popularity with
Giórgo. For Giórgo puts up with an amazing amount of aggravation.

I've seen pickers stumble drunkenly over his chairs, throw food on
his floor, yell obscenities at him and throw punches at each other.
Giórgo keeps a rolling pin in the cutlery drawer and he occasionally
brings it out and waves it around in a vaguely threatening manner.
But I've seen him call the police only once: when a boy got stuck
with his friends' bill and refused to pay it . . . . All of this goes on
without Giórgo speaking a word of English (or French or German)
and with the pickers speaking only execrable Greek. Yet in some curious symbiosis, everybody gets along.

This is decidedly not true for most other Nafplionites. The grievances are legion. Pickers drink too much too fast and pass out in the
street. (This is offensive to Greeks, who pace their drinking with
leisurely eating and wait to get home to pass out.) They squat in

empty buildings, live in caves or camp out in tents like gypsies. They're dirty and they smell. They are widely believed to be on all kinds of drugs and to engage in sexual orgies. They set mattresses on fire for fun and then skip out on the rent. They shoplift and steal. (Again, this is offensive to people here, who leave even their bikes out unlocked overnight.) They're aggressive and belligerent: a French kid was stopped by the police for being in possession of a very large knife, which he insisted he kept with him to open tins. They don't have any manners. Once, when my friend Yannis was enjoying a glass of ouzo and some *meze* (a small plate of appetizers) and got up to go to the bathroom, a picker, in his absence, helped himself to all the *meze*. What offended Yannis so much was that the picker had only to strike up a conversation and Yannis would have happily bought him a whole meal.

The pickers have a point of view of their own. They huddle in a subculture, just like the gypsies, because they do work no Greek would be caught dead doing. For this they are shunned. Within their subculture they cultivate their own values. They may not care much for the Greek values of cleanliness, good manners and sombre dignity, but they do look out for each other, share money and the roof over their heads and invite strangers to their table.

They're gone now, off to pick vegetables in Crete. I went into Giórgo's the other night. There was only me and a couple of old men. Giórgo bustled around me like a maitre d', but we both knew it used to be a lot more fun.

January 15, 1984

I arrived in Greece last November with a self-assigned project to meet some Greek writers of my generation – writers in their thirties. After several false starts, when it seemed that Greeks neither answer letters nor return phone calls, things finally clicked when I met Katerina Angeláki-Rooke. Like anywhere else it's all in who you know, and Katerina is a kind of doyenne of Athenian literary life. She put me in touch with a half-dozen congenial souls and I now have a fair idea of what life is like for a young Greek writer.

Basically, that life is all too familiar. None of the writers I met makes a living from her or his writing. In spite of the fact that Athens is full of bookstores and the country has two hundred fifty publishers, the reading public is small—it can take years to sell out an edition of fifteen hundred copies of a poetry collection. Even where publishing contracts exist – and contracts are by no means standard practice – advances are unheard of; in fact, the vast majority of first-time writers pays their publishers to bring out their work and themselves pass around copies to friends and influential critics, hoping to get a notice. The govenment is making noises about setting up a system of grants, but demands on the public purse are enormous and there is a tendency to believe writers should "suffer" for their art. They can get free-lance work from magazines and radio and television, but the writers I spoke with were curiously reluctant to take up this kind of work. (I've since learned that journalism in Greece is held in very low regard: it is considered barely professional.) So Katerina Rooke supplements her income by selling the pistachio nuts from her family's farm and Jenny Mastoráki translates German novels for the princely sum of four hundred dollars and Rea Gallanáki is writing a film script for a friend, for which she may or may not get paid, and Násos Vayenás teaches literature in a university in Crete where, as an associate professor, he earns six hundred dollars a month. Others, I have been told, live in misery.

Some of their problems are peculiarly Greek. The translation business, for example. Two-thirds of the titles for sale in bookstores are translations, and everybody who's taken a couple of courses at a language institute feels free to hang out a shingle as a translator. This results in a lot of mediocre translations and, according to one critic, the problem of a whole generation of Greek readers wondering what all the fuss is about a Gabriel García Marquez or a Kurt Vonnegut. Greek literary theory is non-existent and the state of book reviewing a scandal. There are seventeen newspapers published in Athens and not one of them has a book columnist. As a result, writers depend on their literary friends for criticism, and you can imagine how honest that kind of criticism is. Obviously, this is fertile ground for a writers' union, and Greece has three of them. One is controlled by a clique of aging academics, the second by the Communist Party, which seems to limit itself to periodic denunciations of American imperialism. This doesn't pay the rent, so a breakaway group has set up shop – small, independent and operating on a shoestring.

And yet, in spite of their troubles, the writers I spoke with positively radiated a sense of mission and purpose. None of them would dream of leaving Greece to "make it" somewhere else. They want to live in their own language. This is both the curse and the blessing of Greek: only the Greeks speak it; it's nobody else's language. As an English-language writer in the shadow of American and British literature, I think I almost envy them.

February 6, 1984

A couple of weeks ago I went to visit friends in the village of Áno Plátanos near the Gulf of Corinth. We were invited to dinner one evening by the village mayor and his wife, and as we were driving back with them from the *taverna*, about one o'clock in the morning, the car's headlights picked out a group of young men feverishly pasting up posters on the wall. An unremarkable-enough scene. Except that the posters, advertising the visit of a member of the New Democracy party (the right-wing party) were being pasted up by youths from PASOK (the socialist party). The mayor, himself a PASOK man, slowed down to have a closer look, but when it became obvious that the young men realized they had been recognized, the mayor's wife grew nervous and urged her husband to pretend he had seen nothing. And so we carried on. I learned later that the posterers had been offered ten dollars each to the job and there would only be trouble if the mayor made a fuss. I mention this incident because it reminded me powerfully of the movie Z, which showed how, in the 60s, right-wing politicians in Greece purchased the services of thugs to attack left-wing politicians.

In the days since the little incident, I've begun to notice a vague creepiness in the political atmosphere. The mayor of Plátanos is being blocked, he says, by right-wing elements in the town, from getting a public library set up. They don't want PASOK to get the credit, and they want to be able to "prove," in the next election, that PASOK didn't do anything for the town. In another town on the Corinth Gulf, friends who teach English have been summoned publicly to a meeting to explain why they've raised their fees. They think the real reason for the summons is that the village mayor, a right-winger, objects to their using, as a classroom, a hall also used by the local Communist youth group. Another friend, who lives in Athens, tells me she has recently become aware of a whispering campaign in her neighbourhood. Little groups of men will suddenly break into very loud and voluble conversation in the cafés, the shops, at the kiosks, denouncing PASOK and prime minister Papandreou in vulgar language. Newspapers tell of roaming gangs of right-wing youths armed with clubs and chains shouting obscenities at passersby. Of a Molotov cocktail thrown through the windows of a PASOK office. Of violent clashes between members of New Democracy Youth and Communist Youth.

But most brazen and bizarre of all is that the jailed leaders of the military *junta* that ruled so violently from 1967 to 1974 still have a lot of supporters, so much so that these supporters have recently launched a political party. Last January, about two thousand people showed up at a luxury hotel in downtown Athens and listened raptly to a tape-recorded message from their leader in his prison cell. He defended the "necessity" of the military coup d'état and attacked the current political parties as "enemies of the country." Some people love this stuff: his message was immediately available on cassettes for sale in Omónia Square, and parades under the banner of the new party feature men in black-leather jackets yelling *"Seig heil!"*

What on earth is going on? Even in Nafplion I've been noticing a proliferation of right-wing slogans, and a friend who works in Árgos, fifteen kilometres away, tells me that it's quite common to run into men there who were once torturers in the secret police of the *junta* and who are now successful and respected businessmen.

I've tried to discuss this with some Greek friends but they just laugh and say that this is the way Greeks do politics. And a *junta*, I suppose, is just another way of "doing" politics?

On the other hand, it says right here in my newspaper that a court in Athens has sentenced a nineteen-year-old student to sixteen months for calling his teacher a "meatball." Now *that's* serious.

February 11, 1984

I was talking the other day to a young man from Portugal. He had just spent two weeks in Turkey and had had a wonderful time. The Turks, he explained, are like what the Greeks were twenty years ago.

This is not the first time I've heard this comparison. Even Greeks, like Dimitri the waiter, compare themselves unfavourably with the people of the Middle East. Dimitri argues that Greeks have become Europeans – "busy, greedy, worried" – and that he will have to go to Libya or Arabia or some such place to find a way of life that's vanishing, even from the Greek villages. I can't help note the irony that westerners still come to Greece, however, hoping to rub up against precisely the lifestyle the Greeks themselves are in a rush to leave behind.

Greece's entry into the Common Market in 1975 seems to have been a turning point. Disposable income shot up and the marketplace became flooded with German stereo equipment, Italian blue jeans, Japanese cars and French cheese. European styles have become *de rigueur*. In Nafplion you can hear trashy French disco music at the Oh-La-La discotheque, drink cappuccino at the Rendezvous café, buy German skin magazines at the kiosk. In this, *the* orange-growing region of Greece, it is impossible to get fresh orange juice, but a tin of Fanta is no problem. The Montreal Pizza House offers a recognizable version of that food; I've been told that "Canadian-style" pizza (introduced by Greek-Canadian restauranteurs who've come back) is the best there is. Although there has been some "Hellenization" of television programming, right now on state television they're running *The Thorn Birds*.

On a more serious note, parents are up in arms about drugs in the high schools (Valium is the current rage), adolescent sex, rebellious daughters who want to go to Athens to find a job rather than settle down into an arranged marriage. Again there's an irony: Greek-Americans and Greek-Australians have been known to send their teen-age children to places like Nafplion, thinking to save them from New World decadence and corruption.

Tourism, of course, has played a large role in these transformations. This year, six million tourists (almost half the population of Greece) are expected, most of them in a deluge in July and August. It is to service them that the Greeks have provided the European-style café-bar (where women are welcome), the night club, the fast-food joint. Yet, while seated at a chic sidewalk café, enjoying their gin and tonic, served by an English-speaking waiter, tourists reminisce about the "good old days" when a café was a *kafenion*, a coffee was a small cup of sludge, an evening's entertainment was a long night in a *taverna*, drinking retsina from a barrel and dancing a *hasápiko* to the sounds of an unamplified *bazouki*. And a Greek was someone dressed in rough woollen clothes, with fierce moustaches, twirling worry beads. Greece still is these things, of course, but now this is a parallel culture to the European one.

How long they can hang on to it is anybody's guess. At a press conference recently to announce the release of his latest album, Mikis Theodorakis (who wrote the music for *Zorba the Greek* and has a lot to answer for himself) complained about the pernicious influence of western pop music on Greek popular music.

A foreigner is on shaky ground here. Who are we, with our central heating and two-car garages back home, our medicare and UIC , our bumper crops and savings bonds in the bank, to insist that the Greeks remain picturesquely impoverished so that, for a couple of weeks a year, we can let our hair down?

"That's the trouble with Greeks," says Yannis, the man who sells birds. "We're so open, so giving of ourselves to foreigners, but foreigners are empty. For centuries Greece has been overrun by empty people trying to fill themselves up with Greekness."

It would be interesting to come back here in ten years, to see just how much Greekness is left even in the Greeks.

February 17, 1984

I first visited Greece in 1969 and for the next ten years I raved about its beauty, the kindness of its people, the glory of its history. Looking back on that visit – I was a hitch-hiker, living on two dollars a day – I can no longer sort out my own romantic daze from what the place was really like. I don't suppose I ever shall. In the past two and a half years I've spent a total of a year here, and that rapture of the North American who sees her first olive grove, hears her first *bazouki*, tastes her first ouzo and receives her first Greek hospitality is gone forever. I know too much about the country now. I'm going through the second phase, common to all outsiders; exasperation. (I'm told there is also a third phase – acceptance – in which the foreigner understands that Greeks are ordinary human beings.)

Let me tell you what exasperates me. Their phenomenal leisureliness: when going for a stroll along the waterfront, you can always tell the westerners; they're twenty paces ahead of the Greeks. *Nobody* walks as slowly as a Greek on a stroll. A Greek can make a small cup of Turkish coffee last an hour. Needless to say there's no such thing as an express lane at the grocery store or the bank; Greeks think of queues as places to visit each other.... The Whipped-Nescafé Syndrome: Greeks believe that if you add just a bit of hot water to the coffee powder and then beat the paste for fifteen minutes before adding the rest of the water you can somehow produce a Nescafé worth drinking. This can be quite a sight: a whole café full of the young and old, the blue-jeaned and the suited, fixedly whacking away at their coffee cups. For some reason, I find this maddening.... Their idea of a concert: first you keep the concert-hall doors locked so a formidable crowd builds up in a crush, then you open only *one* of the four doors and position a guard smack in the middle of it so that the only way to enter is by being spewed forth by the crowd behind. During the concert you allow photographers with flashbulbs to parade around non-stop, taking pictures mainly of the celebrities in the audience; and, at the end, you send up a man in a rumpled suit to throw a bouquet of flowers vaguely in the direction of the artiste, who stoops to pick them up from the floor.... The Spoiled-Male-Brat Syndrome: at least two young men of my acquaintance, well-educated but with little apparent ambition, live very comfortable lives – each has a small flat, a Fiat or VW, a sound system, a holiday in France or Italy – with no visible means of support. They are, in fact, supported by their parents, who wouldn't dream of forcing their darlings to work at some boring job. All that's required of them is to marry a girl with a very good dowry (that is, real estate) and to live thereafter on the rent. First mummy and then the wife will do the cooking, cleaning, sewing.... This is related to the What, Me Work for Somebody Else? phenomenon, in which the Greek disdains to be employed. The result, in a town the size of Nafplion, is a proliferation of small businesses all offering identical goods and services.

In case you think I'm being hard on the Greeks, listen to what they have to say about themselves. "What kind of a nation is this," asked the poet, "where one-half the population is selling lottery tickets and the other half is buying them?" Kostas the barman says that to a Greek it is not important what one *is* but what one *declares* oneself to be. This leads to a great deal of pompous public self-assertion, especially verbally. As an Athenian friend put it, a tendency to "blubber." Greeks are very gregarious, need each other's company, love words and need an audience. A Greek-American journalist complained to me that Greeks think they are the only people to have suffered, and that they have is, of course, always somebody else's fault – the Turks, the British, the Americans. Greeks love to take credit for Classical civilization, but where the Ancients were logical, rational and self-aware, I'd say the modern Greeks are illogical, passionate and self-absorbed.

But I keep coming back here, as do millions of others. The Greeks *do* some things very well. I have discovered, for instance, that one can spend an absolutely satisfying morning simply sitting in the square with a cup of coffee, watching the world go by. I learned that from the Greeks....

Yasou,
Myrna

266

OCCASIONS IN THE LIFE OF A HOST

There was no pattern to the way I wrote the sort of occasional essays for *Morningside* of which this collection is a sample. I wrote for a living long before I started on the radio, of course, and early in my days at *This Country in the Morning* simply kept on with the habit when something in the news or in my own life moved me. Sometimes, I know, my compulsion caused a problem for the producers, for I would arrive in the morning and, after reading the mail and the newspapers, write something that would mean they'd have to rearrange the plans they'd made the previous afternoon. But, by and large, they went along, realizing that my letters to the listeners – for that's really what these pieces are – were as important a part of the program as listeners' letters to me. Here are seven of my letters, out of the order in which they were written but beginning and ending with some personal notes on my own family. Some of the events that inspired me were public, as you'll see, and the news, I trust, will be familiar. At least one had further – and awful – developments. The child I wrote about in January, 1983, turned out to be Sharin' Morningstar Keenan, whose murdered body was found in a refrigerator nine days later. The selection here begins with gentler thoughts.

Boxing Day, December, 1982

I had one of the more pleasant Christmases of my life yesterday, thank
you very much, with rich food, happy memories and the company of
my best friends in the world, my children – or, better, my offspring,
since they are children no longer – and the woman who raised them
with me, who is also, I thank heaven and her, still also a good friend.
We gather, as we always have, on Christmas Eve, and we recreate
rituals and tell tales from times that stretch back to the kids' infan-
cies. We huddle from the world until, as the formal part of the holiday comes to an end on Christmas night, we begin to peel off again
back to our separate lives; only two of the kids are still at home.

Each year, though, things go differently. One of the kids, an accomplished guitarist, had a gig on Christmas Eve and didn't get home till
late on Saturday, and his older sister and I, who now have a private
ritual of midnight Mass, didn't see him until Christmas morning. His
other sister has a man in her life, and after they had shared our opening ceremonies yesterday morning they were off for brunch at *his*
parent's house. There were only a few moments over the weekend
when the world consisted, as it had once always consisted, of the
seven of us alone.

All this is as it should be. Families grow, change, spill over, find
new definitions of each other. John erects the tree now; Mickey
chooses which new record to put first on the turntable. I still carve,
but Peter pours the wine. Alison placed the call to Poland. Maria
buys trinkets for her mother's stocking, and mine. These are new
joys – as it is a new pleasure to know you will no longer win the annual family chess championship (that, in truth, has been true for about
fourteen years, but dreams die hard) or that a sister's present is now
liable to give as much giddy surprise as a parent's.

But still.

We sleep in now, and approach the cornucopia under the tree with
cool maturity. The kids – the young adults – really do enjoy giving as
much as getting, and I, sitting pridefully in my armchair, cannot help
longing for the shining innocence of their swaddling days. Waking
early on Christmas morning and padding down to start the coffee,

careful all the while not to disturb the slumbering guitarist until the appointed hour, I longed for the unexpected opening of my bedroom door, the warm, sweet smell of sleepy skin – and, yes, even the dampened bottom of flannel pyjamas – as someone tumbled into my bed for news of a still-believed-in Santa Claus.

Funny, isn't it, what you miss? John Cheever has written of being homesick for places he had never been; I am homesick for where I was. At Christmas more than other times, perhaps, but still in a way all the time, I miss in my life the presence of someone very young.

There is much I don't miss too. I don't miss 2:00 AM wake-up cries, temper tantrums or having to place all breakable objects more than three feet off the floor. I don't miss doing up snowsuits, changing diapers or, maybe most of all, waiting to make evening plans until we find out if the sitter's free. But I do miss toothless smiles, first words and the incomparable feeling of having someone fall asleep in your lap with her head against your shoulder.

Here's one final funny thing: I would be so much better at it now than I was then. I don't mean I did a bad job – I have five living, handsome, funny proofs to the contrary. But I understand things now that I did not understand when my kids were small, and I wish they were young enough for me to show that to them.

Apology, March, 1983

I have to make a little apology, and, the trouble is, to everyone except the apologizee, it will sound silly and inconsequential. The apologizee is my first-born son, who is also called Peter, and because of that and the unusual last name we also share (proudly, I might add) there is little question in the minds of people who know him and who also listen to the CBC to whom he is related. I can forget this, and forget also that this must be a pain in the you-know to him. He makes light of it. We have some shared jokes, some about me getting dates on the phone with nubile young females and some about him getting offers to host television shows. It amuses Peter to call me here and leave a message for me to call Peter Gzowski.

He is an engineer, as my grandfather was and my grandfather's grandfather too, except where they built bridges and railways and dredged out harbours, he works at a computer and measures, through a technology that remains beyond me, infinitesimally small amounts of poison in the air. It's important work, and my hunch is that he is very good at it. He delights in solving puzzles. He is a pleasant and handsome young man, quite funny, a good third baseman, a good friend. He called yesterday, leaving his usual teasing message, and when I didn't get a chance to get back to him he called again. He had heard about – not heard, but heard about – a remark I made here on Friday, when we were talking about computers. I said he'd been taught mathematics differently from me, and was now able to earn his living in a highly mathematical field without being able to do long division. Well, he *can* do long division, he learned it in public school. That's all he wanted to tell me. Because he and I tease each other so much I didn't realize for a moment that he was serious. But he was. I'd embarrassed him. I didn't mean to. I wish I hadn't, and I apologize.

Awakening, January, 1983

At first, when the police came down the street where I live in Toronto in the middle of last night, I thought one of them had thoughtlessly parked his motorcycle with the radio on. They do that sometimes in the city, and you hear the crackling all night, unpublished news: an accident here, a streetlight out there, someone – probably a loony – suspecting prowlers. Although I have been back here five months now, I still don't sleep as well in the city, where it never grows perfectly dark, as I used to sleep in the country.

Gradually, last night, the sound became louder and clearer. The red digits on my bed-side clock said 2:05. The words began to form a message. A little girl was missing.

The man delivering the message was in a yellow van. High on its prow was a public-address speaker. He was speaking softly but firmly, editing out the emotion, repeating the facts: the girl's name, her age – nine – a description of her long dark-brown hair, and of the clothes she was wearing; brown, quilted knee-length coat, navy-blue and green kilt, white blouse. The police officer had an English accent.

The yellow van rolled slowly past the house where I live. Its headlights were reflected in the dirty freezing rain that had soaked our street. The roof light was on inside the van, and the driver, alone, had his clipboard on his knee. Over and over he read his message: name, age, description. If you have seen her please call the police emergency number. The red digits marked 2:09. The van moved down the street. Lights in the houses flicked on, flicked off.

There was nothing about the missing nine-year-old girl in the early editions of the newspapers I look at when I come to work, although the first local newscasts on the radio had more notes. Her father had gone to pick her up at a park yesterday afternoon and could not find her.

I wonder if her parents heard the van last night themselves, and were made uncomfortable, as we are all wont to do when we inconvenience others. Or if, in their anguish, they even thought of that.

As I came to work this morning, I was still thinking about the girl, and of her parents, and of the cops who steadfastly and unemotionally set about their task in the middle of the freezing rain. I don't, yet, know the names of any of my neighbours in the city, nor they, I imagine, mine. I would guess they talked this morning over coffee about their brief awakening in the misty, imperfect dark and, like me, were curiously moved by it.

Rehearsing, February, 1985

The setting is the dress rehearsal at the O'Keefe Centre in Toronto for the ballet *Blue Snake*, created for our own National company by the brilliant young Montreal-born choreographer Robert Desrosiers, and it is a major event for the National – the world première of an important work by a very exciting artist. There was an air of anticipation around the O'Keefe last night. A National Film Board crew was there, preserving the *Blue Snake*'s evolution for posterity, and some cameras for *The Journal* to make it the boffo arts story of the week. About halfway through the evening I found myself caught up in the excitement, too. A dress rehearsal is an unfair place to watch a ballet, of course, with a couple of hundred people scattered about the seats in the great O'Keefe barn, wearing sweaters and jeans and T-shirts and leather pants instead of the bibs and tuckers they'll all put on for the official debut tonight, and while the musicians and the dancers put out a surprising degree of energy, it is not the real thing; at one point in dancing a sensual and intense Spanish piece called *Canciones*, for example, the incomparable Veronica Tennant reached down under Kevin Pugh's arm and twisted off her pink slipper, which had apparently been chafing her ankle, and flung it into the wings. So the magic didn't always sustain. That said, however, and given my own limited experience at the ballet, the evening was a special one. *Blue Snake*, unless I am wrong, will be a sensation the like of which we seldom see. It is a combination of dance, sound, costume, set design, optics, black-light, special effects, imagination and energy to set you tingling. It includes the most exciting single stage revelation I have ever seen in Canada, and if I had my way the National Ballet would be compelled by law to take it on the road, to show it to everyone who thinks Canadians are dull and, especially, to everyone who thinks we should reduce what we spend on the arts.

The story that caught my eye was almost incidental to that, though not quite. Its heroine is a twenty-three-year-old ballerina called Gretchen Newburger. Gretchen Newburger comes from New Orleans, and has danced in various places around the world, but like a lot of other gifted young people she has found a niche at the National, and in *Blue Snake* tonight she is scheduled to be what the company calls a second soloist. It is obviously a landmark in her life – although her role is not an extensive one, she will be the first person ever to dance it, and she can stick tonight in her memory book forever.

Yesterday afternoon, though, during a sort of rehearsal for the dress rehearsal, she fell trying a difficult move. She landed on her wrist. A bone snapped. Someone from the company, close to tears herself, drove her to the hospital. She was in severe pain.

Frantically, throughout the dress rehearsals of the two other ballets that will hit the boards tonight, *Les Sylphides* and *Canciones*, a substitute worked out backstage. Gretchen came back from the hospital and took a seat among the scattered audience.

At ten o'clock, running behind schedule partly because of the delay caused by coaching and dressing the understudy, the curtain rose on the *Blue Snake*'s breathtaking set. The dance unfolded – the first time anyone had seen it in all its costumed splendor.

Toward the climax, Gretchen Newburger's understudy entered from the wings, dressed in brilliant red and yellow. She whirled with the music. Cameras clicked. Then, at a pause, she stopped, looked down, put her knuckle to her lips in perplexity and shrugged. She was lost. The music rolled on.

From the audience, unheralded, Gretchen Newburger clambered to the stage. She wore jeans, a pale-blue sweater and high-heeled boots. She held her injured wrist in elastic bandage, high above her head. She nodded to the understudy, then stepped into the role and, jeans and boots and all, completed the dance.

I wanted to give her a standing ovation.

When the ballet ended, the feeling of excitement carried on. Ballet people know when they have a hit; they can feel it. So could I. On my way home, I stopped backstage. Gretchen Newburger was with the rest of the cast. They were rehearsing the curtain calls they will get tonight.

Flying, January, 1985

One of my favourite *Maclean's* covers of all time, from the days of a bigger format and paintings instead of photographs, showed a prairie scene at the fall of a summer dusk. In the background, of course, was a glorious sunset, reaching from side to side of that big old magazine cover and, on the painted prairie, from perhaps Elbow to Eyebrow, Saskatchewan. In the foreground was the screen of a drive-in movie, with the cars lined up like Baptists in their pews. And on the screen was a sunset, smaller and less dramatic than the natural show that framed it but, obviously, the focus of attention from the cars. That's all. I can't remember who painted that cover – Franklin Arbuckle would be a guess – but it haunts me still, twenty-five years or so later, an image of how we look at what's around us, or don't.

The movie on the plane that flew me to Vancouver last night was *Romancing the Stone*, an adventure yarn starring Michael Douglas and Kathleen Turner. I didn't watch it, as it happens, not so much because it offends me to pay three-fifty for headphones and then have the airline show me commercials where they used to have cartoons, although it does (I think Canadians are the only people who pay to buy books of matches with advertising on them, aren't they?), but because I'd already seen it. It started about Portage la Prairie, I'd say, and by the time we were over perhaps Camrose, Alberta, Michael and Kathleen – silently, in my headphoneless case, as I peeked up from my book – were rocketing through the northern Andes, pursued by moustachioed villains, their guns smoking.

That's when the guy across the aisle from me pulled up the blind on his window. I don't know what he'd been doing till then. He had headphones, so maybe he'd been following the adventures on the screen. Or maybe not; maybe he'd been listening to Bill Cosby telling old jokes on Channel 8. Or maybe he'd just rented the headphones for the commercials. But when our aircraft started vaulting over the Rockies, he took the headphones off and peered through his window, looking at the snow-capped grandeur below, smiling to himself and not worrying about the spill of grey light that broke the cinematic gloom of our cabin.

Good for him, I say. I wonder, if a generation ago he'd been in one of the cars that modelled for that old *Maclean's* cover, he'd have climbed out when the sunset was on the screen and gone for a walk in the prairie air.

Shipwreck, May, 1984

One of the people I was with when I heard about the *Marques*, the tall ship that appears to have gone down off Bermuda yesterday, was wearing a T-shirt I had bought this winter. Commissioned, in fact. Across the front are the words: I SURVIVED THE VRECK, FEBRUARY 15, 1984.

There are eight such T-shirts in the world; one is mine, a second belongs to the person who was wearing it yesterday; my eldest son and the lady in his life each have one, and the other four belong to the skipper and crew of the *Vagrant*, a sleek, graceful racing schooner that was built in 1914 and almost came to the end of her days on the date the T-shirts commemorate, with the eight of us on board.

The word "Vreck" is an inside joke, what we all hoped was a mildly amusing tribute to our skipper, who is Dutch-born and puts his European accent on the *w* in "wreck." The vreck, or wreck, we survived, happened about fifteen miles off the Caribbean island of Barbuda, where we had spent a lazy sunny morning of beachcombing, and from which we were running before the wind toward Antigua when the mast came down.

Although we were able to make jokes about it later, the wreck did not seem funny at the time. We were, all of us, as frightened as we had ever been in our lives. The sun was shining when the masts came down, but the sea was rolling menacingly high. That's what brought the masts down, suddenly, and silently, falling like trees in a forest. The wrong combination of wind and sea, the power of the great sleek hull smashing into the rolling waves – sixty tons of sailing vessel hitting thousands of tons of water – had snapped a backstay as thin as your wrist, and the masts fell. They were nearly a hundred feet tall each. One just missed the cook, who had been sunning herself on deck, listening to a Joe Cocker tape on what she called her "walk-person."

None of us, thank God, was hurt, although for the next hour and a half our hearts raced as we hurled the smashed masts over the side and cut away rigging and sails. I cut my thumb on a sharp sea-knife, and one of the deckhands broke three of his front teeth when a cable, cut free, struck at him like a coiled snake. The rest of the story was simple endurance, limping back to port, huddled in the cockpit against the now bursting skies, with the seas heaving and the lights of Antigua seeming a lifetime away. It took us six hours in our crippled ship. We sang on the way back and wept a bit when we got home, and had big drinks. The sea can be an exhilarating place to be – the sail back from Barbuda had lifted our spirits – but, as we had been reminded more dramatically than I care to remember in detail this morning, it can be, even in this age of coffee-grinder winches, synthetic sails, radar and rubber life-rafts, a terrifying place to be, dark, furious and primeval; you feel small and powerless when it knocks you down.

It was six days later that I commissioned the T-shirts in Antigua. We hovered in port there after our wreck, part of the yachting scene. I heard about a young man who was making T-shirts to order, to pay for the trip he'd made across the Atlantic. To get to his tiny craft, I had to ask permission and then walk across the deck of a large training ship, moored in harbour while her young crew members worked at refitting her. Then I scrambled down a rope ladder on the other side to visit my artist. I saw him – and the training ship – quite a few times before our deal was done.

That larger ship, tall and beautiful even at rest, was – as you will probably have guessed by now – the *Marques*. I think about her this morning, and of the young men I saw in passing. The news is still coming in. I hope they are all right. I have some small sense of what they have been up against.

The sergeant major, November, 1982

My father died five years ago, red-faced and shaky-handed and forlorn. He was sixty-five when his heart gave out, exactly the age at which he could have retired, if he'd anything to retire from.

He just keeled over, the neighbours said. Someone drove him to Newmarket hospital, and before anyone from the family could get to him he had another attack, and he was dead. They gave me his ring and his glasses, and some pills he'd had in his pocket. We sent his suit to the Sally Ann, organized a small service for him and cremated his body. The newspapers ran something about him, calling him by his rank, sergeant major. Barney Danson, who was the minister of defence then, sent me a warm letter.

I didn't cry. Not then, not now. He wasn't much of a father, if you want to know the truth. He and my mother were divorced not long after I was born. He went up north, mining, and across the prairies, riding the rails, looking for work. Even when he went away to war, I didn't hear from him, and when he came back, although we visited occasionally, we never became close. We didn't have much to talk about. My mother married again, not long after the divorce, but when I got old enough to choose I took his name back and go by it now. He was proud of me, I've heard, although never from him, and I'd probably have said something cutting if he'd told me himself.

He was a helluva soldier. I've heard that, too, although again not from him. Once, when I stayed for a weekend with him and the English bride he'd brought back from the war – that didn't last long either – he had too much to drink, and he grabbed a broomstick and began giving me parade-ground orders. He was rather a comic figure, standing in his undershirt, bellowing out his commands while I shouldered my spindly, imaginary rifle, but I didn't laugh very much.

I thought of him a moment ago, when I heard the parade-square commands shouting in Ottawa.

He'd been one of the first to enlist. *His* father, my grandfather,, had been a colonel of the engineers, but in those days – maybe still now – you couldn't hold a commission in the engineers without a university degree, so my father the gold-miner and occasional hobo was not in contention. But he joined the family regiment anyway, the day after Canada joined the war, and he was quickly off to England. He was an instant NCO. Later, he fought and laid Bailey bridges in Sicily and up the boot of Italy and in Normandy and right across Europe. He married his English girl on a leave to London. Then he went back to fight some more.

Sometimes, later, he'd talk of the good times he'd had, the lasses he'd tumbled in the haystacks of Italy or the wine he'd liberated from the vineyards of France. He didn't talk about the mud or the bullets. He gave me the impression, somehow, that he'd been happiest at war. Afterward, in peacetime, things never quite came together for him. He wandered some construction sites, bellowing his orders and remembering fragments of Italian, but he never stayed long. For a while, he and some friends ran a business called Red Patch Delivery and Shopping Service – the red patch was the symbol of the First Canadian division, or First Div, as they'd say – but the business grew faster than they could handle, and went broke. He didn't seem to care.

When he was blue, he'd go to the Legion, or to a club where other

Sappers – enlisted engineers – told stories. I never went there with him. It was his world, and I didn't know what he saw there.

I don't want to make him sound like more of a hero than he was, on this Remembrance Day. He was a soldier. If he were still alive he might be one of those men in blazers and berets – fewer of them every year – who stand at attention at the cenotaphs today, or who might have sold you a poppy this week. Tonight, he might have gone to the Legion again, and told more stories about when he was young.

I never had to go to war. I'm too old now to answer a call, and my ideas are probably too settled – or perhaps confused – to want to volunteer. Anyway, I won't have to answer the questions he had to answer, and maybe – I pray – my sons, his grandsons, won't either.

I think in his own erect, bellowing way, he had a lot to do with that, he and scores of thousands of others. If he were still around, this would be a good day to have a drink with him, maybe listen to some of his stories and say, among other things, sergeant major, thanks for what you did.

P.G.

THE OTHER SOLITUDE

For different reasons and from very different parts of the country, both Mary McKim, who is married and a mother and who had been living in St. John's, and Mark O'Neill, who is single and had been living in Vancouver, went to Quebec in the fall of 1983, Mary to Quebec City, Mark to Montreal. Each approached us about keeping a public diary as they struggled with their new world. Instead, we suggested they write to each other, as Grace Lane and Ann Pappert had.

October 12, 1983

Dear Mark:

Autumn in Quebec. I smile when I see the ads in the Montreal and Toronto newspapers extolling the delights of an off-season weekend vacation in historic old Quebec City. I've never lived in a tourist attraction before. We live in the house that used to be Montcalm's residence – that makes our house an historic site, and we actually have tour buses come down the street and stop outside the house.

It was partly because we live in la maison Montcalm, and partly because history is so tangible here, that I decided to read up on Quebec history. So I went to the local library and of course all the books are in French except for a few English books in the foreign-languages section. Come to think of it, I don't suppose there are that many French books in the library back in St. John's. I never even thought to look. Anyway, I decided I'd have to *buy* some books on Quebec history, so I searched through several bookstores, and the only English-language book I could find was a Marxist history of Quebec written in the sixties entitled *White Niggers of America*. And then I found the Literary and Historical Society of Quebec. It operates a private lending library, and the books are in English. I suppose it's a retreat from my do-or-die resolve to learn French, but I'm rationalizing by reading books on Wolfe and Montcalm and French colonial history.

Actually I'm beginning to get optimistic about my French. I've done a few free-lance items for various media, and while the interviews were in English, the setting up and arranging had to be done in French. It wasn't too bad. At least people understood what I wanted. However, I've discovered that speaking French requires my total concentration. Driving a car and speaking French is harder than rubbing my tummy and scratching my head at the same time. And lack of concentration can lead to some funny mistakes. Last weekend, Aaron invited a French-speaking school chum to stay overnight. Stumbling around for my coffee in the morning, I figured the two boys should have a good breakfast. But instead of asking them if they wanted eggs –"des oeufs"– I asked if they wanted "des woofs." They both thought that was really funny. There was the time I walked into a bar and instead of asking for a "Cinquante"– a Fifty – I realized I'd coolly ordered a "Soixante"– a sixty. Oh, well, I guess what you need more than anything else to learn to speak French is a sense of humour.

Salut
Mary

October 18, 1983
Dear Mary:

When I was five or six, I believed there were only so many million words in my head and, once they had all been used up, I wouldn't be able to talk any more. I feel much the same after these first few days in Montreal.

From a perfectly good vocabulary of hot-and-cold running nouns, verbs and subordinate clauses, I've been reduced to *oui, non, s'il vous plaît* and *merci*. Language, taken for granted for the past twenty-seven years is, overnight, a frustrating, elusive, invaluable commodity.

The theory of bilingualism has always seemed easy. In fact, I voted Trudeau back in in the heady days of the early seventies because I couldn't help but support the concept of two languages in a country founded by two nations. The theory was reinforced while I was unpacking my suitcases. The CBC was carrying the House of Commons debate on Manitoba's move to entrench French. The prime minister, backed up by Mulroney and Broadbent, couldn't have better timed his endorsement of my decision to double my conversational skills, learn new music, new politics and new literature.

So, armed with the enthusiasm of the federal government, off into my new city. St. Catherine Street is the centre of Montreal's shopping world. There, between the fall sale displays, are a few clues to the reality of Bill 101. Eaton's is *Eaton*. Ogilvy's, a relentlessly English department store, also dropped the s but don't seem committed; you can still see a conspicuous blank where once there was an English possessive. Perhaps they hope it will come back.

Reading store signs is one thing. Actually opening my mouth to spit out the dusty remains of British Columbia high-school French is something else again. The exercise is fraught with the basic fear of an insulting mispronunciation, something everyone so far has either kindly ignored or kindly corrected. What really gives an adrenalin rush is coming so close to correct usage that the subject of the inquiry responds in kind. Thank God "*pardon*" is virtually the same both ways.

Am I painting a picture of a nightmare without subtitles? I hope not, as this first week has been more than anything a lot of fun. My fluently bilingual hosts are helping me decode the "Apartment For Rent" ads in *La Presse*, have introduced me to the non-stop world of Montreal nightlife and took me along to one of the best Thanksgiving dinners ever. In any language.

I think it's going to be hard at times. I'm anticipating moments of severe depression followed by moments of glorious comprehension. Not a bad diet when served with warm croissants, corner-store wine and an actual white Christmas.

I'm eager to hear how you and the family are doing in Quebec City.

Salut
Mark

October 27, 1983
Dear Mark:

I've been in Quebec City three months now and the newness still hasn't worn off. We live in old Quebec, inside the wall. There are four huge cannon just outside our front door, overlooking the city wall and the St. Lawrence River. The streets are narrow. The buildings are stone. On a foggy night it seems as though the people passing in the mist are wearing cloaks and capes and it's a time warp back to the eighteenth century.

But the sense of history here isn't all romantic. The map tells me I'm still in Canada, but everything around me says I'm an alien in a different culture. I can sympathize with your struggles with French. Without the language as the key I can't hope to unlock the door to this new world. And there's so much waiting there to experience. The evidence is everywhere: theatre bills in store windows; notices in the newspaper; a concert by Robert Charlebois, where everyone listens raptly, and cheers wildly, shouting the French equivalent of "right on"–and I don't know what he's said.

You see, I'm the unilingual dummy of the family. My husband, Bob, grew up in Montreal and learned French when he left school and went to work for the old Montreal *Star*. Our ten-year-old-son, Aaron, was in a French-immersion program back in Newfoundland and went right into the next grade in a French-speaking school here. I still feel giddy when I can speak enough French to succcessfully order a new vacuum-cleaner hose at Sears.

All this sense of history strengthens the conviction I had when I came that I have no right to expect people here to speak English. It would be unrealistic for a Francophone to go into a store in St. John's and expect to speak French. But being unable to speak French has affected me in ways I would never have imagined. It eats at my self-image. I've always worked as a news reporter or in public relations. Words and language not only brought me my paycheque; language gives me pleasure and satisfaction. And here I am ... speaking baby talk and getting even that incorrect. For a while I found myself making excuses for not going out of the house because I'd have to struggle with speaking French.

Now I see a new danger: it would be too easy to let myself get entrenched in an English ghetto. I have two new friends–and they're both Anglophone. But how can you be friends with someone if you can't talk easily about this and that and who you are and what you believe?

On the other hand, when we arrived in July I couldn't order a meal in a restaurant in French–and now I can. Someone at a party told me that learning a language is like having a baby–it takes about nine months. He's right, of course, but meanwhile it's so frustrating.

If I've learned anything in the past three months I've learned intuitively that frustrations could bring someone to the point of giving up the struggle to bridge the void between the two solitudes in this country, and how important it is not to give up.

Salut from Quebec

November 2, 1983
Dear Mary:

You say that learning a language is like having a baby – it takes nine months. Well, I'm pleased to report that the rabbit is either dead or dying. The bad news is that my English is falling apart at roughly the same rate I'm remembering how to conjugate verbs.

Most of *my* adventures over the past couple of weeks have been with natives, which is fine, since I still feel a bit like a tourist. I've been taken to some of the noisier attractions: Brac or Beat or Limelight are a great relief from the language gap; music and dancing transcend linguistics and this city is short of neither. As well as escape, I also find inspiration in full volume, stereo Quebec; whenever the frustrations of French get out of hand, I dream of the day Diane DuFreme's lyrics make as much sense as her melodies.

Speaking of dreams, I had one in French last week. I've no idea what it was about but am told it's a good sign. Which balances the appalling discovery of a previously hidden streak of Anglo-imperialism— everyone should be able to speak English when my attempts at their language seize up. Shouldn't they?

Not in my French class. It's a veritable United Nations of new Quebeckers: people from Poland, Hungary, the Philippines, Mexico, China, far-off Alberta, even Westmount. I think most of us enjoy the experience of being part of a minority; it's certainly a novelty for the WASPs in the crowd.

I'm now firmly in residence. It's not quite General Montcalm's bedroom but a cosy old building overlooking Parc LaFontaine in the mainly French east end of the city. My two roommates are both

Quebecois; we've agreed to speak English on the odd-numbered days, French on the even. It this what the royal commision on biculturalism had in mind?

Salut from Montreal
Mark

November 14, 1983
Dear Mary:

It's strange how sixty seconds of noise on a chilly November morning can alter your notions about this nation. On the eleventh hour of the eleventh day of the eleventh month, 1983, nothing much happened. Our French class continued, as did the English group next door; only banks and federal officers were closed. A few hundred stalwart souls placed wreaths at the Montreal cenotaph, dutifully reported by the Anglo media but ignored by most French newspapers. I'd been looking for a poppy-peddling veteran all week long but ended up without that red punctuation mark of history for the first time in at least twenty years. Remembrance Day is not an event in Quebec.

I've always been aware that Quebec was reluctant to join the essentially British wars of 1914 and 1939 and that twice conscription ended the resistance. But, I concluded, surely the magnitude of those wars has overpowered mere Canadian political disagreements. Countless Quebecois must have died in the same battles as English, French, Scottish or Australian soldiers. Surely their survivors and descendants would remember the same way?

Wrong. I don't know why not – maybe it has to do with on-going resentment of promises broken by long-gone dominion governments. Or maybe there is another date that is as meaningful in Quebec memories as November 11 is in English Canada. I'll have to investigate before next Remembrance Day.

It's another small byway in the maze of life in Quebec; a maze in which, I'm constantly learning, language is but one element of the code. Even after learning the letters and numbers, I'll still be a long way from a comprehensive map and the centre of the maze.

Je me souviens,
Mark

November 19, 1983
Dear Mark:

I noticed differences in Remembrance Day ceremonies here, too. Aaron, in grade six, says there were no observances at school. In St. John's his class would go to the War Memorial. There are many differences in the way things are done here, and I'm finding that, if you trace it back, the reason is usually historical. That's one of the exciting spin-offs of my struggle to learn French – I have this feeling of being directly connected to history. It makes it more interesting, but it doesn't make it any easier. And I'm not the one in the family who's having the hardest time with language problems – it's Aaron.

Bob is fluently bilingual. I can generally choose the amount and degree of French I attempt. If I don't feel up to taking the broken toaster to the repair shop and explaining the problem in French, I can put if off till the next day. But a kid in grade six has to go out and wrestle with it every day, and Aaron's finding it tough. Because Bob grew up in Montreal, Aaron could go to an English school. But he wanted to go to a French-language school. It all seemed so idyllic, as if the answer to the problems of the two solitudes could be solved entirely by universally accessible immersion programs in the grade schools. Unfortunately, it's not as simple as that.

When we arrived in July, Aaron had all sorts of confidence in his ability to speak French. But the accent and usage are different, and the speech is much faster than in an immersion class. A lot of the time he doesn't understand, and the result is frustration and low marks in school. He says some of his classmates tell him he should go to English school. Sometimes in my darkest moments I wonder if the reason behind the comment is all sympathy.

If Bob didn't speak French, I don't know what I'd do. But then if Bob didn't speak French, I wouldn't be here. I find it challenging and exciting – just what I needed to jolt me out of the mid-thirties tendency to cling to the security of familiar patterns. I just didn't expect it would be so hard for Aaron. One of the reasons we decided to come to Quebec was to find out how this unique culture was surviving in the North American melting pot. During the past twenty years I've seen much of the distinctive Newfoundland way of life disappear into assimilation. I see the language laws of Bill 101 as a strengthening of the defences against cultural assimilation, as surely as Montcalm saw to the strengthening of the battlements that protected Quebec City so long ago.

My commitment to learn French is based on my belief that there is a place in this country for a unique culture. When I get frustrated by my inability to speak French, I can fall back on my beliefs. But for an eleven-year-old, it all comes down to the fact that he's the new kid who gets low marks. I keep telling myself that in a few years we'll all be bilingual and glad of it, but my heart still aches when Aaron comes home crying at the end of the day.

If I were putting together a bilingualism survival kit I'd put in lots of hugs and hot chocolate.

Bye for now
Mary

December 7, 1983
Dear Mark:

I just spent an interesting week in hospital. That sounds rather bizarre, doesn't it? But like everything else about living here, it's more interesting in two languages, even if it's also more complicated. The reason for the hospital stay was some routine surgery, and I'm home and thriving now. The interesting part was going through all those things that happen in a hospital without the security of having it all happen in a familiar language. I took comfort in the fact that although my doctor is Francophone, she's completely bilingual, and the hospital is the one that serves the English-speaking community of Quebec City, all five percent of us. But one lesson I have learned here is: never expect to get by with just English. So I packed an English-French dictionary with my nighties and toothbrush and off I went. And sure enough: the nurse who came to get me ready for the next day's operation couldn't speak English. Not even a little. Neither did any of the other nursing staff I met that first day. It didn't take long for me to realize that the vocabulary of medical procedures is not what you generally learn in your daily efforts to speak a second language, but between the dictionary, sign language and my limited French, everything got done. But later on, at the end of the evening, I began to worry. I'd had an anesthetic twice before, and I remember waking up afterwards to an avalanche of pain and being barely able to communicate in English.

"This is going to be some kind of test," I thought. "I'm going to have to come out of that ready to translate." And at two o'clock in the morning, alone in a strange hospital room, it was a distressing prospect.

Eventually a nurse came by to see why I had my light on. The name on her tag was Francophone, but she spoke English with an ease that was so welcome I felt as if she were a long-lost sister. I told her about my linguistic worries and she assured me it wouldn't be a problem. And later on, after the operation, I realized she was right. I'm not sure which language I spoke for the first few fuzzy hours, but after a while I realized that I was getting the best kind of medical care you could ever want. I learned later that that wonderful nurse had written on my chart that I was worried about communication and had directed that special effort should be made to speak to me in English. I guess you could say she prescribed English as part of my treatment.

Looking back on the whole episode, I realize that while the language problem made my hospital stay more difficult, it didn't make any difference in the quality of health care I received. Nurses are understanding, knowledgeable, intuitive people and the care they give transcends mere language.

Under the language laws here, there is nothing that says I have the right to medical services in English. It's all part of the philosophy that if you want to live here, you'd better learn the language. And I do want to live here, so next week I'm starting a full-time language course. And speaking of language training, you might want to know what happened to Aaron. In my last letter I told you how unhappy he was at his French-language school. We had the option of putting him in an English school, and we did. It contradicts all the reasons I support the language laws here, but we're doing all kinds of things to see that he maintains and improves his French. And after just two weeks he's a happy kid again. I really think a happy kid will learn French better than a kid who's miserable.

Salut from Quebec
Mary

December 28, 1983
Dear Mary:

The week before I left Vancouver, friends were assuring me they'd see me at Christmas when, of course, I would return home. No, I insisted. December will be too soon and besides I wanted a Quebec Christmas complete with tortière, snow and French carols.

I got all those things, and something I hadn't banked on back in September: large, family-sized doses of homesickness. There were moments during the mostly festive season – in the middle of a sing-along party, toward the end of a well-lubricated office bash, the final carol of midnight mass, the revillion that followed and December 25 itself – when only incredible self-control and a chronic shortage of funds kept me off the next flight to British Columbia.

I spent Christmas dinner with some Quebec friends whose mother had decided to break with family tradition – she cooked turkey! We sat up well into Boxing Day, which really doesn't exist here, discussing the appointment of Madame Sauvé to Rideau Hall (all in favour), the future of Robert Bourassa (the majority against) and who should be the next prime minister (no clear winner).

I guess the best Christmas present of all was a job. The timing was perfect: I began work just after my French course ended and I'll get plenty of opportunity to practice in every-day Quebec conversation. The other day I asked someone to do something and he said why, or at least I thought that's what he said. I explained, until interrupted by a friend who pointed out that "why" is a Quebec version of "oui." Face suitably red, I added another several notes to my file on French-as-she-is-spoke.

Bonne année,
Mark

December 29, 1983
Dear Mark:

Guess what? I'm beginning to understand French! The first time it really happened I was out Christmas shopping in Sears and I felt absolutely giddy with excitement. I still have a long, long way to go to fluency, but this is definitely a breakthrough... and the reason is this French course I'm taking. It's sponsored by the federal government and given by the provincial government and it goes till the end of April. There are fifteen of us, and we sit in a classroom, six hours a day, five days a week – and we speak French. Its exhausting – but it works. After just two weeks, I've improved more than in the previous five months.

I don't know how you did at your French course, Mark, or what approach the course took, but the instructors at this course have let me in on what must be the best-kept secret in French-speaking Canada. The reason I've been having so much trouble understanding the language is that I've been listening for the sort of French I learned seventeen years ago at university in St. John's, and what I've been hearing is Quebecoise. Yes, I knew there was a difference between formal France-type French and Quebec French, but I didn't know what it was. Like, for the words "I am." I knew the French was "je suis," and that's what I've been listening for. Instead, in every-day conversation here in Quebec, people say "Swuis." And for "I am not," which I learned as "Je ne suis pas," what you say is "Swuis pas." I'll never forget the day the teacher explained it. You know those comic-strip panels with the speech bubble with a light bulb? That's just what I felt like. The linguistic lights went on. And when I went to Sears and asked a question in French, I was understood the first time, and got a reply in French, which I understood the first time. Oh, Mark, it really was one of the most exciting moments in my entire life.

I'm glad to hear your first Christmas in Montreal was a happy one. Ours in Quebec City was more like the same old comfortable Christmas we always had in St. John's, with a few important changes. We couldn't gather with the family at Grandma and Grandpa's on Christmas Eve, but we were invited to an authentic tortière supper with new friends. Walking through the old city on Christmas Eve was magic – really cold and still with lots of sparkling and squeaking and smoke rising straight up from the old chimney pots.

But when I think back on my first Christmas in Quebec, I think I'll remember most the candlelight service held the night before Christmas Eve. It was ecumenical, and bilingual, yet still so gentle and familiar though so far from home. It was the first time I'd ever heard the Christmas story with parts read in French. And I understood most of it – partly because of my course, and partly because I know it by heart in English anyway. My favourite part in the Christmas story is where it says "and Mary kept all these things in her heart." It always seemed to me such a comfortable, motherish thing to do. When I became a mother, I found that keeping things in your heart covered a lot of things for which there are no words. And there it was, a familiar friend by candlelight in a church in old Quebec City: "*Marie gardé toutes les choses dans son coeur.*" It's same in French as it is in English – it just sounds a little different.

Bye for now
Mary

March 14, 1984

Dear Mark:

I really feel like running away right now to someplace warm, some-place where I won't have to remember how long it's going to take me to learn to speak French well enough to get a job. When I first started my language course in December I made incredible progress. Now I find I'm grinding along in low gear. Verbs, tenses, objectives and pronouns are beginning to appear in the right place without a dress rehearsal, but to be realistic, even when the course ends in two months I'd be lucky to get a job scrubbing floors.

I didn't realize how political language is here in Quebec City. The inability to speak French isn't accepted as an accident of birth, it's interpreted by the charitable as ignorance and by the militant as an insult. And rightly so, I suppose, given the political and social history of this corner of the world, but a theoretical understanding doesn't help me much in my daily struggle. You see, I'm finding that this learning-French business is bringing out some things in my character that ab-solutely appall me. I should explain that I feel under the gun because my unemployment insurance runs out in June, and I know I have very little chance of improving my French enough by then to get a job. Now, that's not as serious as it would be if my husband didn't have a job, but for a lot of reasons I take my financial independence quite seriously – not to mention my career as a journalist – and I know I'm not going to make it by the end of June. So I'm fighting this rising tide of panic – and discovering some unacceptable things hidden in the dark recesses of my soul.

Back in St. John's I was a home-town girl. I spoke the language and knew my way around. Being relaxed and open is easy when the world's going your way. I guess I'd also gotten used to being reasonably suc-cessful at what I did.

And here I am in a foreign culture with a foreign language, and it's a lot harder than I thought it was going to be. I know some people would say, "Well, what the heck did she expect, moving to Que-bec." Maybe even, "Serves her right." Yes, but what I didn't expect is the secondary struggle inside me, quite apart from the expected effort of learning a second language.

It's hard to talk honestly about this without sounding like a whiny bigot, but I'm going to try, so please give me the benefit of the doubt. I don't like to be an illiterate mute, which is just about what I am in a French milieu. Sometimes I don't want to go to a party where I know everyone will be speaking French, and sometimes I don't want to invite some of my husband's unilingual French colleagues to our house for dinner. Not because of them – not because they're French – but because of me, because of my feelings of stupidity and vulnerability and inadequacy and frustration.

I don't like acting like a dumb blonde who smiles a lot and can't contribute anything intelligent. I think the old-fashioned term for it is "false pride." Some Anglos I know who are now beautifully bilingual tell me what I'm experiencing is not unique; it's one of the recognizable stages on the road to a second language. Ah, but something from another culture that eats away at your self-confidence can so easily become a monster called prejudice or bigotry. It's so much easier to blame everyone else rather than overcome my pride and keep on keeping on.

I'll eventually make it to the Elysian fields of true bilingualism, long after my unemployment insurance runs out. But just for now I'm going to run away and have a long, hot bubble bath. Call me a temporary coward, but these days the bathroom is the only place where I don't have to make a language decision.

Salut
Mary

THE MORNINGSIDE BOOK OF SLIGHTLY AMENDED, NEARLY ALWAYS CANADIAN, VERSE

This all started one day in November, 1982, when I couldn't remember the opening lines of Wilfred Campbell's "Autumn." "Along the line of smoky hills . . ." I started, and then couldn't remember if it wasn't crimson hills and a smoky forest. (I couldn't remember who wrote the lines either, but that was another matter.) I appealed for help. Then, later, I wondered if listeners couldn't improve on those lines and update them. Here are some of the results.

✉ After John McRae's "In Flanders Fields"

In Canada the Liberals roll
Between elections, poll on poll,
That mark their place; in Parliament
The Tories, still bravely clinging, vent
Scarce heard beyond the prairie snow.

Frank Cummins
Cremona, Alberta

✉ After Wilfred Campbell's "Autumn"

Along the track the freight cars move
In ponderous single file
And all the while the traffic's backed
Behind me for a mile.
I watch in apprehension
As the tankers come in view
And pray that none will spring a leak
Before the train's gone through.

Martha Morgan
Saskatoon

✉ After Irving Layton's "Misunderstanding"

We looked
In through
The
Window.

By the way
He held
His finger
We could see
His devotion
To our economy
Was not
Perfect.

Bob Cameron
Georgetown, Ontario

✉ After George Johnson's "War on the Periphery"

My pleasures, how discreet they are!
A little coke, a Mercedes car,
Two little doggies and no strife
Living a small self-actualized life.

My plants and doggies give me heart;
At seven o'clock we kiss and part,
At seven o'clock we meet again;
With a life like this, who needs men?

Gillian Loeb
Toronto

✉ After Wilfred Campbell's "Autumn"

Above the rocks of Sudbury
The belching chimneys rise;
The trees are dead; the rivers reek
With acid from the skies.

The greed of man has nature changed
The birds no longer sing,
The rape of virgin forests brought
The land a silent spring.

Bob Gray
Medicine Hat, Alberta

✉ After Irving Layton's "Song For Naomi"

Who is that in the wolverine parka
Peeping in the windows in the darka?
He's swift, he's silent and he's slick
This Peeping Tom from Inuvik.
Alas, he stayed too long for one last look
And they nabbed the peeper – Tom Tookalook.

Gordon Peters
Caledon East, Ontario

✉ After John Milton's "On His Blindness"

When I consider how much time is lost
Deriding Monsieur Chretien's lament,
I say: It's not a brickbat he tossed
But a subtle (unintended) compliment.
Other nations, short of sight and small of soul,
Content themselves with what's within their grasp;
They settle for the easy, ready goal:
Cheer Cleopatra – and forget the asp.
Inspired by much loftier ideals,
We smell a lemon where they find a peach.
While watching out for fate's banana peels,
We ever strive for stars beyond our reach.
We scratch that ancient existential itch:
They also serve who only whine and bitch.

Margaret Young
Sydney, Nova Scotia

✉ After Pauline Johnson's "The Song My Paddle Sings"

I've stewed the chicken and made the roux.
I've stirred it long but the stirring's through.
My ladle awaits the crucial test –
Oh tangy soup at its tangy best!
Whisk, whisk to reduce the risk
Of lumping. Use a movement brisk!
And now for the joy that good food brings
For smooth is the soup my ladle slings.

Mary Elizabeth Voegelin
LaHave, Nova Scotia

✉ After "Squid-Jiggin' Ground"

Oh, this is the place where the lawyers all gather
Wearing smiles and black gowns and white bands round their
    necks,
All eager for justice and due legal process –
And royal commissions and government cheques.

For it's "Who owns Hibernia?" "Who owns Churchill
    power?"
And "Who owns the cod on the Hamilton Bank?"
And since we already know who owned the *Ranger*,
We'll pay lawyers for four years to find why she sank.

Gordon Inglis
St. John's, Newfoundland

✉ After Dennis Lee's "If You Should Meet"

If you should meet with Jean Chretien
Comfort him with how and when
Then send him on his way again
With empty threats in case of rain.

If you should meet with Marc Lalonde
Ask him where his hair has gone
But if you find it on the rack
Tell him you might not give it back.

And if you meet a minister
Whose name you have forgotten, sir
Don't dwell upon the sinister
Just ask him out to dinner, sir.

If you should meet some mandarin
Don't hesitate to have her in
Concentrate upon her faces
Making notes and saving graces.

Karen Alton
Oakville, Ontario

✉ After John Masefield's "I Must Go Down to the Sea Again"

I have to trim the damn tree again, the too-tall tree on high
And all I ask is a ladder, and no one around to cry.
I also ask to be left alone without that constant yacking
And no remarks or smothered oaths when the ornaments are
    cracking!

I must string up the lights again and find the ones that are out,
The used ones and the fused ones and the ones put away in
    doubt.
And all I ask is no advice – like to know that the tree is wilting,
Or that the angels are upside down and the whole damn thing
    is tilting.

I must decorate the tree again – it's part of the Christmas life
And all I ask is no one's help – and least of all my wife's.
I can do without the smart wisecracks of all the kibitzing
    fellows;
What I really need is a rest and a drink to make my mood more
    mellow.

Nelson Cunningham
Port Carling, Ontario

✉ After Dennis Lee's "The Muddy Puddle"

I am sitting in the middle of a really messy kitchen,
With my dishes on the counter and my housework yet
   undone,

And *Morningside* is calling me to try poetic talents
When I really should be working and not having so much fun.

What I think of in the middle of my really messy kitchen
Is Poetic Inspiration and a contest to be won!

Elizabeth Fleet
Castlegar, British Columbia

MEMORABLE MEALS: THE SECOND COURSE

By now (unless, hungry for more culinary adventures, you have skipped directly to this page from the first collection of responses to my invitation to recall these occasions), you will recognize at least two of the names in this second serving. Ann Meekitjuk Hanson appeared earlier with her notes on spring in the north and Gisela Spier Cohen, to whom I have given the last word here, also presented an argument – arising, as it happens, from the time in her life she recalls here in such a different context.

✉ She walked into my life the way Ingrid Bergman walked into *Casablanca* – tall, cool and poised, with blue, blue eyes and a smile that would make a priest hand in his resignation. When she spoke to me that day on Kitsilano Beach the rain stopped, and so did my heart. I was heading for a fall, and I didn't care.

Somehow, I managed to speak to her; I introduced myself and invited her to coffee. She was busy that day, but I got a promise to meet the next night at a local restaurant. That wasn't my most memorable meal. No, that came a few days later, when she came to my little apartment for supper. I worked all day, cleaning, shining, washing, cooking. The apartment never looked better, and neither did she when she arrived. She was visiting from Germany, with an accent just like Ilsa's at Rick's Café Americain, and I swear I started to look and act more like Bogart as the night went on.

Oh, yes, the meal. I was poor and working, but the dinner seemed so very expensive and perfect next to her; she turned the meal into something heavenly, and my stumbling tongue into that of Cyrano de Bergerac's with her beauty and kindness. The meal was, I suppose, rather plain – chicken roasted with butter and garlic and tarragon, a rice pilaf with mushrooms, shallots and red peppers, carrots with just a touch of horseradish, wine vinegar and tarragon, broccoli with a cheese sauce, no lumps. I don't remember how it tasted – she said it was lovely, and I thought my heart would burst; certainly, it swelled up enough to prevent me tasting the food. Piaf sang in the background and I fell deeply, madly, irreparably in love even before dessert.

I had wanted something special for dessert, something to kindle her love, and finally decided to go with simple elegance: cherries jubilee. I practiced heating, pouring and lighting the brandy twice, and felt supremely confident as I suavely scooped out the ice cream with little flourishes I have never been able to repeat, and arranged the cherries with an eye for balance and form Michelangelo would envy. I smiled my most devastating smile as I retired to the kitchen to pour the heated brandy into the only spouted implement I owned – a large Pyrex measuring cup. The cup had served me well in the past, as a measuring tool, a vinegar cruet and flower vase, and I confidently filled it with warmed brandy. Looking as sophisticated as my twenty-four years would let me, I poured the brandy over the ice cream, and lit it with a taper. The brandy burst into flames with a small pop, and the bluish glow illuminated the face of my dear fraulein. Her admiration for my skill was obvious, until she shrieked, "The tablecloth!" I turned to see the entire top of my table engulfed with a flickering blue flame. I could smell hair burning; later investigation showed my eyebrows to be a little less prominent. Quickly, I patted out the flames with my bare hands, in a cheap Gordon Liddy-Peter O'Toole impersonation, and laughed as I imagined someone who set tables on fire regularly, for a joke, might laugh. "Don't worry, just an old Canadian custom," I said, as lightly as I could. I wondered if I should roll her up in the landlord's carpet, just to be safe, and if I could be liable for the carpet if she was in fact on fire and singed it. If the fire spread, I thought, mind racing out of control, I could dash into the bedroom and puncture my water bed . . . .

Mercifully, the flames soon subsided, and my darling German Schatz had the good grace and breeding not to laugh too hard. Our next supper was at a restaurant.

Mark Leier
Burnaby, British Columbia

✉ The breakfast I'm thinking of was not the kind Adelle Davis prescribes in *Let's Eat Right to Keep Fit* – no vitamins, no minerals, no protein. The menu, as I remember it, was coffee.

The meal was served at the height of a wonderful event in both Toronto's history and my own, the theatre festival in May, 1981, a time of great excitement, exchange, celebration and camaraderie. One morning, after too much such celebration, I woke up beside a new comrade whose name I could not remember. All I knew was that he was a stage manager and that he owned a Hawaiian shirt. I got up to put the kettle on and crept down the hall to my house-mate Jennifer's room. She whispered, "Who'd ja bring home?" I shook my head apologetically "I don't know. You don't remember hearing me *call* him anything when we came in last night?" She laughed; I stood helpless in her doorway.

I headed toward the kitchen to face the music and make the coffee. Conversation was surprisingly easy to make – all theatre festival talk, what-have-you-seen-that's-great, behind-the-scenes gossip and so on. Probably the same conversation we'd had at the gala the night before, but couldn't remember.

The moment of truth came when Jennifer appeared for breakfast and introductions were in order. "This is Jennifer..." I told the Nameless Comrade, hoping that he would pick up on his cue to say, "I'm..." He didn't. We all survived the ordeal; I saw him to his car, wished him well and jumped on my bicycle to go to work.

It was a ride filled with reflection, during which I composed a letter to Helen Gurley Brown.

Dear Madam:

About this Sexual Revolution – the one that sells your magazine.

I don't think you've really thought it *out* very well. It just doesn't deliver the goods!

Why, just this morning, I served breakfast to someone whose *name* I could not remember. That's ridiculous!

You're always linking sex with intimacy – well, I'll tell you, the most intimate moment of this morning's fiasco was that shared by my roommate and me, laughing together at the bizarre situation.

Just thought you'd like to know.

Sincerely,

Ann Davidson

I am quite sure that through exhaustive research, or the grapevine, I could have discovered our Nameless Comrade's name. But I have chose to *keep* him anonymous as a constant reminder of the spiritual malnutrition resulting from a diet of *Cosmopolitan* breakfasts!

Ann Davidson
Toronto

✉ After being shot down on the Menin-Ypres Road in Belgium on November 8, 1917, I spent Christmas in a holding camp in Munich commanded by a retired colonel who had a "Flieger" (son) in a prisonerof-war camp in Gravenhurst, Ontario. According to his father, the son was treated kindly and given ample food.

Promptly at noon Christmas Day, two servant girls brought the six of us a roasted goose with trimmings, various vegetables, a container of Munich lager and a bottle of white wine for each, followed by a hearty pudding with sauce. The colonel must have had a farm or much influence because at that time all Germans were pitifully short of food.

December 19, 1918, I was one of about seventy-five British prisoners of war, mostly flyers, who were repatriated from a camp in the Harz Mountains to Copenhagen to wait for transportation to England.

On Christmas Day, the good citizens of that city arranged a banquet for us in the Javenbranne Hotel and invited a female student from a university in Upsala for each private, NCO and officer. Many of us had been prisoners for four years or longer, living mostly on tinned food supplied by the Red Cross. I had only been held eleven months but like most had some ailment caused by a lack of fresh food.

A small bottle of Danish wine sat at each place. The meal included chicken, pork, seafood, cheese, famed Danish rolls, butter and vegetables, finishing up with Danish confections and a welcoming speech from the daughter of the mayor of Arrhus. What a change for men half-starved for both food and female companionship.

December 25, 1918. I was twenty-one.

H.G. Robinson
Tory Hill, Ontario

✉ In 1957 four of us, university students, were baching in a survey camp in Bow Island, Alberta.

It was a government job and we had a lot of time on our hands, so we began to try to outdo each other in preparing gourmet suppers.

My brother Gary and Danny McDonald had cooked an especially good supper, and Teddy Oshiro and I were wondering how we could top it the next evening.

After supper Teddy was reading an outdoor magazine and saw an advertisement for tinned rattlesnake (six dollars for a two-ounce can).

We looked at each other and without uttering a word began preparing the menu.

In the morning we loaded up our survey equipment and started out to the job site, near Grassy Lake, keeping our eyes and ears peeled for rattlers. Afternoon soon came and Teddy picked a dozen ears of sweet corn from a field we were working by, but no rattlers. It was late August and the rattlers were shedding their skins, and as they shed their corneas with their skin they were temporarily blind and very easily disturbed. We would generally hear one or two every day or so. It was almost quitting time when we heard the loud, pulsating buzz of a good-sized rattler. He was more than three feet long and was buzzing and striking like crazy. Teddy pinned him with a fifteen-foot rod and I despatched him with the stake hatchet.

We cut out a two-foot section from his middle and skinned and cleaned it. It looked very much like a section of fish. We rushed home and started supper. Teddy made a wonderful salad and cleaned up the corn and began steaming it. I worked on the rattler. The flesh was pink and looked exactly like chicken. I cut it into thick, salmon-like steaks, dipped it into spices and flour and began to fry it. No bad odours or anything. Gary and Danny looked into the pan and wondered what kind of fish we had.

We all sat down and ate heartily, except Teddy and I, who were a little picky with our meat course. Finally we told the boys what they had just eaten. They were more than a little upset. But needless to say, there were no seconds for the deep-fried rattlesnake.

Leland Stanford
Spring Coulee, Alberta

✉ It was the summer of 1933. I was travelling west via CPR freight trains from Toronto.

The previous day, the Mounties had cleared the train I was on some seven miles east of Sudbury – a long hot walk. That evening I found an empty boxcar on another westbound freight leaving Sudbury and was curled up asleep when it stopped in the middle of the night. There were several other men in the car, all strangers to me. When the train stopped they jumped out.

Still half-asleep and remembering the Mounties of the day before, I reasoned that the crowd would attract attention while I could escape notice by staying where I was. I went back to sleep.

When I awoke I found that my car was stopped on a siding in the bush. I was quite alone with no idea where I was. I had no watch and, worse, no food.

During the morning some trains passed by on the main track, one going the wrong way and the other moving too fast for me to catch. Eventually another freight, a slow one going in the right direction, came along. I hopped on and climbed up on top of a box car.

There was a family group, a woman and two men, on another car roof further ahead. They were eating a meal and beckoned to me to join them. I jumped from car to car and along the roofs until I reached them.

They were immigrants and spoke very little English, making me welcome with signs and happy grins. They gave me a slice of bread from their loaf, spread with butter and two or three sardines. The locomotive contributed a sprinkling of cinders and ash but that did not detract from the flavour of that sandwich, shared from my benefactors' obviously meagre stock of food. It was absolutely delicious.

J.H. Watts
Sidney, British Columbia

✉ I grew up in Montreal's Anglophone west end, and as a result my knowledge of French was rudimentary. This point was brought home to me during my medical-school training at McGill, where I found myself unable to communicate with my French-speaking patients.

Determined to remedy this situation, I decided to do my medical internship in French, and so, one day, I found myself hired for a year as an intern in a large, University-of-Montreal-affiliated teaching hospital where not a word of English was spoken.

After two months in this environment my French improved dramatically, as did my confidence that I could communicate intelligently in my new second language. One day at a medical conference, when I noticed a very attractive Quebecoise, I found enough gumption to strike up a conversation. She was learning English, and having a point in common we passed a pleasant hour or two together. Encouraged by my success, I asked her out to dinner. To my surprise and delight, she accepted.

The restaurant I had chosen was Spanish and served, I knew, an excellent seafood paella. We began the meal with sangria, moved on to a superb fish soup and opened a bottle of delightful Spanish white wine. My date, who had never had a Spanish meal, was suitably impressed. The conversation was pleasant and friendly, and I was feeling, on the whole, exceptionally pleased. At last the pièce de résistance, the paella, arrived. It looked and smelled heavenly and we both began to eat with relish. But to my dismay I noticed that the tail of my lobster was missing. Now, as everyone knows, the tail of a lobster is the best part. So I discreetly motioned the waiter over.

"This lobster is missing its tail," I said in my new, improved French. "Would you please get me another piece?"

He looked at me as if I were drunk, chuckled and ignored me.

"This lobster has no tail," I repeated more forcefully. "Would you please get me another."

This time I received inquisitive looks from both the waiter and my date.

Seeing that I was still not understood, I repeated even louder, and pointing to the lobster, said "The tail! The tail! There is no tail! Would you please get me another tail!"

The waiter stepped back, shocked. My date blushed, retreated into a corner and made as if she did not know me. Heads turned, men sniggered, women looked askance and comments about my rudeness were overheard. What had I said?

The French word for tail is *queue*. It is feminine and is pronounced "ke" like the *k* in "kettle." I, a typical Anglophone, had said *q*, as in billiard *cue*. Furthermore, I used the masculine form, saying "le cue" instead of "la ke." Normally such minor errors in gender and pronunciation go unnoticed. But not this time, for I had unwittingly said *le cul.* This is a derogatory term for one's bottom parts, a piece of which also means an easy woman.

"The ass! The ass!" I had said to the waiter. "This lobster has no ass! Please get me another piece of ass!"

Although the missing lobster part came, the meal and my evening were ruined. I felt like a fool. My date thought I was one. We finished our meal, I escorted her home, she said goodbye.

Despite this rather inauspicious beginning, we were married three years later. For our honeymoon we went to – where else? – Spain.

John Osterman
Laval, Quebec

✉ I was one of the remnants of an adventurous group of trans-African voyageurs. We had set out from London in January, 1976. Six months later, exhausted and nearly broke, we pulled into Bangui, the capital of the Central African Republic. We had gone less than halfway across the continent. There, our fearless leader up and sold the truck in which we were travelling and flew on to Nairobi, leaving us in the middle of nowhere. The richest of our members flew back to London or on to Nairobi; the rest of us decided to forge on.

We caught a river boat down the Congo River to Kinshasa, the capital of Zaire, and then another boat to Kasai, an important railhead in central-eastern Zaire. From there, we started hopping trains in the general direction of Tanzania. Breakdowns, interrupted schedules and interminable delays hampered our progress all the way. The trains were hot and crowded and uncomfortable, and we were travelling third class, which meant no class. Chickens, goats, lambs and ducks all shared our carriage in a spirit of squawking, braying egalitarianism. It was maddening and frustrating and we had no idea when we were going to reach Tanzania. We were irritable and supercilious with the natives on the train; they, in turn, put up with us in good grace and found our frantic desire to reach our destination rather amusing.

Meanwhile, my money was running dangerously low. I had about three hundred dollars to get to South Africa, so I immediately went on a starvation diet. What did this mean in Zaire? Basically, a diet of bananas, bread, cassava, peanuts and coffee. I acquired a taste for the latter two, and discovered that by quaffing great drafts of coffee and shovelling down mounds of peanuts, I could avoid starvation and live for just pennies a day.

The peanuts were no problem, but making the coffee involved an exercise in logistics. I converted an old soup can into a coffee pot, attached a wire at the top and ended up with something that resembled an Australian billycan. Then I'd build a fire, pour some water in the can, place it over the fire, boil it, throw in some coffee grains, boil it again and voila! – beneath the soot and ashes I had an approximation of a cup of coffee.

It was our third day out of Kasai, and our train was stopped at a remote terminal in the middle of the bush. It was early afternoon and I hadn't had a coffee all day because the train had been moving at a slow but steady pace. My stomach was filled with peanut mash and I had a craving for my coarse campfire coffee. I decided to take a chance.

I found a nice little spot down beside the railway grade and set to work making a fire. It was one of my usual efforts – it coughed and sputtered and smoked but refused to burst into flame. Meanwhile, a few Africans who lived near the station had gathered round me. The children were giggling, but the older natives watched with a great deal of interest. I hardly took notice of them as I cursed the humidity of the tropics and poked my pile of smouldering pulp.

After about ten minutes of fruitless effort I was ready to give up. Suddenly, there were twenty people surrounding me and for a moment I was frightened. They were pointing at my fire and talking in an unintelligible tongue. The women and children started gathering twigs and leaves and brought them back to the pile. Then a couple of the men got down on their knees, re-sorted the pile a little and started blowing. In a matter of minutes they had a crackling fire going. Someone patted me on the back and another let out a hearty laugh. Everyone was smiling.

I filled my can with water and in a few minutes it was boiling. I threw in my coffee grounds and soon I had my can of coffee. Tin cans started appearing from everywhere and I happily went around to each one, pouring in a little coffee. By this point, it no longer mattered that there would only be a little bit for myself; it was the success of the venture we were toasting. I hadn't brought my bananas and peanuts from the train, but there was no need to. The villagers were passing them around to everyone gathered round the fire.

The coffee, by the way was delicious, and the aroma of that coffee is as fresh and pungent today as it was nine years ago by that railroad track in Zaire. The smiling faces, the shared laughter, the dissolving of cultural barriers over a shared repast – shared not only in the eating and drinking but in the preparation – however meagre it may have been, it had in it something in the nature of a holy communion.

Guy Prokopetz
Winnipeg

✉ My aunt Mary and I were cared for by a family who had a winter camp near Lake Harbour. My father had died and my mother and uncle were taken to Hamilton for TB treatment in the early 1950s. Sometimes there were hunger periods when harsh winters prevented our hunters from providing us with food. At severe times there was serious starvation and people did not survive. I remember very clearly that we were going through a hunger period when I was a little girl not more than five years old. We were drinking warm water. There are many things a little girl does not fully understand and one of them is, "Why isn't there any food for us to eat?" I don't know how many days we drank warm water but I do remember a dog team came to our camp and, little as I was, I knew we would have something to eat soon. The sled was so full of things and it seemed to stand so high, the dogs looked healthy, the man smelled alive and full of energy. The dog team was one of the RCMP patrols making winter calls to camps on the southern part of Baffin Island. After the sled was unloaded we must have eaten some food but what I remember the most is having tea – how delicious it tasted.

I have had memorable meals since then with friends, relatives, with royal families, with Prime Minister Trudeau, with Hollywood people, gourmet dinners with good wine, but I can still smell the aroma of that cup of tea many years ago and be thankful that we have enough food to share.

Ann Meekitjuk Hanson
Frobisher Bay, Northwest Territories

✉ One dish evokes a mass of memories for me and at least fifty percent of university students. It is the Kraft Dinner, commonly referred to as KD.

KD was my staple food during the four years I was studying for my undergraduate degree. How one's money supply was lasting was directly proportionate to how many packages of KD there were in one's cupboard. The first term you could observe the occasional blue-and-white box amongst your egg noodles, pâté maison, kaiser buns and canned salmon. But as Christmas approached, all one could see when the cupboard was opened was row upon row of KD. You see, it was cheap and filling.

I once had KD for lunch and dinner on five consecutive days in order to treat myself to a night out at the Rebecca Cohn auditorium to see the National Ballet. The tickets for the ballet were a very steep eleven dollars, which was half my allotted grocery money for that week.

After eating KD for an extended period one can grow quite bored with it. So being the creative and inventive university students we were, my roommates and I devised a cookbook in which each recipe had as its base KD. Tuna casserole à la KD, hamburger deluxe KD style and KD tomato soup were but a few of the delicacies to be found in our cookbook.

My prolonged exposure to KD allowed me to predict with accuracy in what faculty a student belonged by the way that student prepared his or her KD. Business students on the whole preferred their

314

KD very dry and sticky, while fine-arts students preferred theirs quite runny, much like soup. I, being a student of psychology, preferred mine in the middle of these extremes, not too dry by virtue of my humanistic tendencies and not too runny by virtue of my rational scientific training.

I am presently at home taking a year off my studies and I am pleased to report I have not consumed as much as one cup of KD and I have not as yet suffered any serious withdrawal symptoms.

Occasionally, however, when I am shopping for my mom and I make my way down the last aisle of our local grocery store and see that familiar blue-and-white box, I stop and my hand reaches up. I think of my struggling school days and I push my cart a little faster. And I don't look back.

Deborah Lee Aker
Sydney Mines, Nova Scotia

✉ I was hitching from Athens to Holland, and just outside Thessaloniki in northern Greece I got a lift with a German trucker on his way home. Maybe it was his huge load of marble, or it might have been the atrocious Yugoslavian roads, but just across the border the truck developed intestinal problems. We bumped slowly through the fog to a back-water garage. It was early, but two rigs, Dutch and French, were already undergoing surgery. This was a noisy procedure, characterized by hammering, grunts and curses in three languages, soon to be four as my driver tore the guts out of his Fiat. Then another rig pulled up out of the mist, propelled solely by the willpower of its driver, a cheerfully resigned young Greek.

At about noon, they all knocked off in disgust. Indicating to me by the usual gestures that lunch was in the offing, the mechanic brought out a card table and six astonishingly elegant chairs. These he arranged meticulously in the gravelled work-yard, then the drivers repaired to their respective cabs and brought forth vast coolers of grub.

It was an international food fair. Everyone contributed bread and fruit, and each trucker offered the delicacies of his own country. The Frenchman set out pâté, Brie and Camembert, the Dutch chap pickled herring and Edam and my German friend three kinds of sausage and still more cheese. The Greek almost disappeared into his cooler and surfaced with an enormous Greek salad, glistening with olive oil and fragrant with oregano. Then he dived in again and, with the air of a shy conjuror, produced the pièce de résistance: a whole leg of lamb, roasted brown and sweet with herbs and fat chunks of garlic.

Only one thing was missing, but soon the little Yugoslav mechanic puffed, grinning, up to the table, pushing a wheelbarrow full of booze. There were dozens of bottles: beer, rough red wine, some questionable vodka and inexhaustible supplies of slivovitz, the local brandy.

We fell upon the feast with gusto and, at first, conversation was restricted to multilingual thank-yous as the food and drink were passed around. Then, when only a few shreds of meat remained on the lamb bone, we exchanged stories and jokes. This wasn't easy as we shared no common tongue. But the Dutchman and the mechanic were trilingual, so we worked it out. It went something like this: I would relate an anecdote in fractured French to the trucker from Marseilles; the Dutchman translated this into German for my Teutonic friend; then the mechanic reworked it into Greek for the young man from Thessaloniki. It was like the children's party game – Lord knows how the stories changed in the telling.

The hilarity rose with the pile of empties and soon we were laughing just at the translation attempts. Inevitably, our system broke down. The mechanic was shouting in Macedonian to the hysterical Dutchman while I regaled the mystified but giggling Greek with an obscure tale in unrecognizable French.

When the Greek slid off his chair into the cooler, the atmosphere became more emotional. We took turns singing our national anthems, then hotly renounced nationalism and sang the *Internationale*. Just before the mechanic passed out we all swore eternal friendship and, on behalf of our respective governments, signed a non-aggression pact on the table. The Dutchman was completely overcome and cried like a baby.

The next few hours remain a blank, but toward midnight, the German recovered sufficiently to coax the Fiat back to life. After a little shut-eye we rolled slowly away from our slumbering friends, with more reason than ever to curse the bumpy roads.

Hilary Knight
Victoria, British Columbia

✉ It was during World War Two. I was in my early teens, interned in the ghetto of Theresienstadt. One day a group of youngsters was chosen to go into the countryside to pick blossoms of the linden tree, used to make tea, for shipment to Germany. We marched in columns. On both sides of us were Czech guards with rifles. We were delighted to be out of the ghetto in the beautiful Bohemian countryside.

After a while we reached a road that had linden trees on both sides. We started to climb the trees to pick the blossoms. Not far off we could see farmers working in their fields. Suddenly I discovered, on a small fence, a bag with a string. I took the bag, climbed up the tree and peeked into it. Inside were two slices of dark brown bread with creamy butter in the middle. I could not help it. I bit into the bread and butter. I had not eaten butter for years. I got dizzy from the taste. I could see marks left by my teeth. One of the girls saw me. I let her have a bite, then almost finished the bread, high in the tree, not realizing what I was doing. I left a little for the farmer, put the closed bag back on the fence and went back to pick blossoms.

One hour passed. I saw an old farmer walk over to look for his lunch. He opened the bag, then he walked over to our supervisor and told her someone had taken his lunch and that he would report it to the Germans.

Fear engulfed me – I would have to confess if he reported it. It was a long way back to the ghetto.

The farmer never reported me. Until today I can taste the black bread and see my teeth marks in the butter.

Gisela Spier Cohen
Toronto

317

THE LANGUAGE JUDGE

From the outset of my second term on CBC morning radio, I had wanted to find a place on the program for a kind of Canadian language court – a place where Canadians who cared about the way they wrote or talked (as so many of our listeners so obviously did) and who wanted to preserve the subtle differences between our speech and that of Great Britain and the United States could raise questions and hear authoritative answers, and they (and we) could point to errors we noticed and shake our heads and cluck our tongues. The trouble was finding the judge to preside. Our nominee had to have the right blend of snobbishness and wit, of passion about the language and willingness to learn from our investigations. In our third year, and after a couple of false starts, we found him – Charles Haines, professor of English at Carleton University in Ottawa, Shakespearean, and veteran broadcaster. Charles appeared every Monday morning, usually from Ottawa, but in the months he spent as a visiting professor at the University of Hartford in Connecticut, from New York. These appearances from the United States, by the way, led some people to conclude he was not a Canadian. He is – as Canadian as a moccasin. When his first year was up, I asked him to mull over what he had learned and to offer some of his thoughts on speaking Canadian.

There is no doubt that the English language is being abused these days all across the country. It's almost becoming fashionable, at small parties and after-theatre suppers, to comment on the current decline of speech and writing. "Forty percent of English-speaking Canadians are functionally illiterate." You read that sort of thing two or three times a year in the alarmist press. *Functionally illiterate* is a vague and elastic phrase. I know that thousands of people in the country say *flaunt* when they mean *flout*; they say *the reason is . . . because* and they say *They've invited my husband and I . . . .*

That is not functional illiteracy; true functional illiteracy is an inability to wield the language usefully. A functional illiterate has difficulty reading brand names in supermarkets, and greater difficulty writing an address on an envelope that even a case-hardened postal clerk can read.

But let's not be distressed for the wrong reasons. There is worse language butchery than *flaunt* for *flout* – even than *disinterested* for *uninterested* – to be heard: *Attempts will be made to priorize liasing with . . .* and *Meaningful instructional parameters are not easily structured into the today classroom situation.* That is jargon; bloat; inflation of the language as painful as inflation of the money. It is using language to tell a half-lie, to make both the speaker and the listener more important in their own eyes than the subject under discussion would honestly make them: *a classroom situation* is so much more weighty, isn't it, than *a class*?

If thousands of Canadians misuse English daily in one way or another, hundreds (and probably thousands) of Canadians are concerned about all the misusage. They are concerned enough to write to Peter and me at the CBC. Some write short letters, some write four or five pages. Some type, some write long-hand. Some are university professors of English, some admit to having had little schooling but are worried about the state of the language anyway.

Marjory Whitelaw of Halifax sent an interesting two-page typed letter. Among other things, she brought up the matter of *disinterested* and *uninterested*. The misuse of *disinterested* is a frequent mistake these days, and the bad thing about it is that it tends to undermine, not to say eliminate, the useful idea contained in *disinterested* in its true sense. If you are *disinterested*, it doesn't mean you're bored, that you're writhing in place and looking out the window. It means that you are able to decide and to act without favour, without thinking of any personal or professional advantage. It's an idea worth preserving. *Uninterested* means you have no feeling for, no interest in the subject in hand. Let's keep both words and use them correctly. That's not asking a great deal.

Professor James Harrison, Department of English, University of Guelph, quite rightly regretted, in a letter to us, that *goes* and *is concerned* seem to have vanished these days from the phrase *as far as... goes* or *is concerned: As far as Marcel Masse, it seems clear that....* Peter and I agreed with Professor Harrison on air on April 15: you have to add *goes, regards, is concerned, concerns* after *as far as*, but the phrase truncated does turn up often. *Like I say,* or *like he says*, turns up a lot, too. Inez Thompson of Erin, Ontario, wrote in about that one. *Like I say, he's a good mechanic.* That ought to be *As I say, he's....* *Like* is a preposition, *as* is a conjunction – much of the time. The distinction is clear; but you hear *like he says* a dozen times a day. (Why don't people say *like you know: Like you know, Monday's a holiday?* Even the *like-I-say* people, or most of them, would say *as you know* there. Strange.)

Those are three of the more frequently heard mistakes, along with the *lay* for *lie* mix-up, that Peter and I have been asked to deal with – and you can on occasion quite properly end a sentence, as I just have, with a preposition. (I had to defend, on air, very energetically, my having done so in an article I had published in *Canadian Geographic* in October 1984.) Another common blunder I brought up myself on air, unprompted by any letter, in a short series of interrelated remarks I called "The Flight of the Apostrophe." It concerned lawn-signs. Many people have taken to putting a sign outside their house with their family name on the sign. Hemmed in, as we all are, by numbers – postal codes, SIN and a dozen account and credit-card numbers, not to mention telephone numbers and street addresses – I suppose lawn-signs with family names on them are a laudable attempt to re-humanize the atmosphere, or would be if the signs were phrased, were carved, painted, printed in correct English. Many of them, unfortunately, say (for example) The Farr's or The Tolley's when they ought to say, of course, The Farrs and The Tolleys or, if they're trying to emphasize their ownership, The Farrs' and The Tolleys'.

It would be difficult to classify the kinds of mistakes listeners write in about. Some write about spelling, some about pronunciation, some about grammar. Some letters stated, simply, that such-and-such a usage was wrong, and you could hear the flat of the hand hit the table as the writer wrote the letter. Victoria Sansom, of Thorndale, Ontario, was one of those: "It irritates me to hear the word *nauseous* incorrectly used, as it so often is. It does not mean *nauseated*!" I read her letter, and my whole fist hit the table, and I said out loud, "You're so right! Thank you!" Peter and I were on air with *nauseous* on February 18.

Several fists hit several tables very hard when I, ill-advised, said on air in April that "Dawson City is in Yukon, not in the Yukon." I admitted, right after saying it (luckily), that I was not altogether sure about leaving out the *the* but I had heard, I said, that the government in Whitehorse officially preferred to forget the *the*. "We may get letters on this one," Peter said. He was so right. About ten letters, in fact, and five phone calls later, I went back on the air (on May 6) to eat *the* humble pie. Jim McManus and Layla Bevan had written to me immediately: "Damn right you'll get letters on *the* Yukon!... I have not yet lived quite half my life here, but I intend to spend the rest here, and... it will always be *the* Yukon..." and "Nobody up here refers to this place as 'Yukon,' except some government officials, and then only in writing.... No matter what anyone says, this place is *the* Yukon...." Four letters followed this. I called Dawson City and Whitehorse, talked to Peter Menzies and Cal Waddington and to two other people who preferred not to have their names mentioned. Two more letters arrived. The upshot was that those that live there and love the place call it "the Yukon." And so, having learned my lesson, will I.

Unfortunately not all, or even nearly all, the letters we receive get mentioned on air. That is simply because we get so many of them. I have not kept an exact count but I would say that I read at least twenty-five letters a week. Most of them are sent to Toronto, to

Morningside. The *Morningside* office acknowledges them, makes a copy of each and sends the copy to me. I read them all, from beginning to end. I enjoy every line of every one. I'm almost surprised by how eagerly I look forward to getting a fat envelope from Talin – Talin Vartanian, in the CBC Toronto office, is in charge, as it were, of the *Morningside* Good-English item, and she is marvellously cheerful, encouraging, efficient and a user of good English spontaneously herself – and to reading the suggestions and the pet peeves people send in.

I set to one side letters that bring up points Peter and I have just dealt with on air, but the writer happened not to have heard. I set to one side, too, queries about the correct use, and derivation, of four-letter words. Not that I am squeamish: it's just that *Morningside* may not be the right time and place for the analysis of the rougher hayfield and dockside colloquialisms. Some few letters are literally incomprehensible – including one from a university professor in Ottawa: I couldn't tell if he approved or disapproved of several usages he cited. I set his letter and a few more like it to one side. That means that about eighty-five percent of the letters sent in are useable, interesting, justified and air-worthy; and I'm very sorry that time squeezes so many of them out (or should I say I'm... *sorry that time factors impact so negatively on....*)

Occasionally I have been asked by listeners who my authorities are. (For some reason it is the question I am most often asked when listeners telephone me, as they do from time to time.) I have several authorities. The dictionaries I use most frequently are *Webster's New International Dictionary*, second edition (I rarely use the third edition) and the unabridged Oxford dictionary. I consult Fowler (*Modern English Usage*) and Partridge (*The Concise Usage and Abusage*) all the time. I regularly look things up in the *Handbook of Current English* (second Canadian edition) by Moore, Corder and the late Walter Avis. *The Elements of Style* by Strunk and White is useful and delightful. *Modern English: A Glossary* by Lazarus, MacLeish and Smith crams a lot of pertinent information into 462 pages but does move too swiftly over some problems (the subjunctive mood, for one). I turn regularly to the Gage Canadian dictionary and to the *Dictionary of Newfoundland English*. (Though Peter and I do not get very many specifically Newfoundland questions to deal with, the dictionary is a marvellous thing to read, like a good novel.) When a grammar point is very tricky, I go to Jespersen or to Zandvoort. I have read, mostly admiringly, Newman and Simon and when I am in the United States I buy or borrow the Sunday *New York Times* and read William Safire's piece. I reread periodically, with delight and amazement, *The Reader Over Your Shoulder* by Graves and Hodge: they are so hard on beloved literary eminences such as Wells, Shaw, Priestley and T.S. Eliot. From time to time I glance at a number of other English-language books: by Ciardi, Espy, Schur, Jennings, Freeman and Farb. Also I am lucky enough to be able to talk over lunch, say, or a late-night drink, with such users and lovers of good English as Gordon J. Wood, Munro Beattie and Albert Trueman.

I often turn, too – for information about the subjunctive mood, certainly – to my own book on usage: *English is Chaos*. I am not, by the way, giving myself a crafty plug by mentioning the book here, hoping to increase the sales of it. It is out of print and unobtainable. It was written to be a teacher's companion to an English grammar for Italian students of English that I wrote in Italy twenty-four years ago. *Chaos* was published in Italy. I say "my own book." Not quite: Anna Rebora Premuda worked, and worked very hard, with me on it.

I want to quote part of a sentence from the *Chaos* foreword:

> ...there is only one good written English, and it is not the sole property of New Yorkers or of Dubliners or of Londoners: a page well-written in Wellington will be all but identical with a page well-written in Toronto.

But, we go on,

> English is... a welter of exceptions-to-rules, of essential but un-teachable idiomatic phrases, of arbitrary and illogical constructions. English, indeed, is chaos but it is at once a chaos out of which a lively mind can bring the very nicest kind of precise expression....

324

Much of the chaos ... must be ascribed to the fact that English is very much a living language; and thus the chaos is the language's chiefest virtue.

Purists may want to say that "language's" and "chiefest" are questionable usages, if not wrong; but the sentence said then what I believe now. English is very difficult to teach, but there are rules, and I think we ought to know them if only so that we can break them more colourfully. (I am all in favour of bringing the study of Latin back to secondary schools and back into the first year of university.)

Good taste, though, and the educated ear are the most important things to have if you want to use the English language well – and why wouldn't you? Why wouldn't you want to speak clearly, convincingly, interestingly, with colour and with charm? Write that way, too? And the way to have good taste and an educated ear is to love the language.

If you love English, love the sound of a fine line, the beauty and energy of a fine sentence, a fine paragraph, if you love language almost the way you love a fine dish of good food, a tall glass of cold drink on a hot day, if you like to roll good language around on your tongue, then you will read, because you will want to read, the writers who have used the English language well, and their sound will become a part of your sound; and all the *impacted on*s and *liaise with*s, along with *basically* (D.B. Stewart of Killarney, Manitoba, wrote to us about that one), *paranoid* (Keeble McFarlane wrote to complain that "we have cheapened *paranoid* and *massive* and *agony* by overuse") and *prestigious* (one of my own pet peeves) will drop away, as seeds out of grapes, stones out of peaches; and you will surround yourself, your ear and tongue, with true English, pure and undefiled.

Charles Haines
Ottawa

THE THINGS YOU FIGURE OUT

Appropriately, I suppose, the contents of this final exchange between the listeners and the host of *Morningside* are as varied as the program itself. They range, as you will see, from the silly to the serious and from the practical to the profound. Most of them (the last, from Wendi Loome, is an exception) came in response to something I started in the autumn of my second year, when I wrote a series of musings about – well, since my opening salvos are here, I'll let them stand as they were first heard.

One of those musings, though, deserves a footnote. After my show-off piece about how easily I had solved the *Sunday Morning* news quiz, the producers of that program cheerfully named me as one of the winners that week – and, indeed, sent me one of their prizes. But I ought to have known I had not heard the end of it. A year and a half later, when I had had my name on the radio for picking up an ACTRA award, the clues to the quiz were a piece of music I didn't recognize and the words "sounds like the last letter enamoured of a runner." The answer (a z sound, with "awe" and "ski") was me. I didn't get it. Maybe I haven't even figured out the things I thought I had.

I

I passed my forty-ninth birthday in the summer that just flashed by, and next fall I will celebrate thirty years of trying to learn journalism. My beard is grey. I am playing the back nine of life, as someone has said, and the ominous word "veteran" has long since replaced "promising" in the lexicon of people who write about me in the press. You would think, with all that, that I would know a lot of things. In the sense of facts assimilated, I suppose I do. I know what a slough is, and the name of the premier of Prince Edward Island. I know who won the Stanley Cup in 1967 and who wrote the lyrics to "The World Is Waiting for the Sunrise." I can spell *accommodate* and translate most of *Mon pays*. I am flexible, too, and still learning. Although I once worked on a survey crew that measured distances in rods, I can translate miles to kilometres in my head, and I think of the speed limit now as one hundred. I know what time it is in St. John's when it's quarter past ten in Inuvik.

But there is another kind of learning. There are things you figure out as you gain experience. And when I look over my catalogue of *those* acquisitions I am not nearly so boastful as I am about sloughs and time zones. I spent part of my forty-ninth summer, in fact, trying to figure out just what it is I've figured out, and I have come to the conclusion that I need help. So here's what I propose to do. Today, and on each of the next few days of this new *Morningside* season, I will tell you one or two of the things I have figured out. In a few days, I think I can tell you very nearly everything on my list. But in return, I want *you* to tell *me* what *you've* figured out. Not facts. There are already too damn many facts. What we need is wisdom, the benefit of experience, the things you've learned the hard way, or picked up from someone you admire and later figured out to be true. You don't have to be venerable to join in, or even middle-aged. Some of the things I figured out best – that the satisfaction gained from cold beer varies in direct proportion to the exercise you have undergone to earn it, for example – I figured out when I was twenty-three, and some others are just coming in now. Talking this over last week, for instance, with a man I have known for twenty-five years, who is also one of the best editors this country has ever produced, I learned for the first time that cold water, if applied quickly enough, will take those encrusted yellow egg stains off dishes as hot water won't.

What else have I figured out? Well, here's the best egg sandwich in the world. First you chop up some green onions. (In emergencies I've done this with cooking onions, but they're not as good.) Then you fry them lightly in butter, for which, in this case, there is no substitute. Set them aside. Put some more butter in the pan. Break your egg into it as it sizzles. Break the yolk. Sprinkle some Worcestershire sauce into it. Flip the egg while it's still runny and let it fry just enough to be transferable to a plate. Set it aside with the onions. Put still more butter in your pan – lots more. Take two pieces of bread, the fresher the better (though here you're okay with day-old ingredients) and fry them, too, adding yet another dollop of butter when you turn them. Do one side dark gold and the other the colour of Carling Bassett's hair. Slide the egg and the fried onions onto the lighter side and make a sandwich, dark side out. Grab a handful of paper napkins and a glass of icy milk. You will feel wonderful.

II

You can't teach your children anything important. You can teach them the sounds of consonants, how to tie shoelaces, the rules of chess or the manual gearshift. You can give them your recipe for date squares, your dentist's phone number and your barber's name and preference in Christmas gifts. You can enroll them in the schools you went to, introduce them to your best teachers, give them subscriptions to your favourite magazines and keep them up late at night playing excerpts from your cherished collection of records. But no matter how great your efforts and how profound your love, they will learn nothing from what you *try* to teach them. They will, of course, *assimilate* from you – your mannerisms, your gestures, your laugh, your bad habits. They will walk like you and talk like you and you will see parts of yourself, and hear echoes, every time you are with them, but which parts those are, and which echoes – which they have chosen and which they have rejected – will be irrelevent to those you have tried to impart.

They will learn what they *want* to learn from the same place you learned – from life – and they will take, from the part of their life that is you, not what you choose to give them but what they choose to accept.

Is this a pessimistic view of being a parent? I don't think so. I think, in fact, that it is a liberating view. If it means you deserve no credit for what your children know, and are, it also means you take no blame for what they don't know, and what they are not.

When I first started out as a parent, I thought I could teach my children a great deal. I dragged them to worthy afternoons of children's theatre. I guided them through the maze of television and magazines, I took them to Pete Seeger concerts. I showed them the way. Now, they are all adults, or close to adults, and some of them like theatre and some of them don't. Some of them read Alice Munro and some of them read John D. MacDonald. Some like Mozart, some like Big Bill Broonzy and some like the Clash. (None of them, so far as I know, likes Pete Seeger.) And their likes and dislikes, their passions pro and con, appear to me now to bear no relation whatever to the exposure I gave each of them on their way to growing up. They are who they are. I love them all. But I have taught them nothing.

I do not know if this will be forever true. Like everyone I know, I found my own father was at his silliest when I was twenty-one and his wisest as I reached about forty. He died a few years ago, and all I can remember of what he taught me is the secret of his spaghetti sauce, how to read a *Racing Form* and what to do if your partner insists on opening one-no-trump with a doubleton in one of the minors. This is not a bad legacy for a man to have left his son. But he never did tell me – or if he did, I wasn't listening – that there were other things I might have learned. I've figured that out for myself, too, too late.

III

The answer to last *Sunday Morning*'s Headliners – the quiz you hear on our sister CBC radio program – is "Yitzack Shamir." This is not an official announcement, and if you have sent in your answer with another name on it, do not, as they say at the racetrack, destroy your tickets. It is instead something I figured out, and since one of the *principles* I have figured out in my long and richly coloured life is how to solve the *Sunday Morning* news quiz, I will tell you step by step not only how I did this one but how you, too, if you follow my easy lessons (available on cassette for a token price), can figure out the Headliners and win yourself thousands of dollars worth of free Canadian books.

To begin, ignore all the clues that seem to you obscure. The clues last weekend were, first, an intricate piece of fiddle music that I couldn't identify, and then the words "Pahlavi," plus "lake of old." Well, "lake of old" meant nothing to me either, but Pahlavi, I happen to know, is the family name of the Shah of Iran. Thus, *shah* is almost certainly one of the syllables, and it is also almost certainly the first syllable in the last name.

Now comes the key part. You go to the Sunday newspaper or, if you live in a part of the country where there is no Sunday newspaper, you simply review the events of the week as they have been recapitulated on our own "week in the life of the world" – which, to tell you the truth, is the best Sunday newspaper in Canada anyway. Who's in the news with a *shah* in his name? Why, hello. It's Yitzack Shamir, who moved into position to succeed Menachem Begin as prime minister of Israel. Yitzack? I am now reasonably certain the fiddle music was played by Yitzack Perlman. Mir? I honestly don't know – it *sounds* like an old lake, but the *Sunday Morning* quizmaster is more erudite than I, and no doubt when I hear the details this weekend it will all make sense to me.

I get the answers this way all the time. I got Curtis LeMay by knowing only that Tony Curtis's real last name is Schwartz. I got Sidney Jaffe, the Canadian businessman who was snatched into a

Florida jail, by knowing that the man who played Gunga Din in the movie – he was also the old doctor on Ben Casey – was Sam Jaffe. And I got martial law, the week it was lifted in Poland, by recognizing the strains of the old rock tune "I Fought the Law and the Law Won." In each case, that was *all* I knew; the other clues buffaloed me. The newspapers came to my rescue.

Sometimes, mind you, I make a fool of myself. I did not know, or did not remember, that Jane, Elizabeth, Mary, Kitty and Lydia are the names of the Bennett sisters in Jane Austen's *Pride and Prejudice*, so that although I did recognize the showtune "Bill," I spent a fruitless weekend asking various friends if they knew Jane, Elizabeth, Mary and so on and missed Bill Bennett. Worst of all, I was sure the love of Jake Barnes's life was Lady Brett something or other (it is in fact Ashley), but I neglected to perform the rest of my ritual of checking the papers, and on the weekend George Brett was at the centre of the case of the pine-tarred bat, I missed the answer.

Ah well, the system works. It is not much to have figured out in all the years I've been in journalism, but it is something.

One other thing for today. The dates that are stamped onto cardboard milk containers show when the milk is likely to be stale. In every corner store I've ever been in, the proprietor, as I would if I were he, puts the oldest stuff in the front. I've figured out, therefore, that the place to take your milk from is the back of the refrigerator shelf. Smart, eh? It's just that you get no free books for knowing it.

IV

As I try to conclude this series of reflections, and just before I turn the subject over to you, I find myself still somewhat confused. In my life, I have figured out more than I've let on this week. I've figured out how to be a better bridge player than I used to be – I now don't carp at my partners – and I've figured out which part of the turkey I like best: the dark meat. I've figured out that my grandmother was right when she told me to eat a hearty breakfast every day, and that my mother was right when she told me that the way to make a tough decision was to toss a coin – after which, your emotional response to the arbitrary decision will tell clearly what your own real desires are. I've figured out those things, sometimes the hard way, but I do not always *act* as if I have. Similarly, I have figured out a lot of things about men, children, women and friendship. But there is still scarcely a day when I do not find something in each of those categories that I have *not* figured out or which, if I have, I have to figure out again.

When I was younger, I was something of a phenom of the magazine biz. I don't know what readers thought of my work – they could not have enjoyed it as much as I did – but around the office I was known principally for my speed. I once wrote a three-thousand-word cover story for *Maclean's* in less than three days, including research. Now, I write more slowly. *Agonizingly* more slowly. Some of the *sentences* in the book I finished this summer took me longer than that whole *Maclean's* article. But, I think, they are better sentences. The more I write – and, I hope, the better I get – the harder I find writing to do. What I know now that I did not know earlier is just *how* hard it is.

Another example: As a kid golfer, I could putt up a storm. I'd just stand over the ball and hit it toward the hole. Often, it went in. Now, I stand and study. I worry. My hands shake. My forehead breaks into a cold sweat. I jab at the ball. It skitters off independently. I jab again. And so on. Like almost everyone I know, from Arnold Palmer to my favourite partners in Guelph, Ontario, I am a far worse putter in the mature and tranquil years than I was in my carefree salad days.

Golf, of course, is not a metaphor for life. Is writing? In this case, I rather think so. If the work I do now is better than the work I used to do, it is, surely, because I now have some glimmer of comprehension of its difficulty. I think I have figured this out, but I am not sure. Maybe, like my putting, my early work sped toward its target with the certain arrogance of youth.

Thirty years ago, if I had been given a chance to muse out loud about what I'd figured out, I might have gone on for most of a season. Now, I've barely made it to the middle of Friday morning. What will happen, I wonder, when I try this thirty years from now?

P.G.

✉ I used to believe all the ads,
Blindly followed all silly new fads,
A devout Hula Hooper,
A New York pooper-scooper,
Sang along with the crew-cutted lads.

I used only cleansers that bubble;
Trusted Tide with my dirty-clothes trouble.
I greatly loved Lucy,
Chewed gum that was juicy,
The kind with good times by the double.

While striped toothpaste brightened my grin
I watched all the shows where they win,
I stretched with Ed Allen
Used only low-cal in
Decaffed mugs to stay slim.

I always thought father knew best;
Cheered Archie and Edith with zest,
Found *Ford Theater* thrilling,
And *Twilight Zone* chilling,
You can fill in the names of the rest.

Maturity's made me much wiser;
I ignore the TV advertiser,
I snap off the tube;
Throw away Rubik's Cube
Tune in my own synthesizer.

For troubles won't fade when you smoke,
And things don't go better with Coke.
Curl up in a nook,
Find your own favourite book,
Live, love, laugh with your friendly "ain folk."

Audrey Bates
Moncton, New Brunswick

✉ Our fall transplanting gives me mindless work so I have been trying to figure out what it is that I truly know, while propagating plants for next spring's sales. Here's what I know for sure right now:

– Farmers live eternally on hope – the "next-year" concept.
– Without the existence of the next-year concept, farmers would cry
  more often.
– There may not be a next year.

I own two cars and one tractor. Between December 15 and April 1, I know only two vehicles of the three will start and run on the day they are needed; their reluctance to operate is directly proportional to the importance of their successful operation; their reluctance increases geometrically as the temperature decreases.

Doug Green
Athens, Ontario

✉ My son was three years old when my husband was drowned. I was young and so devastated that the only way I could cope was to put him out of my mind. As a result, my son cannot remember his father. I realize now that, had I talked of the things we had done, he would have retained the memory. I hope my mistake will help someone else.

Dorothy Purvis
Manitoulin Island, Ontario

✉ In the bush, should warmth be necessary, it is indeed possible to spend more energy than is prudent in the attempt to make a fire. A fire's consolation is more psychological than practical unless one is soaking wet or unable to move. Covering one's body with leaves, bark and needles, burrowing into the soft silent depths of a snowdrift or burrowing into or under deadfall can all be sufficient to stay warm on even cold nights.

Never use a chainsaw that has more muscle than you. One cubic inch for every hundred pounds of body weight is a good rule of thumb. Should the smallest you can get be a two-and-a-half-cubic-inch job, keep the chain as sharp as possible and never lift the saw above your solar-plexus.

After you've tanned a bear skin, if it's still greasy, spread it out and cover the skin side with a thick layer of fine, dry sawdust. Repeat this process when the dust gets darker in colour; and when it falls off easily, you know the skin won't leave oil stains on your floor.

Matthew Scott
Chester, Nova Scotia

✉ After thirty-six years of trying, I have finally figured out that being a virtuous person is not what I want most in my life to be. So far it has got me nowhere in my efforts to establish myself as a memorable person. Moderation is no longer my motto.

My father was a scamp, a scalawag, a womanizer, a story-teller, a binger and an all-round naughty boy all his life. He certainly never pretended to be a model father. A man like my dad would never have been found among the pages of today's parenting books. He was not virtuous, and yet when he passed away a few months ago he was immortalized in newspaper articles and radio programs and many of his cronies came to the funeral to share with us some hair-raising stories of escapades during his youth and not so youthful days. I only wish I had known of his lack of *virtuousness* during his lifetime. Maybe I could have taken lessons on how to be an adventurer. Maybe I could have figured out long ago that being virtuous is only for those who wish to remain holed up in anonymity, and wish to slide through their short lives rather than bump and growl and snicker through. I plan to stop hiding my naughtiness. The next time the nags are running at Greenwood Racetrack I'm going to spend my whole day there, drinking beer out of plastic cups in a smelly bar, just for the ambience and for the unvirtuous spending of my entire baby-bonus cheque on the triactor. I'll smoke in the mornings, drink as much as I want at parties, stop pretending that I admire the president of the PTA, stay out past eleven with my friends on week-nights and, in short, get rid of all shoulds and shouldn'ts in my life. Maybe then my children will remember me as a great old gal, instead of nice old mom.

Christine Elvin Champagne
Toronto

✉ When I was leaving home to fend for myself in the wider world, my father offered these two maxims: Don't fool around with things that work; and don't drink at the company party.

Doug Smith
St. John's, Newfoundland

✉ When I was a young woman, I gave birth to three beautiful and healthy little girls. I love them now and I did then, but I didn't know much about raising them. I was a strict disciplinarian. Disobedience meant a spanking, temper tantrums or anything of that nature meant a quiet spell spent in their own rooms – behind closed doors. I was flattered when people remarked on my well-behaved children. I didn't realize it then, but they were the image of my motherhood; their good behaviour flattered my ego. I may never have realized my folly, but for a wonderful event.

The year the last little girl went off to grade one, I gave birth to a son. I can't begin to describe my joy. After three little girls who called daddy when in pain or need or moments of great happiness, three little girls, polite, well-mannered and well groomed, I had a son. I was now in my thirties and smarter. From the moment of his arrival, he was a source of constant joy and wonder to us all. There were no confrontations with this child. Things that the little girls were disciplined for he was held and kissed and talked to about. It didn't matter to me what anyone thought of my mothering now – the important thing was this child and our relationship. We discovered a wonderful thing. This child, so aware of the love around him and his own self-worth, had no need to prove himself or justify his actions to anyone. When little friends became aggressive and angry in play, he could be heard gently talking with them, being fair and understanding. When he was four years old, he learned that he would lead a very hard life. He would suffer much pain and even humiliation as his physical appearance would change. He would have to come to terms with life's greatest questions: What is life? What is death?

I have seen nurses weep, not for his pain, but because of his gentle concern for their feelings – knowing that they didn't want to hurt him. One day, noticing he was particularly quiet and knowing instinctively that something had happened, I asked what it was. An older boy had taunted him for having no hair and called him a bald eagle. After a moment, I quietly asked him how he had replied. This was his answer: "A bald eagle is a powerful bird."

Shortly before his tenth birthday, cold mother earth claimed the body of my precious son. His life was short, but the quality of that life was the best. He taught me, and everyone who knew him, a great deal about how to live and how to die. It's not the length of life that is lived but the quality that counts. He also taught me how to raise a child and how to live without regrets.

If only I could start all over with those three little girls.

Joan Martin
Calgary

✉ I'm eighty-three. I've learned to stop ascribing motives to other people's behaviour because I can't honestly assess my own.

Maurice Nichol
Toronto

✉ This translation is for what men say is their timespan for a given chore. They do this to get you to wait, hope and put up with what they want to do. (These are usually preceded by: "give me," "just a," "this will only take," "I'll only be," I can do that in.")

moment	– one to two minutes
second	– three to five minutes
minute	– ten minutes
few minutes	– twenty minutes
five or ten minutes	– one to one and a half hours
twenty minutes	– three hours
half an hour	– half a day
half a day	– three days
two or three days	– three months
a week or so	– six months
three months	– one year
six months or so	– three to five years

Arista Zabal
Port Hardy, British Columbia

✉ Last spring I stood with a seven-year-old nephew waiting to have his hand-made Everest scrapbook autographed by the Everest climbers. One of these incredible men wrote, "Find your own Everest and climb it."

And then he asked the boy, "Do you know what that means? It doesn't mean you have to climb *this* mountain but it does mean you have to find some very big thing in your life and learn to conquer it."

My nephew will never forget this and can tell it word for word yet.

Men who can challenge youth like this deserve praise.

Muriel Dayman
Calgary

✉ You can spit into the wind, if you duck fast.

Judy Thorkelson
North Bay, Ontario

✉ When I was a young girl, I had to walk a long mile to and from school every day. It was in the country: a gravel road with wide, deep ditches on either side. There weren't many farms along the way and they were far apart, with long lanes. A gang of boys had a nasty habit of pestering my younger sister and me. They lay in wait, and teased us belligerently, threateningly. They said they were going to hurt us and we believed them. Once, in winter, they threw us into a ditch deep with snow and held our faces in it. We were very afraid of them. I begged my mother to call their mothers but she said we had to fight our own battles, that we were probably provoking them anyway. One day, utterly fed up, I raised the hand holding my lunch-pail with the aluminum thermos inside very high and smashed the heavy metal box into the meanest boy's face. I loosened his front teeth and gave him a bloody nose. After the phone call from his mother to mine, I was punished severely. My mother said she was angry and ashamed that I would ever display such inexcusable violence. But the boys never bothered us again.

Now I have a daughter the same age and on her school bus was a big boy who annoyed her ceaselessly. No matter how much she warned him, he bothered her; pinching and poking her, tugging her hair, even spitting at her. One day she punched him in the nose very hard. It bled. When she told me, I said, "That's great. Good for you." He leaves her alone now. If I had had the courage and encouragement to behave accordingly, earlier, when I was a child, I could have saved myself a lot of fear and misery.

Laura Hargreaves
Toronto

✉ Several years ago I broke my glasses when I slipped on the ice. I didn't have a spare pair of glasses, so I had to wait three or four days while my own were repaired and a second pair made for another such emergency.

During the waiting period, I couldn't read a word; I had to rely on the radio. It was then I learned how to listen to music. The trick is to concentrate entirely on the music itself. Previously, I had tended to use music as a background to my reading. Concentrate on each note as it comes along, how it is designed to follow the note before and to precede the note that follows. This is not always possible, of course, depending on the complexity of the music. But the goal is to break down the music into the smallest units possible. This will seem to be terribly mechanical and a denial of everything music is supposed to convey to the listener. But by eliminating everything from your mind except the music itself, the music will soon take over – in fact, flood over you – and you will hear it as you never heard it before.

Phil Calder
Toronto

✉ The rather depressing experience of reaching the age of sixty-five was somewhat alleviated for me by a gift containing this advice: "Avenge yourself – live long enough to be a problem to your children."

Margaret Bryans
Vancouver

✉ I heard you and Danny Finkleman crying sour grapes about solo dancers in clubs these days and, as a solo dancer who has been stepping out for four years now, two or three times a week, may I tell you some of the things I've figured out?

1. In most situations, asking a lady to dance in North America is the equivalent of asking her to have sex. Unless you fit her stereotype, you get neither. I travel for a living and rather than risk running in unfamiliar cities, I dance for an hour or two. The rejection wears a bit thin after a while so I dance alone.
2. Most women in clubs aren't strong enough or versatile enough to dance non-stop for an hour or more. One spends more time looking for a partner than dancing. Besides, if there is a great dancer there, she will join you.

3. It's a great ego booster when people clap or, on the occasions when I have been able to dance regularly in a club, the DJ clears the floor for me for a half hour or more. Some people buy me booze.
4. In the hundreds of clubs I have danced in, I can only speak of one hole in Saskatoon that asked me to get off the floor. They said I was keeping other people off the dance floor. Seems strange, as the three waitresses and I made up the crowd.
5. It feels great to move and glide across a floor by oneself if the place is empty, and if it's full, one gets to dance with every pretty lady and great dancer in the place. They all work their way around to you eventually.
6. When the midnight crowd at Tabasco's in Hull gives you the floor for an hour and then applauds, it makes it all worthwhile.

So I suggest you wallflowers get off your egos and strut your stuff. You could be amazed.

Pat Wolfe
Banff, Alberta

✉ I know now that Peter Newman, having greeted every new giant on the Canadian political scene from Diefenbaker through Trudeau to Mulroney with childlike enthusiasm, will continue to do so while always realizing eventually that their advent was not, in fact, the Second Coming, but will each time recover from his disappointment and write a book about it.

Ken Cheetham
Willowdale, Ontario

✉ Education is a continuing thing, from the cradle to the grave. Just last week we bought a lot in the cemetery, just across the road from the edge of our fields. A good friend is the cemetery supervisor, and we found the real estate in a scenic spot with good visibility. "Okay,

Harold," I said, "this is it, and when I land here, be sure that I am heading west so that I can keep an eye on our old home and the community hall."

"No," he says, "you can't do that, for the rules are that everyone is heading east!"

Since learning of this ruling, I have given the subject daily consideration, and have come up with a profound decision, which is: much easier and certainly less costly to change direction of a fella in a box than it would be to change location of our home, woodhouse and community hall. I plan to present this bit of logic to the cemetery council at the annual meeting in February.

Max Banks
Elmsdale, Nova Scotia

✉ I lived in the country when my daughter was born, and one of the first things the doctor added to her diet after pablum was bananas, every day. But the local store didn't always have bananas. I tried the refrigerator. They kept there very well; even if the skins were black a week later, the insides were still in fine shape.

You can so keep bananas in the refrigerator.

Gwen Reaume
Oakville, Ontario

✉ I admire your courage at trying to learn such a complicated task as knitting by following voice instructions alone. So I shall begin by waxing philosophical. There are some definite advantages to being able to knit.

You can make your own socks, mitts, scarves, sweaters and so on, plus gifts for your friends – but this is very time-consuming, as you have already discovered.

You experience the satisfaction of having created something with your own hands. It puts you in the same class as the painter, sculptor and musician.

It is a great pastime. You can knit while listening to the radio or stereo, even while watching TV. I carry my knitting on trips – train, plane, bus or car (so long as I am a passenger) – and I knit at meetings, especially the long, boring ones. That caused quite a sensation at first, but it wasn't long before others joined in. It's a great way to meet people.

If you ever decide to give up the weed, you'll need something to do with your hands. I guarantee you won't have idle hands if you become a knitter.

So much for the philosophy. Now for a few practical points. I taught myself how to knit when I was in my early teens. My grandmother's skill inspired me and my mother's lack of it made me seek help else' where. My "teacher" was a small book called *Learning How Book*. I found the directions easy to follow, the diagrams simple and accu' rate. I still use the basic mitt and sock patterns from this book.

I have since taught other young women how to knit and from that experience, I have found these points to be important:

Don't be afraid to pull apart your work and start over if you've made a mistake. A major error will irritate you every time you look at it if it is left.

Master the art of holding your needles and your wool. Practise until you pick up your needles and wool correctly as automatically as you handle a typewriter. If you don't, you will never learn to knit with any amount of speed and will give up in frustration.

Begin on something small and interesting. *Never* start with a scarf; the boredom will turn you off knitting forever. (Try knitting a skirt for a Barbie doll, if you dare!)

Learn to use four needles as soon as possible. They are necessary for mitts and socks, and there is something about them that makes the knitting go faster. I think it is because you never get to the end of the row!

I hope you learn to knit. It is one of the most satisfying and enduring hobbies I know.

Wendy Caldwell
Ceylon, Saskatchewan

✉ In my early days in Toronto one did not copulate with one's friends' sisters; during the winter months I had a pro on Jarvis Street. She was clean and proficient. She had a nice apartment. Each Tuesday shortly after supper I would put my laundry and mending in a bag and go out. She had cold draught beer at ten cents a glass. (I believe at that time the LCBO sold a keg at four dollars a gallon plus a deposit.) I would copulate with her and leave. On Thursday I would return and repeat the exercise. I would find my wash beautifully clean and ironed and take it home. The charge of three dollars was not excessive. I gave her fifty cents for the laundry and mending.

When I returned from World War Two I found much changed in Toronto. At that time there were no longer any pros visible on Jarvis Street. A German girl to whom I paid five dollars (inflation) told me that most of them had gone to Laval for French immersion. Apparently this was the way that Toronto got rid of what they considered a problem. Also, as in England during the war, competition was fierce.

I solved that problem by getting married. Since she is no longer with me, I may say that she was a delightful Canadian lady.

In my time as a bachelor, we put beer first, then sports; women came next as a necessity, then work.

At my age (seventy-six), one looks over the wasted years. Never refuse a lady's invitation to spend the night with her. If you do you will have remorse in your old age.

H.W. Kirkpatrick
Victoria, British Columbia

✉ I've been a house-husband for about two months now. Both Susie and I have learned a great deal about ourselves and families over the last little while.

We both knew things had come full circle when Susie had not yet arrived by the time I had supper ready to serve at our usual five-thirty meal-time. Her portion cooled on the stove while the kids and I ate. She called at about six, saying she was working and hadn't noticed the time and would be on her way. I told her abruptly that it was too bad for her; that there'd be cold hamburger and clammy

French fries waiting when she got home. The kids told me I was being too mean, but I stood firm: if she'd wanted a late supper, all she had to do was call earlier and let me know.

When she finally arrived I stopped cleaning up and had a cup of tea while she pretended her cold hamburger and fries were delicious. Here I was, coming on like a nagging housewife, and there she was, the income-earner back from work, making feeble excuses for not calling about being late for supper. We were playing out each other's lines, and it was so obvious that we were soon having a good laugh over it.

This was only the latest in a series of minor incidents that have come to the surface since I've been looking after the house end of the family. Susie and I have both been working parents on and off for years, but there's never been a time when it was my "job" to look after the house and Susie's job to bring in the money. In the past I was the major income earner, while she had a teaching job, *and* she carried the major responsibility for the kitchen, daily household maintenance and looking after the kids' needs. It was her job to do all that stuff I am now having to do. Now, after fifteen years of marriage, I'm finding out what's involved in running the house – it's about time! And, do you know what? I'm enjoying it.

There is a richness in this part of family life that I've never seen before. Like being at home with lunch ready when our thirteen-year-old son came in, chin a-quiver, and told me of the shock and upset he had just experienced during his first encounter with junior-high-school hallway violence. I didn't do much other than to listen to him blurt out the story and comfort him as a few tears came; it wasn't much, but it was precious, and something I'd not shared before.

I could go on for pages trying to convey the meat of this new experience, the richness of having insights into my wife's end of our family life, resulting in a new level of warmth and mutual appreciation of each other's worlds. She caught herself pulling one of my old tricks the other evening, leaving a mess on the kitchen counter, with the thought, "Oh, that's okay, Andy will clean it up in the morning." We chuckled and pondered over that one for days. And there are the new dimensions of love and appreciation I sense with the kids, fine, richly embroidered chapters, a feeling that comes from being there when they need somebody or feel like burbling out the seemingly inconsequential news of their daily lives. There are whole chapters of their being that I never knew existed before; fine, richly embroidered chapters that are forming the basis of the people they are in the process of becoming.

There's also the clash of different activities, for the role switch isn't complete. I still do the man's work around the house, keeping the vehicles running, bringing in wood for the stove, cleaning the chimney and so forth. I have found myself at four-thirty on my back under the truck in the driveway replacing a leaking transmission seal, with nothing thawed and ready for supper and children beginning to ask what they'll eat in an hour's time. It takes a lot of work to get the grease off your hands so you can handle food in the kitchen.

Sooner or later I'll be back at work (that is, "outside the home" – I'll have a "job"), but it won't be possible for me just to slip back into the traditional male role (whatever that is these days) and leave the maintenance and nurturing responsibilities to Susie. For one thing, she's not likely to stand for it, and besides, I'm a pretty good cook.

Andy Tamas
Whitehorse, Yukon

✉ A few years ago, I was using a cane to support my MS habit. I am now, at age thirty-seven, in an electric wheelchair, the disease having progressed considerably. When I first adopted the sitting position in 1977, I detected a marked difference in the attitudes of my friends. My wife and I were left virtually alone. Very few people came by to visit any more. I had left my teaching job by that time, so passing the hours grew very tedious. I had too much time to think. The object of most of my thoughts was the reason for my friends' withdrawal of attention.

My initial conclusion was that they were not true friends. I laboured under that assumption for many moons, growing steadily more cynical and unhappy, until a curious thing happened: a very close friend went through a divorce. I knew he needed my support, but because he was such a cherished friend, I felt terribly inadequate and fumbly. Instincts told me to stay clear for awhile, to give him room to breathe. My ineptitude, caused mainly by my feelings of caring and true sorrow over the developments, was better kept away.

As I thought about it, it became clear that I was using the very same rationale my friends were likely using to excuse themselves from seeing me. They did care and were concerned, but my MS upset them. Staying away for awhile was their idea of sparing me the anguish of seeing them upset. The whole attitude was expressed to me one day by one of those whom I felt had abandoned me. I felt ashamed for my presumptuous thoughts.

I wish that I could put this neatly into one sentence. It is, however, something that took considerable time for me to learn. Those things do not lend themselves easily to précis packaging!

So this is something that I came to understand. Many disabled persons already know, but each individual must discover it. No one can tell you.

Paul Gouett
Halifax

✉ I was listening with great interest to your discussion on life and love at fifty or older. I think one thing was not discussed in enough detail, even though you, Peter, snuck in a little sentence. Who cares if you have bags under your eyes and are a little overweight? That's what being older than fifty is all about. Bags are interesting, as they could be a sign of reading later – perhaps to have something to talk about. So you're a little overweight – you've had years to try, experiment and discuss good food. My point is that today's newspapers, books and magazines are always slanted toward youth – while a lot of us just aren't young any more, in spirit and mind maybe, but not in body. But who cares? Sure, youth is interesting and exciting, especially when you watch young people's minds ticking over on some new subject they think they've just discovered, but you've known about for a long time. Yes, I can listen to Tears for Fears or Bronski

Beat for a little while, but give me the comfort of my fireplace, a good book and my Mozart or Beethoven for the long stretch. Yes, young bodies are lovely to look at, but how about the character in an older face that shows a person has lived and knows a thing or two?

If I ever marry again it will not be to someone younger than myself. Older means comfort. Older means not having to worry too much about your stretch marks, those creeping grey hairs, having to hold your tummy in every minute of the day. Older means knowing my feet get sore after walking all day and maybe I don't want to dance all night too. Older means not having to explain to your dearest who Harry Truman was, or Barry Goldwater or Lester Pearson, or Ray Anthony, and older means you've lived through all those wars the kids are learning about in university. Older means patience and understanding. Older means not laughing when I get out my Louis Armstrong records. Older means not having to explain who Dave Brubeck is or exactly how Charlie Parker died. Older means someone who'll rub my back after a nice long walk in the rain. Older means holding hands and dancing slowly and not *having* to rush into bed; you've got time, and at your age you know pretty well what it's all about anyway. Older means knowing how to make a smashing Christmas cake and good jam, being able to knit or crochet and repair almost anything – or know how to get it repaired. And older means loving the young because you've been there yourself and it was very nice, thank you very much.

Don't wish yourself young again, Peter, you're doing just fine the way you are.

Wendi M. Loome
Souris, Prince Edward Island

Index of Authors

Margaret Adams, Coral Harbour, Northwest Territories 147

Deborah Lee Aker, Sydney Mines, Nova Scotia 314

Glen Allen, Montreal 165–174

Karen Alton, Oakville, Ontario 300

Dwight Thomas Atkinson, Vancouver 240

Max Banks, Elmsdale, Nova Scotia 342

Audrey Bates, Moncton, New Brunswick 334

Joan Baumber, Bragg Creek, Alberta 25

Joan Beecroft, Edmonton 51

Inga Benson, Lisieux, Saskatchewan 98

Judith Berman, Montreal 181

Joan Besen, Toronto 205–208

Leslie Bousquet, Montreal 250

Grant Boyd, Thurso, Quebec 30

Chris Brookes, Nicaragua 53–63

Sheila Brown, Waterdown, Ontario 82, 144

Nina Finkelstein Bruck, Montreal 256

Joan Bruce, North Battleford, Saskatchewan 46

Margaret Bryans, Vancouver 341

Phil Calder, Toronto 340

Wendy Caldwell, Ceylon, Saskatchewan 343

Anne Cameron, Powell River, British Columbia 70, 80

Bob Cameron, Georgetown, Ontario 297

Elizabeth Carrell, Minden, Ontario 96

John Chalmers, Edmonton, Alberta 154

Christine Elvin Champagne, Toronto 336

Deborah Chatreau, Thornsburg, Ontario 68

Ken Cheetham, Willowdale, Ontario 342

Jonathan Churcher, Cobble Hill, British Columbia 213

Gisela Spier Cohen, Toronto 78, 317

Roy Conacher, Victoria, British Columbia 230

Emily Cowall, Cannington, Ontario 223

Barney Cummings, Toronto 102

Frank Cummins, Cremona, Alberta 296

Nelson Cunningham, Port Carling, Ontario 301

Kim Dales, Batoche, Saskatchewan 22

Ann Davidson, Toronto 305

Muriel Dayman, Calgary 339

Laura de Cocq, Mill Bay, British Columbia 143

Peter Domin, Calgary 97

Catherine Edward, Belfast, Prince Edward Island 75

F.V. Edwards, Saskatoon 152

Millie Evans, LaHave, Nova Scotia 191

Betty and Art Fish, Winfield, British Columbia 50

Elizabeth Fleet, Castlegar, British Columbia 302

David Foster, Willowdale, Ontario 183

Ben Gadd, Jasper, Alberta 153

Peter Gorrie, Burlington, Ontario 163

Stan Gibson, Okotoks, Alberta 229

Paul Gouett, Halifax 347

Bob Gray, Medicine Hat, Alberta 298

Doug Green, Athens, Ontario 335

Peter Gzowski, Toronto 7–14; 15–22; 87–94; 135–137; 161–163; 175–180; 227–229; 233–237; 267–278; 327–333

Shirley Haid, Anglin Lake, Saskatchewan 222

Charles Haines, Ottawa 319–325

Mryka Hall-Beyer, Scotstown, Quebec 188

Jean Hanlon, Wentworth, Nova Scotia 52

Hannelore, Banfield, British Columbia 150

Ann Meekitjuk Hanson, Frobisher Bay, Northwest Territories 220, 313

Laura Hargreaves, Toronto 340

Katharine Harris, Ganges, British Columbia 225

Catharine Hay, Kenora, Ontario 137, 232

Sue Hemphill, Horsefly, British Columbia 148

M.D. Hetherton, Swift Current, Saskatchewan 40

Mary Eleanor Hill, Glen Williams, Ontario 129, 223

Isabel Huggan, Ottawa 42

Gordon Inglis, St. John's, Newfoundland 300

Alice Issner, Toronto 73

Leslie Jackson, Apsley, Ontario 142

Rick Jamieson, Collingwood, Ontario 39

Carolann Johnson, Calgary 189

Jerry Kambites, Uganda 195–204

Katherine Kelly, Vancouver 94

Brenda LeDrew Keyes, Palgrave, Ontario 35

Margot Keith King, Montreal 192

H.W. Kirkpatrick, Victoria, British Columbia 345

Norianne Kirkpatrick, Armstrong, British Columbia 210

Hilary Knight, Victoria, British Columbia 315

Myrna Kostash, Greece 257–266

Grace Lane, Regina 107–114

Martha Laugher, Elmsdale, Nova Scotia 39

Enerson Lavender, Burlington, Ontario 251

Marie LeBlanc, Little Brook, Nova Scotia 186

Janet Le Febvre, Edmonton 245

Mark Leier, Burnaby, British Columbia 304

Ellery Littleton, Victoria, British Columbia 186

Gillian Loeb, Toronto 297

Wendi M. Loome, Souris, Prince Edward Island 348

Walter Lutz, Holden, Alberta 253

Bill MacLean, Annapolis Royal, Nova Scotia 230

Mary Majko, Albert, New Brunswick 221

Joan Martin, Calgary 337

W.A. Martin, Victoria, British Columbia 76

Tom McEwen, Winnipeg 187

Wayne McKell, St. Chrysostome, Quebec 243

Mary McKim, Quebec City 279–293

Paul McLaughlin, Toronto 48

Norah McRae, Edmonton 100

Jeanne Cuthbert Miller, Thunder Bay, Ontario 105

Beth Minty, White Rock, British Columbia 131

Martha Morgan, Saskatoon 296

Gwen Mortimer, West Vancouver 141

Louise Sheppard Mulhern, St. Hippolyte, Quebec 231

Krista Munroe, Medicine Hat, Alberta 216

Don Myers, Thunder Bay 115–129

Maurice Nichol, Toronto 338

Michael O'Connell, Ottawa 69

Mark O'Neill, Montreal 279–293

Stephanie O'Reilly, Port Hope, Ontario 101

John Osterman, Laval, Quebec 309

Ann Pappert, Toronto 107–114

Peter R. Penny, Plaster Rock, New Brunswick 51

Gordon Peters, Caledon East, Ontario 298

Guy Prokopetz, Winnipeg 311

Dorothy Purvis, Manitoulin Island, Ontario 335

Eugenia C. Ray, Sault Ste. Marie, Ontario 242

Gwen Reaume, Oakville, Ontario 343

Linette Reid, Saskatoon 85

H.G. Robinson, Tory Hill, Ontario 306

Loretta Rosnick, Toronto 30

Cessie Ross, Cobourg, Ontario 140

John Ross, Vancouver 132

Avril Rustage-Johnston, Peterborough, Ontario 237

D.B. Scott, Cambridge, Ontario 47

Matthew Scott, Chester, Nova Scotia 335

Gregory Shea, Montreal 149

Penny Simpson, Tatla Lake, British Columbia 79

David Sims, Toronto 28, 33

Jessie Skinner, Abbotsford, British Columbia 72

Douglas Skoyles, Calgary 145

J.P. Slugworthy, New Westminster, British Columbia 52

Harold Smiley, Enderby, British Columbia 77

Doug Smith, St. John's, Newfoundland 337

Hope Smith, Calgary 23

Margaret Spencer, Lachine, Quebec 229

Leland Stanford, Spring Coulee, Alberta 307

Nancy Staveley, Kingston, Ontario 211

Sandra Steele, Scarborough, Ontario 37

Peter Steele, Whitehorse, Yukon 137

Bill Stephenson, Toronto 246

Sally Swanson, Brooks, Alberta 27

Andy Tamas, Whitehorse, Yukon 345

François Thibeau, Scoudouc, New Brunswick 240

Judy Thorkelson, North Bay, Ontario 339

Dave Trautman, Edmonton 184

Helen Traynor, Toronto 163

Danni Tribe, Sointula, British Columbia 99

Mary Elizabeth Voegelin, LaHave, Nova Scotia 299

Merrily Walker, St. Catharines, Ontario 24

Stephen Watson, Duncan, British Columbia 159

J.H. Watts, Sidney, British Columbia 308

Margaret L. Weber, New Hamburg, Ontario 103

Flo Whyard, Whitehorse, Yukon 249

Joan Wiltshire, Smiths Cove, Nova Scotia 77

Pat Wolfe, Banff, Alberta 341

Lynn Wolff, Edmonton 144

Margaret Young, Sydney, Nova Scotia 299

Arista Zabal, Port Hardy, British Columbia 338